Independent Stardom

Texas Film and Media Studies Series
Thomas Schatz, Editor

« EMILY CARMAN »

Independent Stardom

FREELANCE WOMEN IN THE HOLLYWOOD STUDIO SYSTEM

University of Texas Press AUSTIN

Printed in the United States of America
First edition, 2016
Second paperback printing, 2016

∞ The paper used in this book meets the minimum requirements of ANSI/NISO Z39.48-1992 (R1997) (Permanence of Paper).

LIBRARY OF CONGRESS CATALOGING DATA
Carman, Emily, author.
Independent stardom : freelance women in the Hollywood studio system / by Emily Carman. — First edition.
pages cm — (Texas film and media studies series)
Includes bibliographical references and index.
ISBN 978-1-4773-0731-1 (cloth : alk. paper)
ISBN 978-1-4773-0781-6 (pbk. : alk. paper)
ISBN 978-1-4773-0732-8 (library e-book)
ISBN 978-1-4773-0733-5 (non-library e-book)
1. Motion picture industry—California—Los Angeles—History. 2. Women in the motion picture industry—California—Los Angeles—History. 3. Motion picture actors and actresses—California—Los Angeles—History. 4. Hollywood (Los Angeles, Calif.)—History. I. Title. II. Series: Texas film and media studies series.
PN1995.9.W6C296 2016
791.43082—dc23 2015015797

doi 10.7560/307328

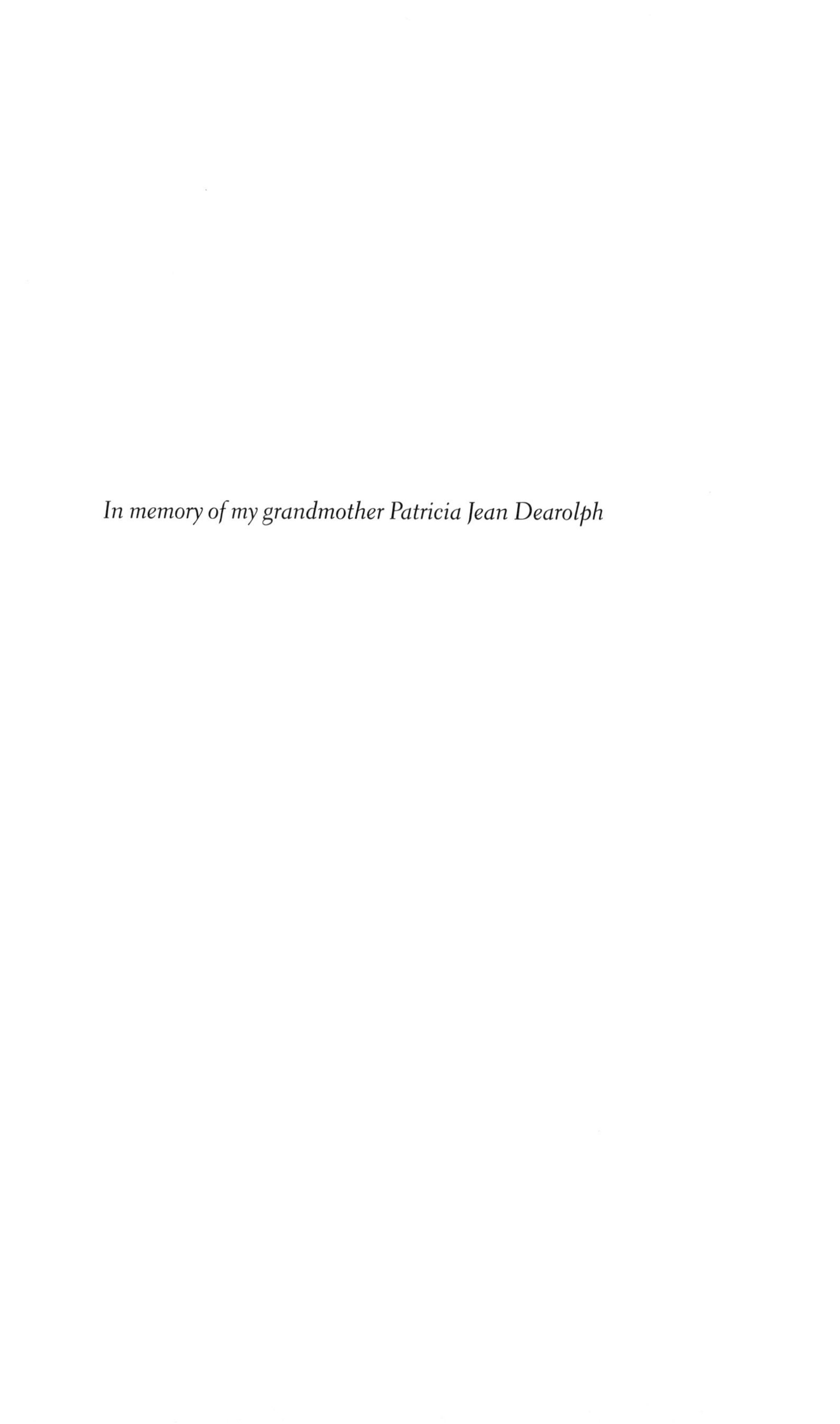

In memory of my grandmother Patricia Jean Dearolph

Contents

Acknowledgments

The process of researching, writing, and revising this book has spanned many life transitions, and I would like to thank the numerous colleagues, family, and friends who have supported me over the years. I'll start by thanking the subjects of the book, the female stars of 1930s Hollywood. Through my journey as graduate student to archivist to professor, my enthusiasm for old Hollywood and its stars has never faltered. Indeed, these women, their films, and their legacy motivated me to forge ahead with this project to its close. To paraphrase Kay Francis and Herbert Marshall in Ernst Lubitsch's *Trouble in Paradise*, it has been glorious, and I feel so fortunate to have written a book on subjects that continue to inspire me.

This book truly began over a decade ago in Vivian Sobchack's historiography seminar at UCLA's Cinema and Media Studies Program, where it became my dissertation. I would like to offer my deepest gratitude to Vivian, who graciously served as the chair of my dissertation committee and taught me so much about critical thinking and writing. I am also thankful for her continued counsel and support. And most of all, she has never failed to appreciate my enthusiasm for film history, the archive, and old Hollywood glamour.

The other members of my committee—Janet Bergstrom, John Caldwell, Kathleen McHugh, and Eric Smoodin—were equally important resources, as were the other professors I studied with at UCLA: Steve Ricci, Denise Mann, Chris Horak, Steve Mamber, and Chon Noriega. In particular, I owe much to Janet Bergstrom's continued mentorship and support, particularly by recognizing and cultivating my primary research skills in the archives. I have enjoyed discussing our mutual admiration for 1930s Hollywood films and having the opportunity to present portions of the book through its long gestation in her graduate seminars at UCLA. John Caldwell has supported my various Society for Cinema and Media Studies conference presentations that featured my book research, while Kathleen McHugh's comments on my dissertation became the initial framework for the book version. Likewise, Eric Smoodin has been a steadfast champion of the project and always envisioned it as a book. Not only has Eric lent his vast knowledge of American cinema in the 1930s to the book, but also his editorial skills. His tutelage from the book proposal to peer reviews to the final writing stages has been tremendously helpful, and I am most grateful for his time and encouragement.

This book also benefited from the insightful feedback of my fellow UCLA graduate student colleagues over the years. My PhD cohort offered excellent suggestions, with a special round of thanks to Chiara Ferrari, Ali Hoffman-Han, Paul Malcolm, and Sachiko Mizuno, while Erica Bochanty-Aguero, Steve Charbonneau, Dawn Fratini, Ross Melnick, Jen Moorman, Mirasol Riojas, Mary Samuelson, Sharon Sharp, and Maya Smukler all listened patiently to my new discoveries, provided astute feedback, and reassured me in moments of frustration. I am also indebted to the research funding that I received at UCLA, including the Summer Research Mentorship Grant, the Dissertation Year Fellowship, the School of Theater, Film and Television Departmental Awards, and the Center for the Study of Women travel grants and dissertation merit awards.

I also acknowledge the inspiration from the professors I studied with as an undergraduate at the University of Florida. Marsha Bryant, Scott Nygren, Maureen Turim, Robert Ray, Stephanie Smith, and Mary Watt all influenced my career trajectory, and I am grateful for the potential they saw in me to pursue scholarly research and writing.

I would also like to thank my faculty colleagues and mentors in the Dodge College of Film and Media Arts at Chapman University, in particular my dean, Bob Bassett, and associate dean, Michael Kowalski, both of whom have provided funding for me to attend important conferences to present my research and to support the writing of the book, and Professor Paul Seydor, for his sustained confidence and reassurance at pivotal moments. Two Chapman Scholarly and Creative Faculty grants have contributed to the book's completion, as well as a Faculty Excellence award. My colleagues Nam Lee, Silvia Kratzer, Federico Pacchioni, Sally Rubin, and Jonathan Wysocki have all provided support as I worked on this project in the years since I joined the faculty. I have the pleasure of teaching a versatile body of students in the Dodge College, from filmmakers to film studies students, undergraduate and graduate students. I thank them for their genuine interest in my work and for all of the inspired film history discussions in our classes that have influenced the book. Thank you to Skylar Harrison, who helped with formatting at a critical phase.

I owe a great debt to the archivists and librarians of the archival collections where I conducted the primary research that was so vital to this book. At the USC Warner Bros. Archives, several curators have guided my research over the years. Haden Guest introduced me to the treasure chest of contracts and legal files of the vast Warner collection in 2004–2005, while I had the pleasure to work alongside Sandra Joy Lee Aguilar in the archive in 2007–2008. After my departure, she and Jonathan Auxier assisted me with important follow-up questions, both in the archive and through email. Ned Comstock of the USC Cinematic Arts Library Special Collections uncovered an array of archival resources that otherwise would have remained unknown to me, while Steve Hanson and Sandra Garcia-Meyers assisted me with accessing and utilizing the stills collection. The UCLA Performing Arts Special Collections provided access to the RKO collection, and I also thank Twentieth Century Fox for giving me permission to examine key legal files from the 1930s. Thanks to Diana King of the UCLA Arts Library for helping me track down some esoteric fan magazines in their collections, and to Mark Quigley for making it possible to view all of the hard-to-see films of my study at the UCLA Archival and Research Study Center. I would also like to thank Barbara Hall and Jenny Romero of the Special Collections at the Margaret Herrick Library, Academy of Motion Picture Arts and Sciences, for all the files they found for me in their wondrous collections, and Faye Thompson for guiding me through the extensive photographic archive. Steve Wilson of the Harry Ransom Center at the University of Texas at Austin kindly answered my detailed emails and assisted me with two research visits to examine the Myron and David Selznick collections that provided pertinent evidence for this book. And thanks to Colleen Montgomery for generously sharing her time to peruse stills on my behalf in the Selznick files. I also thank Rick Jewell for providing some clarifying figures from his extensive research on RKO as well as sharing his expertise on studio-era Hollywood. Deane Albright graciously shared his finance knowledge and accounting skills by helping me fully comprehend the US tax codes of the 1930s and 1940s, and assess the rate of inflation for some star salaries in the book.

Additionally, I am grateful to Edward Branigan, Philip Drake, Jennifer Holt, Eric Hoyt, Paul McDonald, Alisa Perren, Anne Helen Petersen, Janet Walker, and Chuck Wolfe for their continual interest and support. My book has benefited from their multifaceted models of scholarship.

Thanks especially to Cathy Jurca, who took the time to read my manuscript and give constructive suggestions that strengthened it in time for a critical peer review. I would also like to thank Tom Kemper, who has read several versions of this book and seen the project mature over the years. Our stimulating conversations together about savvy agents and stars in 1930s Hollywood reaffirmed my confidence in the integrity of the project. I thank Shannon Kelley Gould for her writing empathy and for providing stamina in the final revision phases. Judy Albright and Noa Bolozky were constant cheerleaders during this project. And a huge thank-you is owed to Melissa Kitchell, my closest friend for over twenty years, who has been a trusted ally throughout the entire process.

The University of Texas Press has tirelessly nurtured this book. Jim Burr has been a kind and generous editor as well as a staunch supporter, and I thank him for guiding me through the editing and review process. I am most indebted to the tutelage of my series editor, Tom Schatz, whose unfaltering support through the book's drafting and revision ensured its completion. It has been a great honor and good fortune to work closely with him on this book, and I extend my deepest gratitude for his counsel, patience, and time. This book has benefited significantly from his model of diligent and original scholarship as well as his enthusiastic expertise of studio-era Hollywood and astute editing. I also appreciate the input from the outside reviewers and their productive suggestions that improved the manuscript as a whole.

Anitra Grisales carefully copyedited this manuscript twice and helped me articulate key points in the book. I thank her for her efforts and prompt responses to my emails when I needed clarification and reassurance. Thank you as well to Dan Reynolds and Nicole Starosielski, who read early drafts of the manuscript and gave me valuable advice. And I owe sincere thanks to my good friend and colleague Rebecca Prime. Our shared passion for primary research spawned many inspiring conversations for the project, and she helped me weather the challenging moments of this book's long journey by encouraging me to soldier on. She is an excellent writer and generously lent her skills to this book with a last round of copyediting.

Special thanks must go to my parents, Jim and Dianne, who have always believed in my ability and in me, nurtured my love of learning, and provided extensive support over the years. They taught me two crucial skills that I utilized for the book: to always give your best effort and to follow through on your commitments. I send my love and gratitude to my siblings, Scott and Cady, and my sister-in-law, Emily, all of whom have cheered me on throughout the years, and to my grandfather David

Dearolph. Perhaps the most significant influence in fostering my passion for learning, writing, and old Hollywood was my maternal grandmother, Patricia Jean Dearolph. When I was a child, her gifts of film history books, star biographies, and movie memorabilia, as well as trips to the libraries and video stores, left an indelible mark on me. She always encouraged my aspirations to be a writer. This book is dedicated to her memory.

Finally, I feel the deepest heartfelt gratitude to Michael Albright, who has personally watched this book progress, from beginning to end. He has attentively listened to my ideas, contributed his intellectual input to the project, redesigned my workspace for optimal ergonomics, and bolstered my stamina with much needed emotional and moral support at every phase. He has stood by me patiently as I labored through the revisions and stepped in with valuable feedback in the final stage. Throughout this entire process, his confidence in me never faltered. Now that the book is finished, I look forward to our future together.

Independent Stardom

Introduction

INDEPENDENT STARDOM IS BORN

By the late 1930s, the actress Carole Lombard had achieved A-list film stardom through what appeared to be an unconventional path in the Hollywood studio system: freelancing. As a freelancer or "free agent" (in the industry parlance of the time), Lombard chose her own film projects and negotiated individual deals with multiple studios. Moreover, her freelance contracts contained numerous provisions that guaranteed her creative control over her career and star image.[1] She retained the power to choose the director, cinematographer, costar, producer, screenwriter, story, costume designer, makeup artist, hairstylist, and even her publicist. She also negotiated a "no loan-out" clause, meaning the studio could not outsource her contract to another studio.

In addition to ensuring that Lombard was one of the highest paid actors of the period, these provisions enabled her to reach the apex of her career. She cemented her reputation as Hollywood's top comedienne in *Nothing Sacred* and *True Confession* (both released in 1937, the first directed by William Wellman and the latter by Wesley Ruggles) while also establishing her ability as a dramatic actress in *Made for Each Other* (John Cromwell, 1939). All of these films were part of three-picture deals that she negotiated concurrently with Paramount Pictures and Selznick International Pictures (SIP). By the time she negotiated with RKO Radio Pictures in 1939 for another freelance deal, Lombard not only earned $100,000 per film but also got a cut of her film's box-office profits. Reflecting her unusual status within the industry, Lombard's high earnings and professional accomplishments appeared to generate as much public interest as her love affair with Clark Gable (who became her second husband). Indeed, in 1939, the popular film fan magazine *Photoplay* extolled the actress's freelance achievements before her personal life, noting that Lombard "freelances, she draws approximately one hundred thousand dollars per picture, plus profit percentage. Last year her income totaled nearly half a million, and, in addition, Hollywood's most box-office screen lover [Gable] is also [the] number one man in her life."[2]

Lombard was in the vanguard yet again when in 1940 she and her agent, Myron Selznick, crafted a "contract like no other" with RKO that included a new profit-participation deal.[3] For her last two films in this agreement, the actress relinquished her $100,000 flat-rate fee in exchange for a $25,000 advance *against* her projected $150,000 interest in the film distributor's gross, which equated to instant earnings for the actress as soon as these films were released.[4] This "percentage deal" contract, personally negotiated by Selznick and RKO president George Schaefer, also included a number of specific terms such as story approval and a billing clause that she could only costar with an established leading man; it specifically designated the fourth picture as a "Lombard-Hitchcock" collaboration (*Mr. and Mrs. Smith* in 1941, the only Hollywood comedy directed by Alfred Hitchcock).

Perhaps the most interesting aspect of Lombard's new percentage deal was how it safeguarded the actress's gross earnings from Hollywood's monopolistic distribution and exhibition practices. Her 10 percent share included earnings from both domestic and foreign box-office receipts, including any specialty (i.e., higher-priced) road-show screenings at RKO theaters, and an arbitrated share of the studio block-booking packages of her films.[5] Her renegotiation proved to be a worthwhile financial move, with her total earnings amounting to approximately $133,000 for *Mr. and Mrs. Smith* and $91,000 for *They Knew What They Wanted* (Garson Kanin, 1940), roughly the equivalent of her usual $100,000 flat fee.[6] In addition, these earnings were taxed at the capital gains rate of 25 percent versus the 77 percent tax rate for personal income at the time. Indeed, Lombard's keen apprehension of industry know-how extended to production as well as contract negotiations. Kanin called her "the best producer in the business since Irving Thalberg." He also explained, "She has great intuition for which writer to get on a script. She knows what kind of story to do and can give pointers to its structure. And she's a great saleswoman. She has one of the best agents in the business but she really does not need one. She makes her own deals and does as well as anyone could."[7]

Lombard's remarkable career, and the exceptional degree of control she exerted over it, runs counter to conventional narratives of the Hollywood studio system, which depict film stars as studio property and de facto indentured servants. It also challenges the commonly accepted periodization that locates the development of Hollywood talent freelancing within the postwar era by emphasizing two key events: the California Supreme Court's 1944 "De Havilland Law,"[8] which ruled in favor of actress Olivia de Havilland in her suit to end her contract with Warner Bros.; and the innovative percentage deal that Lew Wasserman negotiated for actor James Stewart for *Winchester '73* (Anthony Mann, 1950).

Carole Lombard was far from alone in her successful freelance labor practices; indeed, she was part of an overlooked but significant trend of female independent stardom in 1930s Hollywood. Constance Bennett, Clara Bow, Claudette Colbert, Irene Dunne, Janet Gaynor, Katharine Hepburn, and Miriam Hopkins all participated in "net"-only profit-sharing deals similar to the one that would make headlines for Stewart fifteen years later, earning a percentage of their films' *overall* gross profits after the initial production costs had been recouped.

Independent stardom is the term I use to describe this alternative freelance path in 1930s Hollywood. This not only resulted in better salaries for these actresses, but also garnered them more control over their careers. In addition to the actresses mentioned above, Ruth Chatterton, Dolores del Río, Ann Harding, Ida Lupino, and Barbara Stanwyck all achieved varying levels of economic and professional independence through their active negotiations with film corporations over the course of the 1930s and, in some cases, into the 1940s. To minimize the risks of freelancing (giving up the job security of a long-term studio contract, along with the status conferred by association with a major studio), these women employed a number of strategies. They worked with prominent, prestigious, independent producers such as David O. Selznick and Samuel Goldwyn, as well as with the shrewd talent agents Myron Selznick and Charles Feldman; they remade their on-screen images by personally choosing to "off-cast" themselves in new and different leading roles; and they made multiple pictures at a time for a variety of studios.

The omission of these women from the narratives of Hollywood history is striking and raises important questions in regard to film historiography and American cinema. The phenomenon of female independent stardom in pre–World War II Hollywood presents a rich field of investigation for several reasons. Significantly, it offers scholars the opportunity to rethink the experience of star "serfdom" in the Hollywood studio system as a process of collaboration and negotiation with producers and major studios that afforded women tremendous professional opportunities. It likewise proves compelling from the perspective of film historiography, as it constructs an alternative experience of Hollywood, principally in regard to gender and contract-labor conditions. These were business-savvy women who challenged the hierarchical and paternalistic structure of the film industry. They took a proactive role in shaping their careers through their freelance labor practices, thereby dynamically participating in what Thomas Schatz has called (quoting André Bazin) the "genius" of the studio system: its fusion of art, human labor, and commerce on a massive scale.[9] What is particularly striking about these female stars, however, is that they worked independently during a time when studio heads and producers presumably controlled and manipulated stardom as part of their oligopolistic business practices. Consequently, independent stardom changes the way in which we think about stardom, gender, and power dynamics in 1930s Hollywood, and calls for a new perspective that recognizes the place of women and their pioneering freelancing in American cinema and US labor history.

This book's methodology mobilizes a broad spectrum of archival research—studio contracts and legal documents, industry trades, newspapers, and fan magazines—to unearth the story of independent stardom in Hollywood. I make extensive use of contracts and studio memos pertaining to stars' film contracts and their negotiations with agents, studio executives, and producers to attain them. The financial nomenclature of contracts and studio legalese tends to be relegated to footnotes in most studies on stardom and classic Hollywood, but here they are foregrounded as crucial to our understanding of the contractual, cultural, and legal terms of independent stardom. This multifaceted archival approach also raises the issue of access to studio archives as they relate to questions of film historiography, specifically which studios' historical legal and production materials are available for this kind of research. In this regard, of the major Hollywood studios, the Warner Bros. Archives (WBA) at the University of Southern California is the only accessible archive, housing the production, distribution, and exhibition records that document the activities of a vertically integrated studio.[10] It should come as no surprise, then, that a great deal of scholarly work on studio-era stardom focuses on Warner Bros. stars—especially James Cagney, Bette Davis, and Olivia de Havilland.[11] Moreover, these stars' very public battles with the studio over its oppressive suspension policy and binding long-term contracts generated a great deal of press in the industry trade magazines, *Variety* and the *Hollywood Reporter*, both of which are readily available digitally or on microfilm. Given this visibility and ease of access, it is not surprising that these events have been well documented.[12] However, as Tom Kemper notes in *Hidden Talent*, his insightful study of talent agents, these three Warner Bros. stars' careers "betray poor management, a dimension that is generally elided in most histories on classical Hollywood."[13] Thus, they are far from exemplary cases, making the attention they receive in most film histories somewhat misleading.

Among my goals in *Independent Stardom* is to cast the widest net possible in terms of accessing archival studio collections that contain substantial contracts, legal records, studio memos, or payroll cards using readily available collections as well as those that are less utilized or incomplete. Looking at a variety of stars (employed at or by various studios) as case studies across a range of primary sources contributes to what Eric Smoodin calls the "textuality of the historical field" by supplying "new subjects and modes of historical inquiry."[14] In addition to WBA, this study makes use of the legal files of the Twentieth Century-Fox Collection;[15] the employee payroll cards of the RKO Radio Pictures, Inc., Studio Collection (1922–1952) housed at the UCLA Performing Arts Special Collections; and the legal files and studio memos from the David O. Selznick Collection (which also contains documents from his business partner Jock Whitney and his brother, talent agent Myron Selznick) at the Harry Ransom Center at the University of Texas at Austin. The Margaret Herrick Library houses some MGM legal department records as well as Paramount production materials, select contract summaries, and an impressive array of popular fan magazines from the 1930s, while the United Artists Collection at the Wisconsin Center for Film and Theater Research contains the company's corporate records from its founding in 1919 until the early 1950s.[16] The USC Cinematic Arts Library's Archives of Performing Arts contain a sampling of records from MGM, Universal, and Twentieth Century Fox.[17] The consultation of a wide array of primary materials enables us to recast the Hollywood star story from one of servitude to free agency.[18] *Independent Stardom*'s "rewriting" of American film history seeks to interrogate past historical assumptions and create a nuanced understanding of how independent stardom functioned in the studio system and provided an opportunity for female empowerment in Hollywood.

RECASTING HOLLYWOOD INDEPENDENCE

In addition to establishing the historical significance of the overlooked phenomenon of independent stardom, this book also asks the crucial question of why this "traditional" historical narrative has dominated. To begin to answer this question, we need to revisit the two celebrated markers of star independence in studio-era Hollywood: Olivia de Havilland's legal victory over Warner Bros., and James Stewart's profit-sharing deal at Universal. These events have been misrepresented in histories of American cinema as the initial flashpoints of freelance Hollywood, when in actuality they are the culmination of the self-determining actions and negotiations of women in the 1930s. Indeed the California Supreme Court verdict that became known as the "De Havilland Law" signified an important victory for top stars and a substantial setback for film corporations, as studios could no longer prevent an artist from "sitting out" a contract to become a free agent.[19] Nor did stars have to resort to lengthy court battles as the most viable way to win control over their careers at the expense of their screen exposure. (De Havilland herself remained off-screen for nearly three years while her case went all the way to the California Supreme Court.)

Likewise, female independent stardom in the 1930s preceded what has often been lauded as the pivotal achievement of actor independence in studio-era Hollywood: the deal-making tactics of James Stewart and Lew Wasserman, his maverick agent.[20] In 1950 Wasserman negotiated a lucrative freelance deal with Universal Studios for the actor to make *Winchester '73*, winning him a sizable percentage of the film's box-office earnings. We might ask why this is considered the first significant instance of profit sharing among Hollywood stars given the fact that numerous prominent female stars had freelanced and negotiated for a percentage of their films' profits a decade earlier.

To understand this lapse in American film history, we must juxtapose the contractual terms of Stewart's deal with those of the top female stars in the 1930s. What made Stewart's agreement so remarkable is the exceptionally large salary that he earned from his 50 percent cut of the net profits from his Universal films *Winchester '73* and *Harvey* (Henry Koster, 1950), which amounted to more than $600,000.[21] This deal enabled the actor to reduce his exorbitant personal income tax, as his percentage was taxed at the much lower capital gains rate; this strategy also protected Universal from additional financial risk by not having to supply the actor's salary up front, ahead of the production.[22] The generally accepted ramifications of Stewart's deal in 1950 are that it generated the most lavish sum of money for a freelance actor's profit-sharing agreement, signified the demise of long-term contracts for talent, and substantially altered talent salary negotiations in Hollywood. However, while we should not dismiss the significance of Stewart's *Winchester '73* deal as a reflection of postwar star muscle, it did not garner major headlines in the industry trades, nor did it send shockwaves around the film industry in 1950.[23] Its overstated importance seems more of a manufactured publicity story engineered by the legend of postwar, agency-driven Hollywood rather than one of historical actuality.

In fact, such deals had been a long-standing practice for powerful stars as far back as 1919, when Charles Chaplin, Douglas Fairbanks, Mary Pickford, and D. W. Griffith all self-produced and distributed their films after forming their own studio, United Artists (UA), as an alternative to the emerging, vertically integrated studio-system model.[24] This move guaranteed that any profits from their films would go directly to them. Even after the major studios solidified their monopolistic control over Hollywood filmmaking after the transition to sound in the late 1920s, there remained autonomous avenues in the star system. For instance, upon their arrival in Hollywood, the soon-to-be screen stars Irene Dunne and Barbara Stanwyck (both Broadway actresses) rejected long-term contracts with major studios. Stanwyck worked at an array of studios from the very beginning of her career (UA, Columbia, and Warner Bros.), while Dunne negotiated a two-year contract with RKO that retained her right to return to New York to act in plays between film productions.

Independent Stardom's historiographical intervention also extends to star studies and our understanding of Hollywood stardom. As Paul McDonald notes, there has been a tendency in academic star studies to separate the stars' images from the film industry that employs and sustains their labor.[25] While there is significant literature on individual stars in relation to their screen performances and their cultural images (most prominently, Richard Dyer's seminal text *Stars*), these works tend to eschew issues of contract labor—in particular, freelancing—and how a star's individual agency impacted her career and public persona.[26] Similarly, most studies of screen actors' labor in the 1930s, particularly Danae Clark's *Negotiating Hollywood*, emphasize collective-bargaining labor organizations like the Screen Actors Guild (SAG) and focus less on the efforts of individual stars and the strides they made toward professional independence in Hollywood, in addition to omitting any discussion of gender.[27] The studies that do focus on individual stars and their place in the industry tend to concentrate primarily on their failed attempts to get out of their seven-year standard contracts. By default, these historical accounts have depicted Hollywood as an all-powerful "grand design" business structure that dwarfed the individual efforts of stars to attain agency within the studio system.[28]

Furthermore, these works do not fully consider the impact that freelance women had on the star system during the 1930s. In this regard, the phenomenon of independent stardom and the opportunities it afforded women in Hollywood extends the vibrant discourse of feminist film historiography in its focus on the underemphasized achievements of women as editors, directors, screenwriters, and producers during the 1910s and '20s.[29] Furthermore, this vein of scholarship also underscores the importance of primary research in constructing these histories, including written memoirs, fan magazines, audience studies, advertisements, and screenplays. Yet these studies tend to stop short of examining women's contributions to Hollywood cinema during the sound era and beyond, after the film industry became a big-business enterprise. On this point, Karen Ward Mahar, in her book *Women Filmmakers in Early Hollywood*, contends that by the mid-1920s female star power had "diminished, the independent movement had ended, and the gendered studio emerged" to produce a thoroughly masculinized film industry that minimized women's opportunities for the creative crafts behind the camera.[30] However, they were a mainstay *in front* of the camera in the following decade of sound cinema, when female stars truly did rule the Hollywood screen as top box-office attractions.[31] Thus, if we probe further and go beyond the screen to examine the behind-the-scenes negotiations, we find that star autonomy remained intact for some women in the 1930s. In many ways, *Independent Stardom* picks up where Mahar's book leaves off; the "independent movement" had not ended, nor had the "gendered studio" snuffed out female autonomy in Hollywood, especially if we examine the occupation most available to women during this time: acting/stardom.[32] As *Independent Stardom* argues, women's off-screen agency persisted in the 1930s, especially because of the freelance career choices that enhanced their professional opportunities, all of which are illuminated in the studio contracts and legal documents examined in this book.

STARRING IN A DIFFERENT STORY

Independent Stardom delves deeper into the careers, depictions of stardom, and audience fascination with these freelance actresses of the 1930s. *Professional agency* is the phrase I use to refer to how these stars used the legal terms of their labor as actors and their unique creative public personae—their "celebrity" images—to attain increased professional visibility in the Hollywood film industry. They did this by bargaining with major studio executives and producers more on their own terms. Together with their contract labor and screen images, their independent stardom engendered a new kind of image (and commodity) in the Hollywood market: the female free agent.

Along these lines, *Independent Stardom* also explores the plausible reasons as to why women were the ones to dominate independent stardom at first. Chapter 1 considers the industry milieu of 1930s Hollywood to highlight how female stars negotiated the independent avenues made available to them in the studio system. At the time, the industry presumed that women moviegoers made up the overwhelming majority of the motion picture audience in the 1930s; as a result, films were tailored to female consumers and thus gave privileged status to female actors. Likewise, as chapter 2 underscores, women outnumbered their male star counterparts in the freelance realm, thereby making independent stardom in studio-era Hollywood truly a female phenomenon. This is illustrated by the remarkable freelance career trajectories of key female stars over the course of the 1930s, which can be traced in the terms of their individual contracts. Janet Gaynor, Miriam Hopkins, and Carole Lombard each began as studio employees who had long-term option contracts by 1930, but they all decided against re-signing long-term studio contracts in order to become free agents from the mid-1930s onward.[33] In contrast, Constance Bennett, Irene Dunne, and Barbara Stanwyck signed limited, non-option contracts beginning in 1930 and were freelancing at several studios by the middle of the decade.

Independence, however, meant different things for different women. In this regard, *Independent Stardom* considers the flipside of independence in the studio system, as freelancing was not necessarily the ideal choice for working Hollywood women. Indeed, the combination of steady employment and a dependable weekly salary guaranteed by a long-term studio contract was a desirable option to many aspiring actors during the 1930s. (In fact, the major studios employed approximately 500 actors on such contracts.) While the top Hollywood talent bracket had the discretion and leverage to choose freelance employment over a long-term contract, most did not have this option. Chapter 2, then, also considers the reverse experience of Hollywood freelancing through the case studies of the Chinese-American actress Anna May Wong and Mexican actress Lupe Vélez. While freelance labor was liberating for Anglo A-list stars, actresses of color often experienced an imposed independence that was not necessarily their ambition or personal preference, but was instead determined by Hollywood's institutionalized discriminatory business practices. Put simply, free agency was a hindrance, rather than an advantage, to their film careers.

But for those women who benefited from freelancing, independent stardom represented the opportunity to take ownership of their off-screen images as well, mainly through advertising campaigns, film fan magazines, and studio publicity, as well as in national newspapers and magazines. In this way, they effectively became architects of their images by correlating their contractual agency with their creative-image commodity. This is the focus of chapter 3, which analyzes how these texts depict a synergy between these women's careers and their star personae by reporting on their freelance contracts alongside the more traditionally "feminine" aspects of each star's career—that is, glamour and romance. Thus, the fan and popular press characterized these Hollywood women and their impressive careers as an average experience for the modern working American woman in the 1930s. I argue that these women's self-promotion of their freelance personae in the popular press reveals how this type of labor became a significant characteristic of their star celebrity that, in turn, further "sold" them to their fans.

Independent Stardom reveals the challenges, merits, and stakes of independence that female stars experienced in 1930s Hollywood. Ultimately, the book aspires to dispel the notion that there was no true agency available to working women in studio-era Hollywood. In fact, this was quite the contrary for a cadre of A-list actresses in the 1930s.

ONE

1930s Hollywood

THE GOLDEN AGE FOR TALENT

In 1937, the *San Francisco Chronicle* observed the talent boom in the US film industry, noting that in this "golden age for talent . . . major studios and independent operations are in frantic competition, signing every available name and possibility."[1] The newspaper also highlighted the growing number of freelance actors who "prefer to make their money a little less consistently" in order to "retain the right of approval of roles, something that is denied them when they are under contract" to a studio.[2] The article went on to discuss the growing importance of the talent agents who crafted freelancers' deals and the independent producers (and major studios) who employed them. In sum, the *Chronicle* identified several factors of the 1930s star system that had propelled the move toward independent stardom: the power of stars in the film industry, the malleable nature of the motion picture talent contract, the mediation of talent agents, and the growing number of independent producers. These four facets of Hollywood stardom provided the impetus for greater creative freedom and career agency in the 1930s studio system.

Although the long-term studio contract remained a cornerstone of the industry star system that favored the producer over the artist, the contract could be negotiated to ensure increased creative control and financial reward for stars through special provisions. In this regard, the experiences of Ruth Chatterton, Claudette Colbert, and others are telling. Furthermore, savvy stars and their agents mobilized loan-outs to score new roles at different studios, thereby "recasting" their personae and bolstering their star agency (here again Colbert was key, as were Bette Davis and Carole Lombard). Along these lines, A-list stars utilized the top talent agents Myron Selznick and Charles Feldman as third-party negotiators to deal directly with studio bosses to attain these provisions. Finally, ambitious stars such as Barbara Stanwyck sought out projects apart from the dominant major studios by working with creative, risk-taking independent producers such as Samuel Goldwyn and David O. Selznick, who landed them in prestigious productions that enhanced their critical reputations and their stardom. These alternatives were distributed by United Artists (UA), the studio dedicated to putting out creative, independent productions in the 1930s. By analyzing these four attributes of independent stardom that emerged over the course of the decade, we can discern how freelancing became a viable alternative for A-list talent during this period, thereby challenging the presumed "standard" for contracting with the major studios in the 1930s.

With women dominating the Hollywood star system in the 1930s, there was also an on-screen "fascination with female power," as Sarah Berry has noted.[3] This, I argue, correlates with the box-office power and off-screen agency of freelance female stars that emerged during the studio era. Freelance stars such as Constance Bennett, Miriam Hopkins, and Barbara Stanwyck, among others, portrayed ambitious gold diggers in films such as *The Easiest Way* (Jack Conway, 1931); working women (in both the public and private sphere) in films such as *Baby Face* (Alfred Green, 1933); and sexually adventurous social climbers in films such as *Design for Living* (Ernst Lubitsch, 1933). They then mobilized their star power to bargain for more creative incentives in their contracts and were in the unique position to do so because of the prominence of female stars in 1930s Hollywood. This chapter will show how these women flourished in the studio system, both on- and off-screen across the decade, pioneering the path toward independent stardom.

WOMEN RULE HOLLYWOOD

With the advent of sound cinema, Hollywood wooed several Broadway actresses to the screen—including future freelance stars Irene Dunne, Ann Harding, Barbara Stanwyck, and Miriam Hopkins—and incorporated the stage's focus on female heroines into film narratives in an effort to cater to women audiences.[4] Accordingly, popular female-oriented film genres prominently featured female protagonists in 1930s Hollywood. Of particular interest was the "woman's film," which accounted for more than a quarter of the movies in *Film Daily* exhibitor polls as well as *Variety*'s top-grossing films lists, particularly in the early 1930s. "The woman's film" typically refers to "a type of motion picture that revolves around an adult female protagonist and is designed to appeal mostly to a female audience"; it covers a range of genres, including fallen-woman films, romantic comedies and dramas, Cinderella romances, and gold-digger and working-woman stories.[5]

First introduced as a production trend in the 1910s to bring women into the theaters, the woman's film was enriched by the transition to sound cinema and flourished in 1930s Hollywood. *Anna Christie* (Clarence Brown, 1930), Greta Garbo's sound debut; *Daddy Long Legs* (Alfred Santell, 1931) starring Janet Gaynor; *Back Street* (John Stahl, 1932) with Irene Dunne; and the female-dominant cast of *Little Women* (George Cukor, 1933), headlined by Katharine Hepburn, are films that garnered high financial returns. Moreover, 50 percent of the *Motion Picture Herald*'s annual "10 Top Box Office Stars" throughout the decade were women (including Marie Dressler, Norma Shearer, Bette Davis, Myrna Loy, Claudette Colbert, Joan Crawford, Janet Gaynor, Greta Garbo, Shirley Temple, and others).[6] In July 1936, the freelance female stars Irene Dunne, Carole Lombard, and Barbara Stanwyck also ranked among exhibitor polls as "The Fifty Best Money Stars," according to the *Hollywood Reporter*.[7]

Whether women did, in fact, make up the majority of film audiences in the 1930s is impossible to ascertain, but it is quite clear that Hollywood assumed that women were its primary and most financially lucrative market.[8] As Melvyn Stokes has observed in his study of film audiences of the 1920s–1930s, the male executives of the film industry presumed that for a film "to be profitable, it had to appeal mainly to women."[9] This assumption can be traced back to both the fan and trade press in Hollywood; for instance, in 1924 the fan magazine *Photoplay* estimated the female audience to be 75 percent, and in 1927 the exhibitor trade journal *Motion Picture World* projected the proportion of women even higher, at 83 percent.[10] Consequently, this opinion had "a profound effect on the way that American cinema developed during the 1920s and 1930s" in that it targeted a female audience.[11]

Anecdotal evidence from both the industry trade press and fan magazines reaffirms this industry assumption of a female-dominant film audience. For instance, a *Variety* article from June 16, 1931 ascribed the rise in sordid themes in films that featured "fallen" women and gold diggers—at their most popular in the early 1930s—to female moviegoers, claiming "Dirt Craze Due to Women."[12] Explaining that women made up the majority of film audiences, *Variety* claimed, "Women are responsible for the ever-increasing public taste in sensationalism and sexy stuff. Women who make up the bulk of the picture audiences are also the majority of readers of tabloids, scandal sheets, flashy magazines and erotic books."[13] Producer Samuel Goldwyn also noted the importance of the female audience to the film industry and film fan magazines in his March 1935 article, "Women Rule Hollywood," in *New Movie Magazine*. The independent producer reasoned that it would be "professional suicide" to dismiss the preferences of women in motion pictures, especially given that, by his estimate, the average film audience was "*more than 70 percent feminine*."[14] The producer stressed that women, much more than men, also shaped the star system by patronizing films headlined by female stars:

> It is women who are largely responsible for the so-called "star system" in the studios. They are much more inclined than men to become dyed-in-the-wool fans of the sort who idolize their favorite screen personalities, and flock to see the pictures made by those stars. . . . Such fans are the backbone of the motion picture industry. . . . Not only "matinee idols" of the masculine persuasion but almost all outstanding feminine stars owe their stardom to women in the audience. Women, even more eagerly than men, flock to the screen's beautiful women.[15]

The producer identified Norma Shearer, Gloria Swanson, Greta Garbo, and Joan Crawford as the most popular "woman's [*sic*] stars" that female audiences supported through their movie patronage; indeed, they were some of the industry's most coveted stars. Goldwyn's article elucidates the presumed importance of the female audience that influenced industry practices in the 1930s. Representing that point of view, these articles from *Variety* and *New Movie Magazine* explicitly attest to how Hollywood in this period designed, produced, and marketed films with women in mind. They also demonstrate how a sustained demand for female talent helped independent stardom thrive for female stars as a viable career option. At its zenith during the 1930s, the star system sustained their independent careers as a key component of the film industry.

NOT-SO-EXCLUSIVE AFFILIATIONS

The female-driven star system thus became the economic underpinning of the larger industrial apparatus of Hollywood during the classical era, and as the major studios consolidated their monopoly over the American film industry after the transition to sound cinema.[16] As Paul McDonald and Janet Staiger note, Hollywood's capitalist business structure organized its labor around the "principles of specialization and hierarchal power," and stars were part of this system as the elite class of Hollywood laborers.[17] The Hollywood business practice of vertical integration—in which the major studios produced, distributed, and exhibited their films—operated under the assumption that actors were the industry's currency, and A-class productions were designed around a particular star's persona.[18] For example, MGM would shape a film entirely around Garbo's screen image, from story (often historical melodramas like *Anna Karenina* [Clarence Brown, 1935] and *Camille* [George Cukor, 1936]), to wardrobe (made for the actress specifically by studio designer Adrian), to crew and talent (Garbo worked exclusively with cinematographer William Daniels). Likewise, in distribution, the studios marketed each film around a star, and often her image and name dominated the publicity campaigns. Finally, at the exhibition level, film fans and spectators helped fund stars' extravagant salaries and validated the star system by paying the ticket price. These star vehicles also sustained the studios' block-booking practices in that theater owners accepted a year's supply of pictures unseen (much of them B movies with lower production values) in order to secure the A-class films with big stars.

The long-term option contract also allowed a studio to develop and promote a stable of stars who epitomized the company's signature style as a visual trademark. Studio-branded stars of stature included Errol Flynn and Bette Davis at Warner Bros.; Garbo, Joan Crawford, and Clark Gable at MGM; Claudette Colbert and Gary Cooper at Paramount; Shirley Temple and Tyrone Power at Twentieth Century-Fox; and Katharine Hepburn, Fred Astaire, and Ginger Rogers at RKO.

From its inception, the talent contract was a pliable document, as the standard actor's agreement was generally structured on a long-term basis, by renewal, and determined by the studio. In the 1920s, the typical Hollywood studio contract for actors was limited to a five-year term. Then, in August 1931, the California State Senate officially approved a law extending the civil code in regard to personal-service contracts to seven years.[19] While this law clearly applied to the film industry, the bill did not explicitly reference it. The only clue that it pertained to the film industry is in its definition of personal service: "to perform or render service of a special, unique, unusual, extraordinary, or intellectual character, which gives it peculiar value."[20]

This language is reminiscent of the terminology used in studio talent contracts, which define an actor's talent as a unique and invaluable commodity. For example, provision 12 in actor Ronald Colman's 1935 con-

By

SAMUEL GOLDWYN

as told to Eric L. Ergenbright

WOMEN RULE

"WHY do you emphasize romance and glamour and beauty so heavily in your pictures? Why do you invariably favor love stories when there are other human emotions just as suitable for drama as love? Why do you stress emotionalism? Why do you avoid grimness and cruelty and sordidness and all of the other harsh but ever-present aspects of everyday life?"

If I have been asked such questions once, I have had them put to me a thousand times. And the answer is very simple:

Women rule Hollywood!

Any producer who disregards the established preferences of women is committing professional suicide. His pictures may be the product of genius. His actors may have the talent of Bernhardt, his director the finesse of Reinhardt, his scenarist the power of Shakespeare—but, unless the finished picture possesses that elusive quality called "feminine appeal," it is certain to fail at the box office.

I am ready to grant that life can be grim and cruel. In fact in my own experience I have too often found it so. But women are idealists, not realists. They are emotionalists, not analysts. And, since I have no wish to be a professional suicide, I try to produce pictures which will suit their tastes. Like most veteran showmen, my first instinct is to please the women in the audience. Women have always ruled "show business."

The average motion picture theater audience is *more than seventy per cent feminine!* In the average matinee audience, women predominate by an even larger majority. These figures, which are the findings of actual surveys and not haphazard estimates of my own, speak for themselves. Without the steady patronage of women, theaters and studios could not survive.

Still more important in establishing woman's rule over the motion picture industry is the fact that women almost invariably are the arbiters of their families' entertainment. Wives select the shows that their husbands take them to see. Unmarried girls dictate the shows for which their escorts buy tickets. Mothers select the screen entertainment for their children. And, in every case, the picture selected reflects the woman's tastes.

It is the woman who cons the drama page and reads the theatrical advertisements, while her husband, after glancing over the financial section, turns to the sports pages and checks up on his favorite football or baseball team. He knows from experience that his wife regards a motion picture as *her* outing and that she will determine which show they shall see. Show me the husband whose occasional objections have not been overruled in some fashion as this:

"I didn't say one word last Sunday when you wanted to play golf. I think you might at least take me to the show that *I* want to see!"

Naturally, most theater owners and most producers, being convinced from first hand experience that such an argument is irresistible, "slant" their advertising to attract women. Check up on the theater ads in your current newspaper and note how many feature the words "love" or "romance."

"Please the women and they will bring the men to the theater"—that is one of the oldest and most dependable rules for theatrical success.

It is women who are largely responsible for the so-called "star system" in the studios. They are much more inclined than men to become dyed-in-the-wool fans of the sort who idolize their favorite screen personalities, and flock to see the pictures made by those stars without bothering to ask what the pictures' plots may be. Such fans are the very backbone of the motion picture industry. Hollywood produces, each year, approximately 600 feature length films and it is difficult to find that many worthwhile stories. Without the feminine tendency to consider personalities first and plot second, picture making would be far more risky and far less profitable.

Men, no matter how much they enjoy seeing pictures, are by nature, and by training and habit, much more analytical. No matter how brilliant the cast, they are quick to detect and condemn story flaws. Instead of asking, "Who's the star?" they are more apt to demand, "What's the picture about?" The average man likes a western . . . or a costume picture . . . or any other type of story which appeals to his particular taste; the average woman likes *any* picture in which her favorite stars appear.

Not only "matinee idols" of the masculine persuasion but almost all outstanding feminine stars owe their stardom to the women in the audience. Women, even more eagerly than men, flock to see the screen's beautiful women —especially if those stars are pronounced intriguing by Mr. Average Man. "What makes them glamorous?" . . . "why do men find them intriguing?" . . . and women rush to the theaters to seek the answers to those questions.

Norma Shearer, I believe, is the greatest "woman's star" in screen history. For every one man who is her ardent fan, she owns the allegiance of at least five women. Norma Shearer, poised, intelligent, superbly gowned, sophisticated, beautiful, is to the average woman the very epitome of feminine charm, the personification of all the qualities which the average woman longs to possess. Furthermore, her pictures have been deftly and deliberately tailored to appeal to women. On the screen, she has moved continually through an ultra-glamorous world of sophisticated romance. She has challenged, in her pictures, the convictions which most women obey—and secretly resent. She has starred in dramas based upon the problems which are understood, felt and shared by most of the women in her audiences. Of course, she has many masculine fans—but the majority of men, I believe, have resented such pictures as "Strangers May Kiss." But, resentful or pleased, they nevertheless have seen them—for women select the family's entertainment.

Greta Garbo is another star who appeals far more to women than to men. Test my statement by taking a straw vote in any mixed gathering. You will find that almost every woman present will list her as a prime favorite—but that few men will include her name. Women like her because her pictures, like Norma Shearer's deal with *their* problems, and because her personality suggests exotic romance. The average woman's life is so cramped by the four walls of her home that she longs for an escape from routine and finds it, vicariously, in such

(Extreme left) Chaplin, Cantor, Lloyd . . . deans of comedy because their pathos makes women want to "mother" them. (Center) Anna Sten has uncanny ability to stir women's emotions. (Above) Gloria Swanson did it with gowns.

Men see the show

18

The New Movie Magazine, March, 19

"Women Rule Hollywood," penned by Samuel Goldwyn, from *New Movie Magazine* (March 1935). Courtesy of the UCLA Arts Library; copyright holder Tower Magazines, Inc., 1929–1935.

HOLLYWOOD

If the men had their way, we'd have more slapstick comedy and adventure stories on the screen. Perhaps we'd have a different kind of star altogether from those shown below. If you're tired of love and problem pictures, blame Mrs. and Miss America!

Norma Shearer . . . greatest women's star ever.

It is women, too, who adore the exotic Garbo.

Joan Crawford . . . giving glamour to the girls.

pictures as those which Garbo has made famous.

Gloria Swanson was a great woman's star and she was shrewd in strengthening her appeal to women by wearing lavish costumes. Thousands of women stood in line to see her pictures—and her clothes. Thousands of women, every day, attend theaters—and conscript their husbands as escorts—because they want to see the styles which are being created by Hollywood's designers. And never think that motion picture producers, knowing the preponderance of feminine theater attendance, are blind to the importance of "dressing" their stars. A beautiful star, who has the knack of wearing beautiful clothes to the greatest advantage, is a recognized asset coveted by every studio.

Joan Crawford would be listed as a "favorite star" by many men, yet I think that she owes her tremendous popularity to the fact that she is an idol of the world's working girls. She represents the girl that they want to become—and her own life story, which is one of struggle and achievement, confirms her hold on their admiration. Recall and analyze her most successful pictures and you will find that they were tailored to fit, that they dealt with, and lent glamour to, the problems of America's working girls.

Anna Sten, I think, is destined to become one of the great women's stars, for she has uncanny ability to awaken emotional response in women. To date she has appealed to women more than to men.

In what, principally, do the screen entertainment tastes of men and women differ?

Chiefly in the fact that women are idealists and men are realists. Women are more concerned with the emotion than with the sequence of dramatic situations which give the emotion birth. They see pictures with their "hearts," whereas men see them with their "minds."

Both men and women are interested in love stories, for love between the sexes plays an important part in every normal life. Yet, in the life of the average woman love looms larger than in the life of the average man. The masculine audience does not demand love as the central theme of every picture; the feminine audience does. If men, instead of women, comprized three-fourths of the screen's audience, you would see the screen flooded with stirring adventure stories, many of them entirely lacking in love interest.

The magazine rack in every corner drug store reflects the difference in feminine and masculine entertainment tastes. The hundreds of "pulp" magazines are published for masculine consumption. Their stories drip action and adventure. Few of them contain any mention of love. Their heroes are red-blooded, two-fisted go-getters. The women's magazines, on the contrary, favor stories in which love is the predominant theme—and love, in every story, is idealized. Compromising the two extremes are "general" magazines. They bid for popularity with both sexes—and that, of course, is just what Hollywood tries to do in selecting its screen material. But Hollywood never loses sight of the fact that women are its greatest audience, and, in every case, the canny producer favors their established tastes.

Traditionally, men love comedy. Being realists, they are quick to detect and appreciate exaggeration. They laugh at "slap stick" which leaves the woman's sense of humor untouched.

Yet, even in its comedy-making, Hollywood defers to woman's rule. The great comedians in screen history are those who have appealed to women, and, in every instance, you will find that the secret of their appeal is the flavor of pathos which is ever-present in their fun-making. Charles Chaplin, Harold Lloyd and Eddie Cantor are the deans of screen comedy because women like them. There is a wistful, pathetic, helpless quality in their portrayals which arouses in the average woman the "mother complex." They are funny, yet lovable. They exaggerate, yet in (*Please turn to page 53*)

women pick. Women audiences make and break the stars

tract with Selznick International Pictures (SIP) nearly replicates this parlance: "It is mutually understood and agreed that your services are special, unique, unusual, extraordinary, and of an intellectual character, giving them a peculiar value."[21] Furthermore, overhauling the talent contract was one way the major studios attempted to reassert their dominion over the star system, especially given the climate of fiscal uncertainty during the Depression. In extending the long-term contract to seven years with the renewal option at their discretion, the studios steamrolled the empowered and financially lucrative contracts that popular, money-making stars of the 1920s (such as Gloria Swanson and John Gilbert) had previously enjoyed. Not surprisingly, this amendment to the standard studio option contract perplexed Hollywood's acting community. These sentiments were voiced in the industry trades, as a *Variety* article, "Objections to the 7-Yr. Contract," underscored:

> New California law allowing seven-year contracts is not looked on favorably by talent, who see it only as an advantage to the producer. It gives the film company a chance to shake the player at option time, but binds the artist for full length of time, according to the players' side. Present five-year contracts are called only that in name because of the semi-yearly options to be taken at the producer's preference. Adding two years to these would only lengthen the agony, these contractees contend.[22]

Here *Variety* illuminated the clashes over the contract between producers and actors at play in the early 1930s, as both existing and new laws favored the producer over the actor in regard to exercising renewal options. The change in the law extending the talent contract from five to seven years also provides insight as to why, in the 1930s, some stars began to seek out freelance and non-option contractual agreements with producers and major studios.[23]

Nevertheless, the seven-year, long-term "option contract" became the key document engineered by studio executives to control their high-priced talent employees, as the document reserved the studio's exclusive right to "option" an actor's services every six months. On this aspect, Tino Balio notes, "Every six months the studio reviewed an actor's progress and decided whether or not to pick up the option. If the studio dropped the option, the actor was out of work; if the studio picked up the option, the actor continued on the payroll for another six months. . . . Note that the studio, not the star, had the right to drop or pick up the option."[24] What is more, these contracts enabled a studio to develop a star's image and employ his or her services for a seven-year period.[25]

The exemplary case in studio-era Hollywood is Bette Davis, who was under a long-term contract to Warner Bros. for nearly two decades in the 1930s and 1940s. Cathy Klaprat explains that as Davis's star ascended, critical acclaim brought only minor concessions from Warner Bros., and only her salary rose.[26] She first signed with Warner Bros. in 1931, in a five-year option contract agreement at a salary of $400 a week with a renewable term every six months for the first year, and yearly thereafter, which gave the studio the authority to drop her from their roster at any point.[27] Davis finally had the opportunity to showcase her talents on loan to RKO, delivering a critically acclaimed performance in *Of Human Bondage* (John Cromwell, 1934). Although this role garnered her a new contract in 1934 back at her home studio, more advantageous provisions remained minor: a raise in salary to $1,350 per week from $1,000 and featured (but not star) billing.[28] It was not until four years later that Davis would fully attain star billing and receive a weekly salary of $3,500. Nonetheless, this later contract did little to bolster the actress's creative agency, as she "had to perform and render her services whenever, wherever and as often as the producer requested."[29] Even as Davis became more famous, Klaprat notes that she "never did earn the right to choose her roles or to have a say in her publicity."[30] Davis's case can be understood as *dependent stardom* in a long-term contract, one that was contingent upon an exclusive affiliation with a major Hollywood studio that made all the creative and career choices for its stars. Hence, this exclusive affiliation with a studio could restrict a star's autonomy. Thomas Schatz notes, "The more effectively a studio packaged and commodified its stars, the more restrictive the studios' and the public's shared perception of a star's persona tended to be."[31]

If there was a dispute about roles or salary, these long-term option contracts allowed the studios to prevent many stars from becoming free agents by suspending them without pay. This happened at Warner Bros. with Davis, as well as James Cagney and Olivia de Havilland, when these contract stars attempted to get out of their agreements or asked for an increase in salary and creative input.[32] As Jane Gaines points out, "Suspension effectively stopped the seven-year contract clock, thus adding more time to the actor's required employment for every day he or she was laid off. Actors who wanted to be free to work for other studios on scripts of their own choice felt trapped by the compulsory extension of their contracts."[33] Understood in this context, movie stardom was a "dazzling illusion to the degradations of servitude" for actors working in the film industry during the 1930s.[34] What emerged during this time was a paradox between the stars' "glamorous" images and their material labor as contractually obligated workers; although they were well compensated, stars still had to conform to the decrees of studio bosses and the hierarchy of their assembly-line production practices.

Davis's experiences at Warner Bros., and the long-term option contract in particular, were neither ubiquitous nor exemplary for all actors working within the 1930s studio system. As Richard Jewell has asserted, studio records often contradict Davis's well-publicized battles, showing that most motion picture actors "could and did turn down parts they did not like," even at Warner Bros.[35] Indeed, stars could attain independence and career control during this time. Such was the case with actress Ruth Chatterton, who came to Warner Bros. in 1931 in a practice known as "star raiding," which enabled stars to exercise their contract options to renegotiate for more money should they receive a better offer from a rival studio. An actor could then nullify his or her contract at their existing employer and accept this counteroffer to renegotiate a better contract with the new studio, thereby overriding the legality of the old contract.

Agent Myron Selznick instigated the practice of star raiding when he bargained for new contract deals on behalf of his clients, which included Chatterton, Kay Francis, and William Powell—all of whom were Paramount stars in the early 1930s. Selznick negotiated new contracts for more money because Warner Bros. was in need of high-profile talent after the advent of sound. Chatterton received an astonishing salary of $8,000 a week; Powell signed at $6,000 a week; and Francis made $4,000.[36] Even so, Chatterton's deal far surpassed those of Powell and Francis in terms of contractual agency. The actress's contract awarded her a substantial amount of creative control, including costar, director, and story approval; sole star billing; and control over the use of her image (in that the studio could not use her photograph in advertising without her approval).[37] This contract was limited to a two-year period in which she would make no more than three films per year for $975,000 per year (a remarkable salary that was parlayed before the effects of the Depression fully impacted Hollywood).[38] Moreover, Chatterton's agreement was negotiated after the seven-year contract-extension law in October 1931. Her box-office popularity, coupled with Hollywood's demand for Broadway talent after the inauguration of sound film, provides some insight as to why she was able to eschew any binding, long-term contract. Female stars such as Chatterton

Ruth Chatterton in the early 1930s. Courtesy of the Margaret Herrick Library, the Academy of Motion Picture Arts and Sciences; copyright holder unknown.

played a substantial role in the famous star raids of the decade, and they usually commanded respectable salaries as a result.

Likewise, Kay Francis also bargained with Warner Bros. for greater control over her image after she arrived at the studio in the Paramount star raid. Although her contract paled in comparison to Chatterton's, Francis lobbied for and won control over her image use four years later, after she and agent Myron Selznick renegotiated her contract and successfully lobbied the studio to refrain from using her name in any advertising or product merchandising in connection with Warner Bros.[39] This decision resulted from a disagreement between Francis and the studio in 1933, when she protested its use of her image in a Compo leather shoes ad campaign for her film *The Keyhole* (Michael Curtiz, 1933).[40] This ad appeared in

Photoplay in May 1933, at which time her contract sanctioned the studio's use of her image in connection with product tie-ups and merchandising. Her new, renegotiated contract in 1935 prevented Warner Bros. from using her likeness without her permission and granted her greater legal control over her own image.[41]

After the famous star-raiding controversy of 1931, the major studios distrusted agents: Selznick's innovative practice had broken the "non-proselytizing agreement" between the major studios that had been in place since the silent era.[42] This unofficial agreement stipulated that no studio would hire actors away from another, even after their contracts expired; this allowed studios to keep their contract stars, forced actors to remain with the same company, and basically ensured that the industry would remain an oligopoly. But Selznick defied this agreement in 1931 when he arranged for his clients to move to Warner Bros. in an effective "raid." Thereafter, non-proselytizing agreements lost their merit, and stars, assisted by their talent agents, had more versatile contract options as studios competed for their services.[43] The studios tried to eliminate star raiding, cap star salaries, and bar agents from intervening in the contract process via the 1933 National Industrial Recovery Act (NIRA), signed by President Franklin D. Roosevelt on June 16, 1933. NIRA was "one of the programs established by the president's National Recovery Administration (NRA) to stimulate growth and promote inter-industry cooperation."[44] However, as Danae Clark explains in *Negotiating Hollywood*, NIRA engendered an industry paradox in Hollywood, sanctioning government assistance for both management and labor. Clark notes, "Industry was sheltered from anti-trust laws (which protected monopolistic practices such as price fixing and block-booking) and labor was guaranteed minimum wage and maximum hours as well as the right to organize and bargain collectively with representatives of their own choosing."[45] As I discuss in more detail later in this chapter, motion picture actors mobilized in reaction to the studios' oppressive use of NIRA by organizing the Screen Actors Guild (SAG) to defeat these clauses.[46]

Myron Selznick's impressive star raid and NIRA merit an extended discussion of talent agents and their role in designing contracts and molding the star system. As Tom Kemper has persuasively argued, one of the most important assets to stars seeking independence in Hollywood was the talent agent, who served as the chief interlocutor between the star, the studio executives, and the producers in contractual negotiations.[47] Agents became the "middlemen" in the industry by lobbying the studios and improving their clients' labor conditions. By doing so, they became a permanent (albeit at times controversial) fixture of the film industry.

The efforts of Selznick to build the careers of numerous A-list stars best exemplifies how talent agents bolstered star power in their contractual negotiations with the studios, especially when stars went freelance. By 1932, Selznick had become the Hollywood film industry's "most prosperous nemesis" because of the shrewd business deals that he hustled for his clients.[48] Selznick mobilized his agent status to aggressively lobby the major studios on his clients' behalf, and he was known for his trademark line during contract negotiations: "It isn't enough." Yet as Kemper explains, for all of the agent's "inflammatory oppositional rhetoric" and "his posture as an opponent of the studios," he (along with fellow talent agents Charles Feldman, Leland Hayward, and others) forged "strong routine relationships with studio executives, a mutually beneficial and reinforcing network."[49] Myron Selznick maintained solid business relationships with MGM producer Hunt Stromberg and independent producers Kenneth MacGowan and Walter Wanger. These were, of course, crucial to his success in building Hollywood's top agency of the decade. Furthermore, Selznick was a key investor in his brother David's independent production company, SIP, in 1935. This move, Schatz contends, was motivated by "utter pragmatism" rather than "fraternal piety," since "the investment would be returned by many times over" when Myron's freelance clients paid him 10 percent of their SIP salaries.[50]

Selznick's client list boasted much of Hollywood's top talent in the 1930s. Indeed, he represented many of the freelance women of primary interest to this study, including Constance Bennett, Janet Gaynor, Miriam Hopkins, and Carole Lombard, as well as freelance actor Fredric March and other major stars, including Fred Astaire, Vivien Leigh, Myrna Loy, Merle Oberon, Ginger Rogers, and Loretta Young.[51] With a keen understanding of how to translate art and culture into the bureaucracy and economics of the studio system, Selznick "militated" for his star clients' control of their craft.[52] Moreover, his representation elevated their professional standing because the studios respected the prestige of his agency as a "competent and reputable thoroughfare for talent."[53] He worked with only the top tier of Hollywood talent. Although, at times, he exacerbated already strained contractual labor relations between stars and their studio employers, he was also key in helping actors become more independent and win creative discretion, all while whittling away the studios' authority.

By contrast, Selznick's main rival, Charles Feldman, could not be more different in persona and style. Kemper maintains that "While the jaundiced Selznick seemed frustrated in the role of embattled agent, Feldman took a cool and integrated approach to his business."[54] Counter to the agent stereotype, Feldman enjoyed long-lasting friendships with movie moguls Darryl Zanuck, Samuel Goldwyn, and Jack Warner, and he mobilized his legal background to become a "probing reader of contracts and writer of nuanced and inventive provisions."[55] This skill was crucial in bolstering independent stardom for his clients, including actresses Claudette Colbert, Sylvia Sidney, and Irene Dunne; actor Charles Boyer; directors Michael Curtiz and Anatole Litvak; and many others in the ranks of Hollywood top talent.[56]

Charles Feldman's approach is most apparent in the deals that he negotiated for Dunne, who recognized the importance of a good agent in negotiating an advantageous deal with a major studio. Once Dunne teamed up with Feldman in 1932, the agent renegotiated her RKO contract, which doubled her salary, awarded her story approval, and gave her a 25 percent cut of all her films' gross receipts.[57] Feldman's influence in Dunne's career also demonstrates the important role that agents played in cultivating independent stardom, in particular with "off-casting" and remaking a star's image. At Feldman's prodding, Dunne ventured into comedy with the screwball hit *Theodora Goes Wild* (Richard Boleslawski, 1936). Kemper explains how Feldman encouraged the actress to expand her acting range, and how *Theodora* led to subsequent projects: "The film's success led to roles sculpted for Dunne's idiosyncratic brand of comedy, screwball but always in control of a discerning but empathetic intelligence."[58] Her independent stardom brought more than just money; she also received Academy Award nominations for Best Actress in *Theodora* and *The Awful Truth* (Leo McCarey, 1937). Dunne's comedic persona was hailed by the *Los Angeles Times* in its review of the latter film, noting her "top-notch class" acting in this "masterpiece" screwball comedy directed by McCarey, which they likened to the phenomenon of *It Happened One Night* (Frank Capra, 1934).[59] Feldman's agency strategy—encouraging clients to manage various freelance, non-exclusive contracts—presented another challenge to the supposedly ironclad, long-term contract system.

LOAN-OUTS AND OFF-CASTING

Star raiding, coupled with the skilled interventions of agents, allowed stars to have more input in renegotiating their studio contracts by mobiliz-

Irene Dunne being pampered by costar Melvyn Douglas and director Richard Boleslawski on the set of *Theodora Goes Wild*. Courtesy of the Cinematic Arts Library, the University of Southern California; copyright holder unknown.

ing their economic power. And as the case of Irene Dunne attests, multiple studio agreements created opportunities for stars to reinvent their personae through off-casting. In an attempt to counter star raiding, the studios developed their own alternative solution with a star "loan-out" policy. By loaning out their high-priced talent, the major studios kept idle stars busy working, recouped their overhead expenses, and shared their contract stars with rival studios and independent producers by devising various agreements on a per-deal basis.[60] Examples of loan-out deals include charging a studio a minimum fee of four weeks' salary plus a surcharge of three weeks' salary for a star's services, or charging a producer the star's basic contract salary for however long she was needed, plus a 25 percent surcharge. But any profit made from the deal went solely to the studio and not the star, who received his or her standard contract salary.

These loan-outs, however, were not necessarily detrimental to stars, especially those under long-term studio contracts, because they could also function as a means to secure challenging parts elsewhere. In this context, the loan-out presented an opportunity for long-term talent that mirrored the off-casting strategy that Feldman advocated for his freelance client, Dunne. In fact, many actors did not attain major stardom until another studio borrowed them for a particular project. For ambitious women studio players who wanted to ascend the star ladder, establish their talent, and/or win important roles, the loan-out was key. For instance, Bette Davis established her reputation as a skilled dramatic actress in *Of Human Bondage* after she lobbied her home studio, Warner Bros., to loan her out to RKO.

A *New York Times* review titled "Sensational Hit Made by Bette Davis" illustrates the critical praise her work garnered. Reviewer Norbert Lusk lauded the actress, noting "the profound impression" her performance left, one that has been "ratified by the public to the extent of depositing nearly $100,000 in the box office of Radio City Music Hall. . . . [T]he picture is notable in every respect, but the acting of Miss Davis gives it the added advantage of bringing to light a startling discovery."[61] Interestingly, Lusk correlated the film's box-office popularity to Davis's acting ability: "In short, she has made a hit and there is nothing the public loves more . . . her performance is as brave as it is brilliant, and always arresting and irresistible."[62] This artistic achievement can be attributed to the actress's foresight and desire to demonstrate her dramatic skill. In response, Warner Bros. did invest in Davis's talents, providing her with plum roles in films such as *Dangerous* (Alfred Green, 1935), for which she won her first Best Actress Oscar, as well as *The Petrified Forest* (Archie Mayo, 1936) and finally

Jezebel (William Wyler, 1938), which was completely designed around her persona and won her a second Academy Award for Best Actress. Even so, the studio was slow to stop assigning her second-rate roles in movies such as *Satan Met a Lady* (William Dieterle, 1936) or featured parts second to male stars (as with Archie Mayo's *Bordertown* in 1935, for which she was billed under Paul Muni and after the title credits). Her case demonstrates how some major studios (and agents) did not necessarily rush to fully develop their talent on long-term contracts.[63] It also highlights how this lack of professional recognition could motivate former contract players to take a freelance career path, which was the case with Carole Lombard.

Similarly, Lombard found her most successful critical and commercial opportunities on loan-out deals away from her home studio, Paramount, which had cast her in glamorous, clotheshorse roles in second-rate films. Conversely, Columbia's *Twentieth Century* (Howard Hawks, 1934) and Universal's *My Man Godfrey* (Gregory La Cava, 1936) showcased her talent for screwball comedy, proved her to be a box-office commodity, and inadvertently led her to take ownership of her career to ensure the best professional opportunities. This often compelled her to campaign for lead female roles even though they were at less prestigious studios.

Cast opposite John Barrymore in *Twentieth Century*, Lombard saw in this particular part (that of independent and high-spirited actress Lily Garland) an opportunity to achieve leading-lady status. Lombard's instinct proved correct, as the film was a critical success and revitalized her career. Critics raved about the "New Lombard," as this praise from the *Los Angeles Times* attests: "Carole Lombard . . . succeeds in showing an entirely new and different side of her personality as well as her ability. Coolly intelligent and calculatedly alluring in former pictures, in this she vibrates with life and passion, abandon and diablerie. So completely it is the best performance she has ever given."[64]

Lombard's metamorphosis from glamour girl to screwball comedienne was extolled again for Universal's *My Man Godfrey*. The *New York Times* noted in its review of her zany character, Irene Bullock (a "cow-eyed girl that has a one-track mind with grass growing over its rails"), "It is not a fair portrait of Carole Lombard, but she rises beautifully to the role."[65] Likewise, *Variety* noted the novelty of Lombard's comedic talents in *Godfrey*, which it predicted would generate a "nifty return" at the box office, and observed that the actress "has played screwball dames before, but none so screwy as this one, from start to finish, with no letdowns or lapses into quiet sanity."[66] Furthermore, it underscored how Lombard's role was more difficult than that of her costar William Powell, and noted how the actress had reached the apex of her career because her part "call[ed] for pressure acting all the way and it was no simple trick to refrain from overworking the insanity plea in a many-sided argument."[67] This off-cast role brought Lombard her sole Best Actress Oscar nomination, solidified her reputation as Hollywood's top comedienne, and reaffirmed her decision to freelance.

The success of Davis and Lombard underscores how career-wise stars used loan-outs to their own advantage. Another example is Claudette Colbert, whose renegotiated 1934 and 1936 Paramount contracts stipulated that the studio "could not lend" her services without her "written consent."[68] These contracts, however, also outlined her right to do outside pictures for specific studios, independent producers, and/or directors. For example, her 1933 Paramount contract outlined that she would do one picture for Warner Bros., two for director John M. Stahl, and two for Columbia, with story and director approval (specifying either Frank Capra, Frank Borzage, or Lewis Milestone, all top directors), and that she should receive star or costar billing. The latter loan-out, outside-picture approval with Columbia resulted in her Oscar-winning role in *It Happened One Night,* in addition to two more films for that studio. Compare Colbert's deal for the film with that of costar Clark Gable, who was loaned by his MGM boss Louis B. Mayer as supposed "punishment" for being "difficult." In contrast, Colbert's loan-out to Columbia was negotiated by her agent, Charles Feldman, at her behest and showcased the actress's professional agency at the time.[69] As these three cases demonstrate, female stars undermined oppressive studio labor policies, including loan-out deals and contract clauses, to their professional advantage, thereby more proactively participating in the Hollywood star system.

A major movement toward independent stardom that transpired alongside star raiding and loan-out tactics in 1930s Hollywood was the collective unionization of motion picture actors that resulted in the formation of the Screen Actors Guild (SAG). It was founded on July 12, 1933, by a group of freelance actors, including Ralph Morgan, Alan Mowbray, Boris Karloff, and Kenneth Thomson. Danae Clark has historicized the SAG labor struggle as part of the sociopolitical "New Deal" discourse that emerged in the 1930s, arguing that the economic unrest caused by the Depression exacerbated labor-relations anxiety in Hollywood, particularly between actors and the major studios. The cash-strapped studios used NIRA—the aforementioned federal emergency relief program created by Roosevelt's NRA program—to cut labor costs and tighten control of production in the "name of economic conservation."[70]

Carole Lombard on the set of her breakthrough film, *Twentieth Century*, with director Howard Hawks and costar John Barrymore. Courtesy of the Margaret Herrick Library, the Academy of Motion Picture Arts and Sciences; copyright holder unknown.

Carole Lombard on set with fellow *My Man Godfrey* freelance cast members Mischa Auer and William Powell, and director Gregory La Cava on the right. Courtesy of the Margaret Herrick Library, the Academy of Motion Picture Arts and Sciences; copyright holder unknown.

In accordance with NIRA policy, the studios drafted a "Code of Fair Competition" on behalf of the film business with the goal of providing economic relief and reviving the overall industry. In their draft of this code, the studios attempted to blame their financial woes on extravagant star salaries, but they failed to mention the decline in theater attendance and their debt from expanding theater chains after the conversion to sound. The major studios also used NIRA to further cement their control over actors by capping their salaries, curbing the activities of talent agents, and eliminating star raiding. This prompted high-profile acting talent—including George Bancroft, Charles Butterworth, James Cagney,

Gary Cooper, Jeanette MacDonald, Robert Montgomery, Frank Morgan, Chester Morris, and Paul Muni, as well as future freelance stars Ann Harding, Miriam Hopkins, Fredric March, and Adolph Menjou—to join SAG in October 1933 in order to collectively bargain and negotiate the terms of their employment with the studios.[71] Through the personal campaign of SAG president (and good friend of President Roosevelt) comedian Eddie Cantor, Hollywood actors won Roosevelt's support and defeated the studios' three actor-discriminatory clauses: salary curtailment, agent control, and anti-star raiding.[72] However, NIRA was declared unconstitutional in 1935, which stalled the full galvanization of SAG. Both SAG and the Screen Writers Guild (SWG) then functioned on the margins of the film industry until Louis B. Mayer (head of production at MGM) formally recognized them in 1937 as having official bargaining power, with the other studios soon following suit.

The formation of SAG signified that, in the 1930s, Hollywood actors officially recognized themselves as "workers," even if SAG did not significantly alter labor-management relations in the film industry. With this decision, motion picture actors rebelled against the "paternalism of studio execs" and placed their loyalty with each other and in the acting profession itself, not with producers and studio executives.[73] Through SAG, actors combated and circumvented the exploitative power of the major studios and executives who ran Hollywood. This movement toward independence—along with star raiding, agents, and loan-out negotiations—was yet another tactic that stars used prior to freelancing to attain professional agency in the 1930s. There was, however, one alternative studio within the system that helped provide and sustain independence in Hollywood.

UNITED ARTISTS AND "PRESTIGE" INDEPENDENT PRODUCERS

Through the emergence and maturity of independent production in Hollywood, beginning with United Artists (UA), the studio-system movie "factory" was able to maintain independence for A-list stars and talent.[74] The distribution-only studio founded in 1919 by Charles Chaplin, Douglas Fairbanks, Mary Pickford, and D. W. Griffith operated in the 1930s as a haven for independently minded artists and producers, and worked in tandem with the vertically integrated Big Five studios. The founding of UA was part of a larger "star frenzy" trend that had taken the film industry by storm in the late 1910s, when even moderate and second-tier stars could

Mary Pickford (center) with her fellow United Artists founders: Douglas Fairbanks, D. W. Griffith, and Charles Chaplin. Courtesy of the Mary Pickford Foundation; copyright holder unknown.

garner lucrative contracts.[75] Nonetheless, Mary Pickford's contributions to UA and her Hollywood legacy are important for laying the groundwork for female independent stardom in the 1930s.

With a business acumen that made her one of the most powerful players in Hollywood by the mid-1910s, Pickford's shrewd comprehension of contracts enabled UA to succeed in Hollywood alongside rival, vertically integrated studios. Indeed, Chaplin noted that it was Pickford's film business knowledge that kept their fledgling production company afloat: "She knew all the nomenclature: the amortizations and deferred stocks, etc. She understood all the articles of incorporation, the legal discrepancy on Page 7, paragraph A, Article 27, and coolly referred to the overlap in contradiction in Paragraph D, Article 24."[76]

In the silent Hollywood era, prior to the cementing of the vertical integration that shifted the power balance to the major studios and their big-business enterprise monopoly, stars could still form their own independent production ventures. In the 1920s Pickford took advantage of this by co-founding UA, and she became a model of professional agency for female stars seeking their own form of independent stardom in the changing financial climate in the 1930s. After the conversion to sound film and after the economic hardships inflicted by the Depression had fully impacted Hollywood, independent production had become a precarious move for stars. Furthermore, the studios effectively used the climate of fiscal uncertainty to eliminate the empowered and financially lucrative contracts that popular stars like Pickford had enjoyed in the silent era, reorganizing their business practices vis-à-vis vertical integration.

Thus, independence in the studio system for A-list talent now translated to working with independent producers and UA, which was a viable alternative to signing long-term option contracts with major studios. As Matthew Bernstein points out, there have always been various types of "independent production" in Hollywood, from its inception to the present day.[77] In the 1930s the independent system resulted in two kinds of productions: the "prestige" brand epitomized by Samuel Goldwyn, David O. Selznick, Walter Wanger, and other producers who often distributed their films through UA; and those made by low-budget, independent studios, including Republic, Monogram, Mascot, Liberty, Majestic, and Chesterfield, which came to be know as "Poverty Row." While the term does not refer to any real physical location, many of these studios were clustered together in the Hollywood neighborhood. Though Poverty Row independents made roughly 300 films annually, translating to about 75 percent of the overall Hollywood pictures produced during the 1930s,[78] my focus here is on the "prestige" independent productions and the major talent who formed their own companies, employed their own talent and technicians, and produced high-budget films for national distribution through one of the major studios. This is most relevant to the crystallization of independent stardom, as most A-list film stars worked on these prestige productions.

As Thomas Schatz observes, going "independent" in 1930s Hollywood, especially for talent who desired to work in top features, invariably meant working at UA.[79] The emergent freelance stars of the 1930s all worked there during the decade. For example, Constance Bennett made two films on the UA lot in 1934 (produced by Darryl F. Zanuck's independent production company, Twentieth Century, prior to its merger with Fox), while in the late 1930s both Janet Gaynor and Carole Lombard had individual multipicture deals with Selznick's SIP. Starring in an independent production in Hollywood was more than an economic incentive to freelance talent: it not only facilitated financial incentives such as profit-sharing distribution deals, but also allowed for what Bernstein defines as "individualistic and innovative approaches to narrative structure, plot resolution, and film style."[80]

Goldwyn and Selznick represented a new breed of first-class independent producers who headed their own production companies (Samuel Goldwyn Studios and SIP, respectively) at UA during the 1930s. They produced high-profile films in return for a UA distribution contract that guaranteed the promotion and selling of a given picture in both the domestic and key overseas markets.[81] Although Goldwyn and Selznick modeled their operations on the major studios' A-class productions in order to tailor their films to the first-run market, they differed from the Big Five studios in their approach to the filmmaking process by providing the opportunity for enhanced creative autonomy. Additionally, the British producer Alexander Korda, along with Americans Howard Hughes and Darryl Zanuck, all produced films at UA at different times across the decade.[82] Many former studio executives became independent producers, including Jesse Lasky and B. P. Schulberg (previously at Paramount), Selznick (former production head of RKO and unit producer at MGM), Wanger (who produced at Paramount and MGM in the late 1920s and early 1930s), and Zanuck (former production chief at Warner Bros. until 1933 and later production head of Twentieth Century-Fox in 1935). They went into business for themselves for both financial and creative reasons. These producers disagreed with specific studio management policies (Zanuck at Warner Bros.), found the studio system too alienating (Selznick at Paramount, RKO, and MGM), or felt that independence would allow them to take more creative risks than the majors would permit (Selznick and Wanger).[83]

Independent producers also benefited from signing freelance A-list stars. While the major studios valued long-term talent contracts in order to maximize their financial profit and film output, prestige independent producers could not maintain such a lengthy star roster because they made only a few films per year and did not have the finances to offer numerous long-term contracts. Thus, freelance stars and independent producers stood to mutually benefit each other. The stars had more creative control, earned a flat-rate salary for one film at a time, and participated in the production process, while producers had A-list talent with box-office popularity without long-term investment or having to compete for studio stars with loan-outs from major studios. Independent production was also a source of quality product for the major studios' first-run, more profitable theaters, since UA releases and other independents also brought revenue

Barbara Stanwyck in *Stella Dallas*. Courtesy of the Cinematic Arts Library, University of Southern California; copyright 1937, Samuel Goldwyn.

in distribution fees to the Big Five.[84] However entrenched independent production remained in the studio system, these producers represented a viable alternative for Hollywood talent who aspired to independent stardom.

This discussion of independent production in 1930s Hollywood suggests why certain stars would follow the example of these producers to seek unorthodox career paths—apart from the often narrow and rigid options available at the major studios—and gain a professional advantage over stars under long-term studio contracts. Off-casting is relevant here as well, as stars could tackle challenging roles with independent producers more often than at major studios (especially when they were on long-term contracts with little authority over which roles they played). The outcome could redefine an actor's reputation and expand her range. For example,

Barbara Stanwyck won the lead role of *Stella Dallas* in 1937, directed by King Vidor and produced by Goldwyn, who screen-tested close to fifty actresses for the part. Goldwyn had initially thought that at age twenty-nine Stanwyck was too young to play a mother who ages almost twenty years in the course of the film, but he changed his mind when she personally campaigned for the role.[85] *Stella Dallas* was a tremendous critical success for Stanwyck; much like Bette Davis's performance in *Of Human Bondage*, it confirmed her talent as a dramatic actress. Reviews like this one from the *Los Angeles Times* reinforce this view, as it lauded "the spectacle of Barbara Stanwyck in her finest performance."[86] Likewise, *Variety* observed that Samuel Goldwyn's remake of his 1925 film was so well done that the producer has box office "socko on his hands," and it underlined the actress's performance in the lead role.[87]

Stanwyck's critical reputation was significantly enhanced by her *Stella Dallas* performance, for which she received her first Academy Award nomination for Best Actress. Yet unlike Davis, Stanwyck's freelance status enabled her to continue to choose compelling roles and maintain her reputation as a dramatic actress. Stanwyck's newfound agency was quickly recognized when she returned to RKO to complete her agreement with the studio. The *Los Angeles Times* noted how RKO had assigned its Oscar-winning writer Dudley Nichols (for John Ford's *The Informer* [1935]) to "make sure that Stanwyck was thoroughly supplied with potential picture subjects" as an appropriate follow-up to *Stella Dallas*.[88] The freedom to off-cast oneself and redefine one's career and screen persona was a significant advantage of going freelance and working with independent producers.

THE SEEDS OF INDEPENDENCE ARE PLANTED

As Giuliana Muscio astutely observes about the 1930s American film industry, "beneath the monolithic and glamorous surface," there were "continuous tensions and struggles" that can help historians reconceive the classical Hollywood studio system not as a "static model," but as "a dynamic process of adaptation" that faced different cultural and economic pressures.[89] As this chapter has made evident, independent stardom was a strategic position that some actresses chose to take in search of professional autonomy in the star system. Given the industry's presumption that women made up the bulk of the domestic film audience, Hollywood, in turn, was compelled to adapt. Even with the studios' streamlining of long-term contract and loan-out practices, actors rallied to maintain agency over their careers. A few top stars turned these studio policies around to their advantage.

In sum, Irene Dunne and Claudette Colbert made effective contracts with major studios through the wheeling and dealing of their talent agent, Charles Feldman. And through off-casting loan-out maneuverings, Bette Davis and Carole Lombard demonstrated their acting range—even when their home studio largely neglected to provide them with adequate film assignments. And through SAG, motion picture actors challenged the monopolistic practices of the film industry that attempted to stymie their salaries, ignore their talent agents, and prevent them from seeking out employment opportunities at rival studios. With the help of Roosevelt's New Deal policies, actors were guaranteed that the major studios would recognize these rights, and all of them became key to achieving and maintaining independent stardom in Hollywood. Finally, career-savvy actresses secured greater creative control by making films with prestige independent producers at UA. As Stanwyck's experience with *Stella Dallas* makes clear, individual freelance deals with indie producers such as Goldwyn provided new creative opportunities that actors were often denied at the major studios.

So while the seeds of independence were sown and germinated in the 1930s star system, independent stardom blossomed during the decade through the actual contractual negotiations with the studios. The contracts themselves outline the compromises, gains, and struggles that these female stars experienced in their pursuit of greater career autonomy and freedom from studio domination and exploitation. As the following chapter will show, these freelance contracts differed from the studio option contract and benefited the artist more than the producer, enabling actresses to attain independent stardom in Hollywood.

TWO

The [Freelance] Contract in Context

Although SAG membership, loan-outs, and long-term exclusive studio affiliations could bolster a star's professional agency, many A-list actresses took additional steps to forge a freelance career on their own terms. As established box-office attractions, these women mobilized their screen images and leveraged their popularity in order to negotiate major studio contracts that guaranteed a certain degree of creative control and favorable working conditions. Their success in doing so speaks to the female-driven star system of the era and helps explain why women outnumbered men in the new freelance class that propelled the independent stardom movement in 1930s Hollywood.

David O. Selznick, for example, extolled the initiative that Carole Lombard showed in her negotiations with Warner Bros. on behalf of his independent production studio, Selznick International Pictures (SIP). He wrote:

> Carole Lombard has what I think is a swell idea. . . . She says that Warners are after her hot and heavy for a picture and she suggests that she make a deal with them on the condition that they let us have Errol Flynn for one of the pictures she is to do with us here. I think this idea of the stars themselves getting into trading for the benefit of their pictures is new and valuable, but very rarely will you find anyone with the initiative and cooperative spirit of Carole—so let's take advantage of this.[1]

The producer's enthusiasm highlights the sense of collaboration between talent and producers that was burgeoning by the late 1930s, as evidenced by the contractual negotiations of freelance stars.

This chapter examines the contractual discourse of elite freelancers in order to catalog the range of experiences encompassed by independent stardom in the 1930s. In doing so, I argue that the influence and economic power of the movie industry's A-level talent during the studio years has been seriously underestimated in favor of a conception of the star as indentured laborer.[2] This misperception is especially apparent in the case of women. Recall Bette Davis's previously discussed *dependent stardom*—that of the unhappy star whose career was hindered as much as it was helped by her exclusive affiliation with Warner Bros. In this chapter, I take a closer look at how female stars negotiated their deals—particularly freelance contracts and profit-sharing percentage deals—with major studios and independent producers, challenging the assumption that female stars worked in a state of virtual servitude. Although it was true that long-term contract stars like Davis had only limited story approval in relation to scripts, and even less creative input in relation to actual production, those who attained independent stardom in the 1930s enjoyed far more creative agency in terms of story selection, script development, cinematography, and choice of principal cast and crew assignments. By bargaining for these provisions in their contracts, these women effectively became creative agents who molded their own self-representation onscreen by choosing the craftsmen and talent to collaborate with and selecting the projects in which they would star.

The myriad advantages of freelancing appear patently obvious in the contracts of Constance Bennett, Irene Dunne, Barbara Stanwyck, Clara Bow, and Miriam Hopkins. Some of these women used their independent stardom to their financial advantage by initiating the profit-participation "percentage deal," a pioneering business tactic that became standard practice for Hollywood talent in the 1950s. Likewise, stars who maintained an exclusive, long-term affiliation with a studio—Ann Harding, Claudette Colbert, and Katharine Hepburn, for example—negotiated for higher salaries and increased creative control as they proved their market value, thus engineering a *semi-independent stardom*.[3] Others, like Janet Gaynor, went freelance after less-than-gratifying experiences with their parent studios' management of their careers and initiated their freelance stardom with David O. Selznick's SIP. Finally, perhaps the most demonstrative case of independent stardom was Lombard, who emerged as the highest-compensated and savviest freelancer of Hollywood by the end of the 1930s.

A freelance career did not, however, always lead to personal liberation and better roles, especially for actresses of color. The careers of Anna May Wong and Lupe Vélez illuminate the flipside of independent stardom: a *minimum independence*, whereby freelancing represented the only available form of employment in the absence of long-term studio contracts.[4] Consequently, their forced independent path did not provide as advantageous career opportunities. By highlighting the various contractual terms of independent stardom, we can discern how women achieved professional agency as freelance stars, thus laying the groundwork for Hollywood talent's innovative deal-making tactics in the studio era and beyond.

DEALS ON THE SIDE: BARBARA STANWYCK AND CONSTANCE BENNETT

Barbara Stanwyck and Constance Bennett used their contracts to secure professional agency from the very beginning of their film careers. They also continued to freelance even while under studio contracts, using the outside interest to bolster their standing. As such, Stanwyck and Bennett used the creative provisions in their freelance contracts in the 1930s (and, for Stanwyck, into the 1940s) to control the evolution of their star images. A careful analysis of these legal documents shows how female stars used contracts as a source of empowerment in the studio system.

Stanwyck arrived in Hollywood in 1929 in the company of her husband, the stage star and Warner Bros. recruit Frank Fay. She quickly found freelance work with United Artists in *The Locked Door* (George FitzMaurice, 1929) and was then signed to a joint contract between Columbia and Warner Bros. from 1929 to 1933. During that time Stanwyck established her reputation as a capable dramatic actress in films like Frank Capra's *The Miracle Woman* (1931) and *The Bitter Tea of General Yen* (1933). Her husband, who had wanted to retain the ability to return to Broadway, initially advised her to pursue limited, non-option contracts. That advice may have contributed to the contract dispute that arose between Columbia Pictures and Warner Bros. Studios in mid-July 1931.

Claiming that she had already fulfilled her three-picture commitment to Columbia, Stanwyck moved to Warner Bros., stating that she would return only if she received a raise that reflected her rising box-office value.[5] In response, Columbia's head of production, Harry Cohn, sued Stanwyck for "jumping" studios before completing her contractual obligations.[6] Meanwhile, Warner Bros. argued that it was "spending $8,000 a day standing by" for Stanwyck and was anxiously awaiting her return to the picture she had already begun filming.[7] Thus the actress had two major studios battling over her services, despite the fact that she had not signed a long-term

Barbara Stanwyck dining with her agent, Zeppo Marx, and his wife, along with Robert Taylor, circa late 1930s. Courtesy of the Margaret Herrick Library, the Academy of Motion Picture Arts and Sciences; copyright holder unknown.

contract with either one. Although Columbia won the suit, and Stanwyck was ordered to complete the remainder of her contract, she did receive a raise from Cohn, who increased her salary to $25,000 (from $20,000) for her next film, *Forbidden* (Frank Capra, 1932), as well as for her remaining two pictures at the studio.[8] Furthermore, she kept working at Warner Bros. while completing her contract with Columbia. Stanwyck learned from this experience and made sure to negotiate for the right to do outside pictures in subsequent contracts. This practice, making multiple pictures at an array of studios, became a mainstay of independent stardom.

Stanwyck's next contract with Warner Bros., which she negotiated in 1932, granted her special provisions such as sole star billing, story approval, and the right to decline any project within a thirty-day period.[9] It also enabled her to personally select films such as the notorious fallen woman film *Baby Face* (1933), in which the actress played the juicy role of Lily Powers, a working-class gold digger who manipulates men for economic prosperity at their expense during the height of the Depression. In 1935 Stanwyck, encouraged by her agent, Zeppo Marx, signed a dual one-year contract shared between RKO and Twentieth Century-Fox to make two pictures for each studio.[10] Her contract included an option that enabled RKO to renew her services beyond the one-year period; however, Stanwyck still retained the contractual right to do outside freelance films at other studios, including for Paramount (in the contemporary hospital drama *Interns Can't Take Money* directed by Alfred Santell, 1937) and MGM (the historical romance *His Brother's Wife* directed by W. S. Van Dyke, 1936, the first film in which Stanwyck appeared with her future husband, Robert Taylor), in addition to her Fox and RKO projects. In each of her contracts the actress secured story approval, star billing, and the right to make outside freelance deals. These deals appeared to vex Fox, as the studio bemoaned the actress's outside freelance deals when she negotiated to make *Stella Dallas* for Samuel Goldwyn at United Artists in 1937, forcing Fox to postpone one of its own productions featuring Stanwyck.[11] Fox producer E. C. de Lavigne complained, "RKO seems to be adopting a policy of allowing Miss Stanwyck to make her own deals on the side."[12]

Stanwyck's cultural capital in Hollywood directly benefited from her freelance wheeling and dealing. She followed her lauded turn in *Stella Dallas* with versatile performances in films made for some of Hollywood's top directors and studios: the Western *Union Pacific* for Cecil B. DeMille (Paramount) and the screen adaptation of Clifford Odets's play *Golden Boy* for Rouben Mamoulian (Columbia) in 1939, as well as screwball comedy *The Lady Eve* for Preston Sturges (Paramount) and comedy/drama *Meet John Doe* for Frank Capra (Warner Bros.), both released in 1941. In 1943 she even became the highest paid woman in the nation, as reported by the US Treasury, with an annual salary of $323,333 from her combined work at Paramount, Universal, and United Artists.[13] Her 1944 freelance agreement with Warner Bros. reveals how the actress retained her independent status through her contractually guaranteed creative provisions and financial incentives, just as she had with the studio in the 1930s.

Stanwyck's contract with Warner Bros. gave her the right to make two outside pictures concurrent with her tenure at the studio; outlined her $100,000 per film salary; and also contained a unique stipulation in which the studio pledged to directly negotiate with Paramount to allow their chief costume designer, Edith Head, to design Stanwyck's costumes for *A Christmas in Connecticut* (Peter Godfrey, 1944), the first film under her new contract.[14] After her positive experience working with Head in comedies *The Lady Eve* and *Ball of Fire* (Howard Hawks, 1941)—in which Head's costumes helped revamp her image as a bona-fide sex symbol—Stanwyck insisted that Head personally design all of her onscreen wardrobe.

In *The Lady Eve*, Stanwyck not only revealed her glamorous side

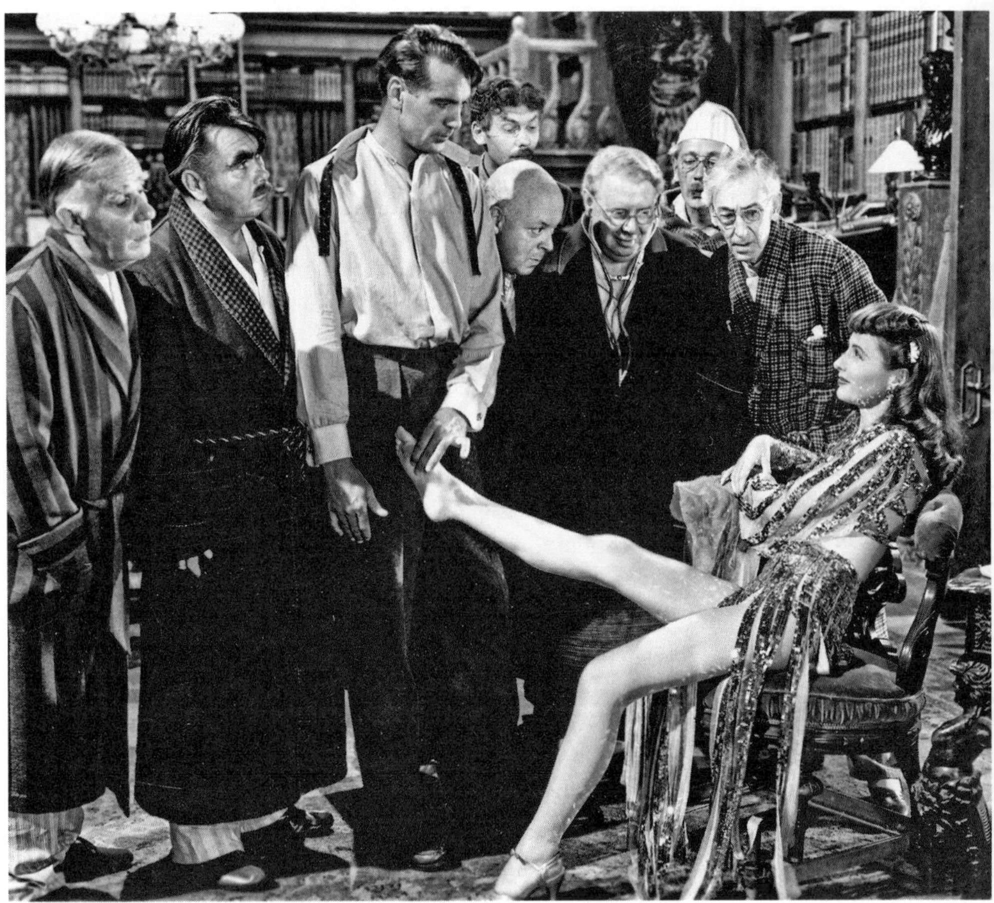

The "new" Stanwyck in *Ball of Fire à la* Edith Head's costuming. Courtesy of the Margaret Herrick Library, the Academy of Motion Picture Arts and Sciences; copyright 1941, Samuel Goldwyn.

thanks to Head's alluring gowns, but also her talent as a witty screwball comedienne. We see here how Stanwyck's free agency directly correlated with her ability to off-cast herself and redesign her star persona, just as she had with *Stella Dallas* four years earlier. Stanwyck's free agency impacted her career by giving her the ability to choose projects at various studios and to demonstrate her range as an A-list dramatic actress and comedienne who worked with Hollywood's best directors (Hawks, Sturges, DeMille, and Capra, among others). Furthermore, her ability to negotiate for special provisions like costuming directly correlated to redefining her screen image, so that by the 1940s she was also a sex symbol and glamour icon.

Like Barbara Stanwyck, Constance Bennett maintained ownership of her star persona from film to film, regardless of which studio employed her. Bennett hailed from a famous acting clan: her father Richard had been a luminary of the New York stage in the early twentieth century, but his fame was eclipsed by that of Constance and her sister Joan when they became Hollywood stars in the 1930s. Although MGM had offered her a contract in the 1920s, Bennett did not initiate her screen career until after the transition to sound in 1929, when she signed with Pathé (purchased by RKO in 1928).[15]

In 1931, with the aid of her agent, Myron Selznick, the actress clandestinely arranged to make two films at Warner Bros. in a ten-week period during her vacation for an astounding salary of $30,000 a week.[16] In addition to the standard creative provisions that empowered stars demanded, her Warner Bros. contract gave her the right to employ her cameraman of choice, John Mescall, A.S.C., and guaranteed Bennett top producers, noting that she would be "supervised directly" by Darryl Zanuck, and should he be unavailable, by a manager directly designated by Jack Warner.[17] Her specific control over her cinematographer gave her more control over her onscreen image, and designating head of production Zanuck (Bennett's personal good friend) ensured her an A-class quality production at Warner Bros. Bennett's cumulative $300,000 salary generated a great deal of press, and, in fact, an outraged RKO only learned of the deal when it was announced in the industry trades. *Variety* noted on January 28, 1931, "Warner may face a court battle over the signing of Constance Bennett. Belief is that RKO does not recognize the Warner contract with the star and RKO execs are making no secret of the fact that they intend to fight to keep Miss Bennett exclusive for RKO."[18] Bennett's exorbitant salary concerned other studios, who feared their top stars would demand similar salaries for short-term deals.[19] Although RKO protested the validity of her Warner Bros. deal, it ended up recognizing the contract and working with the other studio to coordinate production schedules for Bennett's films.[20] Her decision to make films for a rival studio during her twelve-week vacation from RKO was unorthodox for a star in an exclusive studio contract. But in a resolution similar to the dispute between Stanwyck, Columbia, and Warner Bros., the actress and her employers mutually agreed to sanction her deals and work around each other.[21]

Bennett continued to work independently for several studios, where she tried off-casting to refashion her star image. In the early 1930s at RKO and Warner Bros., she often played fallen women in films such as *Bed of Roses* (Sidney Lanfield, 1933), which cast her as an ex-prostitute who, after

Constance Bennett dining with her employer and personal friend, Darryl Zanuck, and his wife, Virginia, circa mid-1930s. Courtesy of the Margaret Herrick Library, the Academy of Motion Picture Arts and Sciences; copyright holder unknown.

serving time in prison, must choose between true love with a barge owner or remaining the mistress of a millionaire. These roles often exploited her sex appeal but limited her acting range. However, after signing with the independent production company Twentieth Century Pictures in 1934, she chose serious dramatic roles designed to expand her screen persona in different genres. In her first attempt, Bennett appeared as the Duchess of Florence in the historical epic *The Affairs of Cellini* (Gregory La Cava, 1934). Emboldened by this experience, she later tried her hand as a comedienne in the Hal Roach produced *Topper* (Norman Z. McLeod, 1937), in which she played a recently deceased ghost who "haunts" her friend to loosen up his uptight lifestyle. As the *New York Times* observed in its review of the film, Bennett's earlier roles required little more of her than to be "glamorous" and "haut-monde," whereas in this supernatural screwball comedy the actress delivered an "animated, whimsy" performance.[22]

Bennett's 1934 deal with Twentieth Century Pictures was also noteworthy for its percentage-deal provision that the studio pay a cut of Bennett's films' box-office profits directly to her own company, the Bennett Pictures Corporation.[23] On *The Affairs of Cellini*, she would earn 5 percent of the film's distribution profits until the total film gross reached $1,200,000.[24] Her contract further specified that if her personal share of the gross did not amount to $75,000 within nine months of the film's general release date, the difference from her advance salary of $60,000 would be paid to her at the time.[25] By arranging for a portion of her salary to be paid through the film's gross, Bennett's income from this film would be taxed not as personal income but as capital gains.

THE PROS AND CONS OF THE PERCENTAGE DEAL: IRENE DUNNE, CLARA BOW, AND MIRIAM HOPKINS

Bennett's percentage deal was not an anomaly in Hollywood at the time; this salary alternative became an attractive option for A-list stars given the US tax structure. In 1936, changes in US tax laws raised the taxable percentage of income for the country's upper earning brackets. Thus, individuals making more than $70,000 were taxed at a now unimaginable rate of 75 percent.[26] Not surprisingly, many of Hollywood's top earners sought to sidestep these taxes through provisions like percentage deals. As Thomas Schatz explains, stars grew "wary of long-term contracts and salaried income," and instead "pursued profit-sharing and one-picture deals whereby their salaries could be invested into a picture and taxed as capital gains at a rate of only 25 percent."[27] As a crucial contractual provision that correlated to greater professional agency, profit participation had obvious appeal for artistically inclined, business-savvy stars working in the studio system because it increased their involvement in the creative and financial components of filmmaking. As Tom Kemper points out, Hollywood itself stimulated these deals through various changes in its business practices, such as the introduction of independent production companies, the growing power of talent, and the rise of what he calls an "emboldened studio system that, ironically, allowed for a certain assured flexibility in its operations."[28]

This kind of "percentage picture" arrangement also had advantages for the struggling majors RKO and Universal, as well as for independent producers such as David O. Selznick and Walter Wanger. All of them sanctioned percentage deals throughout the 1930s and into the 1940s. In an effort to turn a profit by mid-decade, RKO and Universal were compelled to pursue cost-cutting strategies; one solution was to limit the high cost of keeping talent under long-term contracts. Freelance percentage-deal contracts not only enabled these two studios to minimize up-front production costs, but also allowed them to feature A-list talent.[29] Similarly, percentage deals for talent lowered the overhead for independent producers, who had to secure funding without the backing of a powerful major studio and also lacked the cash flow to employ A-list stars on a long-term basis. Hence, cash-strapped studios and independent producers were willing to experiment with freelance contractual agreements and profit-sharing deals. Freelance stars, in turn, leveraged their salaries contingent upon their box-office earning power, so both producer/studio and talent stood to mutually benefit (or lose) from these deals.

Irene Dunne, Clara Bow, and Miriam Hopkins, in addition to Constance Bennett, received a share of their films' distribution profits through contractual percentage deals that crystallized their professional agency in different ways. Dunne's experience shows how a clearly articulated percentage deal could be a gold mine, supplying earnings long after production of the film had concluded. By contrast, Bow arranged for her Hollywood comeback at Fox through a promising percentage-deal bonus that ultimately was never paid to her due to contractual distribution provisions that favored the studio. Lastly, Hopkins's apparent lack of interest in her percentage deal illuminates how her freelance career suffered in the long run.

Irene Dunne began her screen career as an independent actress and negotiated profitable contracts with several major studios to maintain her professional agency throughout the decade. A reputable actress on the Broadway stage by the late 1920s, and with a musical background in opera, she first came to work at RKO in 1930 to star in their Western sound spectacle *Cimarron* (Wesley Ruggles, 1931). Her two-year contract contained special provisions that were quite unconventional for an actress who had yet to prove her worth at the box office. However, her acting and singing talents, coupled with her Academy Award nomination for Best Actress in *Cimarron*, were a coveted commodity in Hollywood. Moreover, Dunne's move to motion pictures also represents a synergy between theater and the film industry in the early 1930s, which her 1930 RKO contract reflects. Because the studio was in need of stars after the transition to sound, it sought out Broadway talent to fill the void. The contract gave Dunne the right to return to New York to act in plays between films, which enhanced her reputation as a skilled dramatic actress of both stage and screen.[30] She even reprised some of her noteworthy stage performances for the screen, most prominently in James Whale's *Show Boat*, released by Universal in 1936, in which she played the lead female role, Magnolia, a gifted singer.

Dunne's contract also gave her featured billing, and in the event that the studio loaned her out, RKO would pay her "half of any amount [it] received" for such services over and above her weekly salary (which began at $1,000 a week in 1931 and culminated in $2,000 a week at the end of the agreement).[31] When she renewed her contract in 1933, Dunne hired Charles Feldman to be her agent, and he negotiated a lucrative one-year, four-picture deal that included 15 percent of the third film's gross receipts once it had recouped twice the amount of the film's budget.[32] The definition of "gross receipts and proceeds" varied depending on the specific studio and/or producer in a star's contract, which clarifies why percentage deals differed case by case. With regard to Dunne's deal, RKO defined gross receipts as any earnings "received from played or paid bookings of said photoplay by RKO Distributing Corporation or any other distributor in its stead" (including RKO Pictures Australia, Canada, and Great Britain).[33] The third film that she made in this agreement was *Roberta* (William A. Seiter, 1935), costarring with the box-office powerhouse duo Fred Astaire and Ginger Rogers (neither of whom had a percentage deal). Dunne continued to collect a respectable salary years after *Roberta*'s initial 1935 release from the film's ongoing distribution, with her percentage earnings reaching a grand total of $157,948.50 by November 1941.[34] Thus Dunne's profit-sharing deal with RKO was far more lucrative than the $45,000 salary she received to make the film in 1934.[35]

Based on her success with *Roberta*, the actress made subsequent distribution percentage deals at RKO as well as future deals, including at Universal in 1937.[36] To make the screwball comedy *My Favorite Wife* (Garson Kanin, 1940) at RKO, Dunne dropped her flat-rate salary from $150,000 to $100,000 for ten weeks of work in exchange for a cut of the film's total distribution gross, which—counter to her *Roberta* deal—meant that she received earnings on the film as profits came in from the very beginning of the film's release. Her percentage term specified that she would receive a $50,000 salary from the distribution gross of the film (which would be taxed at the lower capital gains rate) as well as 7.5 percent of the gross once the film amassed more than $1,750,000 in box-office receipts.[37] *My Favorite Wife* performed well, with a world gross totaling $2,057,000 and generating a profit for the studio of $505,000; thus Dunne earned an additional $139,056.20 for the film in 1940-1941 alone, doubling her initial salary.[38]

Director Garson Kanin and costar Cary Grant look on as Irene Dunne plays piano on the set of *My Favorite Wife* (1941), another lucrative picture for RKO and the actress. Courtesy of the Cinematic Arts Library, the University of Southern California; copyright 1941, RKO Radio Pictures.

Dunne also used her contracts with various studios to improve her critical standing in the industry by securing creative stipulations that she believed would improve a project's artistic integrity, especially by securing film deals with respected directors. Her 1937 Universal agreement specified John Stahl as director in at least two of three films; it also stated that the studio could not loan her out, and granted her story and script approval.[39] Dunne collaborated with director Leo McCarey again when she starred in the romantic tearjerker *Love Affair* (1939), a freelance deal for

UA that earned her a fourth Oscar nomination. The actress's savvy use of the contract underscored "the autonomy that Dunne exercised within the studio system."[40] Through her distribution percentage deals, she bolstered her critical reputation in the industry, becoming more selective with her projects and retaining more creative discretion in the film's production process.

By 1943 Dunne had maintained freelance status in Hollywood for more than thirteen years, and she remained in high demand at various studios, all of which were contractually obligated to honor the actress's various agreements and thus arrange production schedules around her availability. This was challenging for the studios to comply with at times, and resulted in some corporate bickering. In January 1943, when a litigious situation emerged between Dunne and two studios with which she had freelance deals, Columbia and MGM, Columbia tried to prematurely force her starting date for the first film in their agreement, even though it conflicted with her prior contract with MGM. In a January 20, 1943, letter, Dunne's agent, Charles Feldman, reprimanded Columbia, arguing that the studio could not apply the "standard" contractual terms to the freelance actress's situation, especially in regard to her starting date. Feldman explained:

> At no time since the date of her said agreement with you has Miss Dunne entered into any "term contract." You know very well that the phrase, "term contract" is clearly understood in the industry to mean a contract upon a weekly basis and it is clearly distinguishable from a contract which would prevent her from performing her services under your contract since she is specifically permitted under your contract to enter into other picture commitments and Paragraph 22 of said agreement recognizes her right to refuse a starting date given by you if it conflicts with any prior commitment for another picture.[41]

Dunne's contract with Columbia sanctioned her simultaneous freelance agreements with other studios, in this case, with MGM for the war/action romances *A Guy Named Joe* (Victor Fleming, 1943) and *The White Cliffs of Dover* (Clarence Brown, 1944). Feldman's letter went on to chastise Columbia, stating that they would be held "strictly accountable" should they compromise her professional reputation.[42] In the end, Columbia was forced to start its picture with the actress *after* she had completed her films for MGM, as her contract explicitly outlined. Hence, closer scrutiny of Dunne's contracts over a decade demonstrates how she not only secured important creative-control provisions but also used the percentage deal for financial benefit in the long term, all while remaining gainfully employed as a top Hollywood freelance actress.

The percentage deal could also help restore the reputations of "has-been" stars looking to make a comeback in Hollywood, as was the case with the "It" girl, silent film superstar Clara Bow. As Paramount's most valuable star in the late 1920s, Bow had made a successful transition to sound in *The Wild Party* (Dorothy Arzner, 1929). However, the studio then haphazardly cast her in a series of mediocre productions, including *True to the Navy* (1929) and *Her Wedding Night* (1930), both directed by Frank Tuttle, which sought only to exploit her substantial box-office draw. Bow's image had also been tarnished by the very public scandal in 1931 engendered by the civil suit *People v. DeVoe* against her former secretary, Daisy DeVoe, who exposed much of her former employer's colorful off-screen antics and personal life on the stand. After the box-office disappointments of her 1931 films *No Limit* (Frank Tuttle, 1931) and *Kick In* (Richard Wallace, 1931), Bow lost a plum lead role in Rouben Mamoulian's gangster crime drama *City Streets* (1931); it went to Silvia Sidney (then the mistress of B. P. Schulberg, Paramount's head of production). Later that year, Bow and the studio mutually agreed not to renew her contract.[43]

Analyzing the contracts for Bow's return to the screen two years later reveals that she did not leave Paramount in disgrace due to her inability to make the transition to sound film, or for her dwindling box-office allure.[44] In fact, nearly every major studio offered Bow a film deal after she left Paramount.[45] Instead, after her bitter experience there, Bow put her career in the hands of independent producer Sam Rork.[46] In the fall of 1931, she and Rork negotiated with Columbia for a one-picture deal in which she would be paid $100,000 plus an additional amount equivalent to 10 percent of the net profits the producer earned or received from the sale or distribution of the film.[47] This deal unraveled, however, after Columbia approached Rork to "option" Bow's services for two additional pictures and tried to lower her salary to $75,000 per film. While Bow agreed to the reduced salary, she never approved the final agreement between Rork and Columbia, and by January 1932 she had initiated talks with Fox for a two-picture deal.[48]

Bow leveraged her former star power to secure creative autonomy and a lucrative salary in a non-exclusive contract with Fox. For her comeback in 1933, she received $75,000 for the film—plus script, director, and co-star approval—and negotiated for a closed set during filming to make an

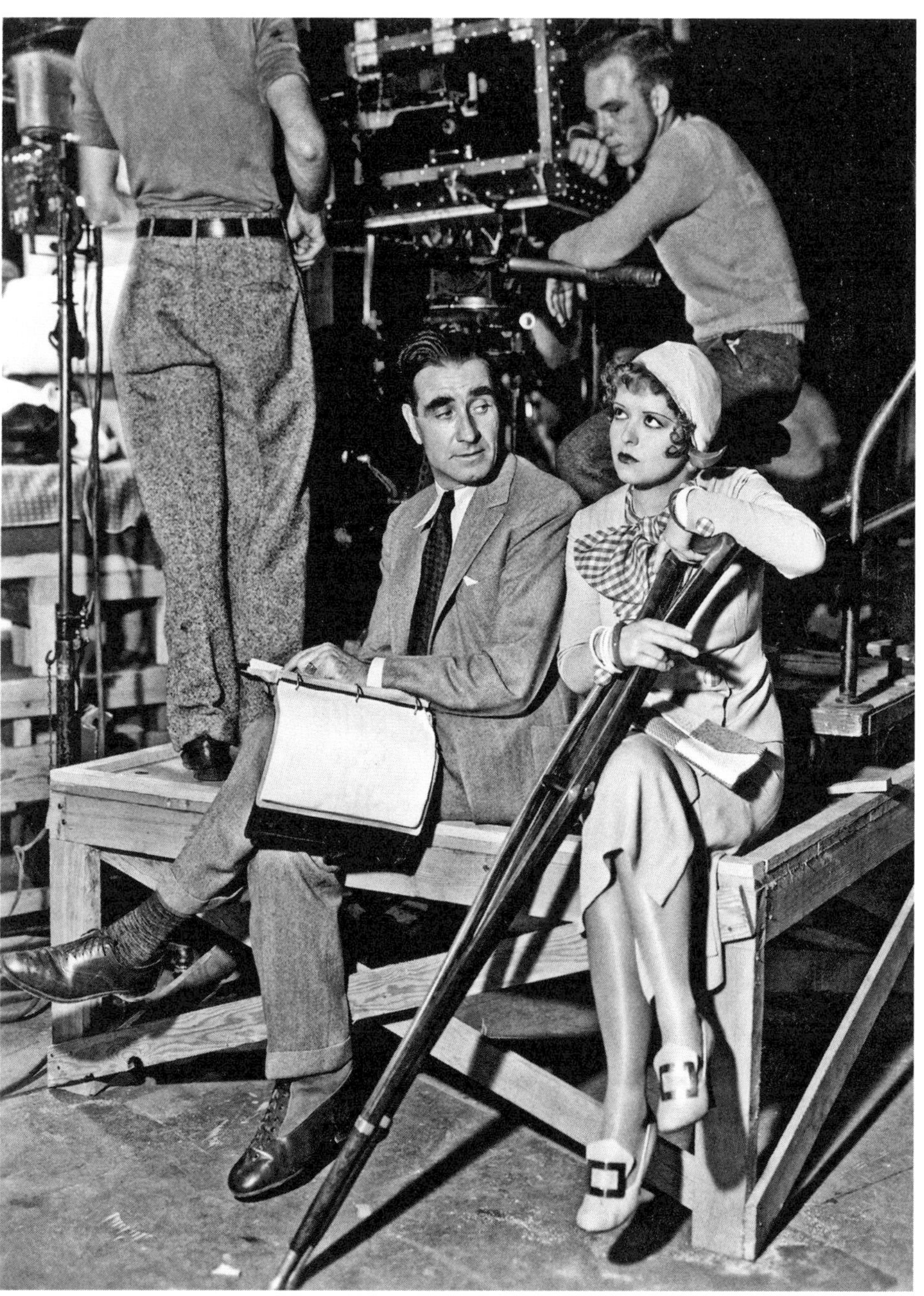

Triumphant comeback: Clara Bow consulting with her hand-picked director, John Francis Dillon, on the set of *Call Her Savage* in 1932. Courtesy of the Margaret Herrick Library, the Academy of Motion Picture Arts and Sciences; copyright 1933, Fox Film Corporation.

adaptation of Tiffany Thayer's best-selling novel *Call Her Savage* (John Francis Dillon, 1932), a story that Bow personally selected.[49] Bow played the fiery Texan heiress Nasa Springer in a sensational tale featuring a range of subjects then considered taboo, including interracial love, incest, promiscuity, sadism, and lesbianism. Despite the film's exploitative material, Bow's creative control finally enabled her to take ownership of her screen image and showcase her dramatic talent and range alongside her sex appeal. The critics and industry trades also recognized this, with *Variety* noting, "Bow's greatly improved acting technique is an added element of strength" to *Call Her Savage*.[50]

Per her contract she was to receive a $25,000 bonus should the picture gross over $800,000 in profits—a shrewd arrangement for a star who had been out of circulation for two years after uneven performances. By contrast, Paramount, which had considered Bow "washed up" two years before, went into receivership that year with a $15 million deficit and fired her former boss, Schulberg. Hence, Bow's decision to leave Paramount and return as a freelancer restored her professional standing in Hollywood, gave her the discretion to choose her production terms, and demonstrated that she was still a top box-office draw. Although Fox wanted to extend her employment, and other studios made additional offers, Bow's comeback was short-lived; she retired from acting in 1934 to focus on raising a family with her husband, Rex Bell, himself a star of B-movie Westerns.[51]

Bow's deal at Fox also illustrates how the interpretation of a film's distribution gross varied from studio to studio in the 1930s, and it emphasizes why freelance stars had to articulate very clearly the terms of their profit-sharing agreements. Bow's percentage was different from Dunne's in that she received a bonus only if each film grossed over $800,000. Both *Call Her Savage* and *Hoop-La* (Frank Lloyd, 1933) were solid box-office successes, and Bow tried to collect her $25,000 bonus in October 1935, arguing that these films did indeed earn $800,000 in profits. But Fox itself was bombarded with financial problems, in receivership, and in the process of merging with Twentieth Century Pictures. Darryl Zanuck and Joseph Schenck, the new heads of Twentieth Century-Fox, claimed that her films had not reached this amount due to apparent "deductions" in preparing her film for foreign exhibition. Because the distribution gross terms were loosely defined in Bow's contract, the studio had the upper hand in determining whether or not she would receive her percentage bonus.[52] By contrast, Irene Dunne's participation in the distribution profits were delineated specifically in her contract in terms of payment schedule and the amount of earnings that she would receive.

Whereas the percentage deal served to bolster the career of Irene Dunne and reignite that of Clara Bow, the case of Miriam Hopkins illustrates the perils of the tactic if stars did not realize the increased personal responsibility necessary to maintain independent stardom in Hollywood. The actress initially used the percentage deal to gain more financial security on what she perceived to be a risky production, *Becky Sharp* (Rouben Mamoulian, 1935), Hollywood's first major live-action, three-color Technicolor film (produced by the independent production company Pioneer Pictures). This film marked the inception of her independent stardom in 1934, after she asked Paramount to release her from her long-term contract.[53]

For the *Becky Sharp* deal, Hopkins's non-option, one-picture contract gave her approval of her director and supplemented her flat-rate $60,000 salary with a 10 percent cut of the film's gross receipts after it had recouped the negative cost of the film's production, $800,000.[54] Her agent, Myron Selznick, justified his client's percentage as compensation for the career gamble that this live-action color film represented, as audience reaction to three-color Technicolor had yet to be determined. Furthermore, Hopkins carried the film as its lead star, and thus its success (or failure) would largely be attributed to her. To make sure that the Pioneer accountants were keeping accurate records, Hopkins's contract also retained her right to have her accountants audit the percentage earnings.[55] *Becky Sharp* did go on to gross over its base production cost of $800,000; curiously, however, Hopkins sold off her share of the profits in 1936 for a flat rate of $2,500 with 7.5 percent interest.

Evidence from Pioneer Picture's interoffice memos suggests that Hopkins was not enthused about the publicity work required to help promote *Becky Sharp*. Pioneer employee Lowell Calvert vented his frustration at Hopkins's endless "excuses" and lack of cooperation in the film's publicity campaign, which was critical to its long-term box-office success. Calvert contended that her cooperation would benefit not only Pioneer and RKO (the film's distributor), but also the actress herself as a freelance artist:

> In spite of it all, we still feel confident that we will get by with some publicity, but with the clause in Hopkins's contract, which to her is exceedingly favorable if the gate receipts are good, she should be breaking her doggone little neck to do anything and everything which would cause favorable publicity to ooze forth from all of the magazines, newspapers, trade papers, etc.[56]

All eyes on Miriam Hopkins on the set of *Becky Sharp*, which required more off-screen promotion than the actress realized when she signed her contract. Courtesy of the Margaret Herrick Library, the Academy of Motion Picture Arts and Sciences; copyright 1935, Pioneer Pictures, Inc.

Calvert's dismay with Hopkins highlights how her freelance contract differed substantially from the standard long-term option studio contract, in which a star would be contractually obligated to cooperate with publicists and advertising for the film.[57] Moreover, Hopkins's percentage deal remained one of the most lucrative aspects of her freelance contract with Pioneer, and thus she also stood to gain (or lose) directly from her film's distribution and exhibition. However, her apparent apathy about working the publicity circuit diminished her cut of the film's gross and eventually her ability to maintain a freelance career.

Consequently, independent stardom hindered Hopkins in the long run and led to the loss of the stellar status that she had attained at Paramount in the early 1930s. Compounding her indifference about publicizing her films was the fact that those she made for Samuel Goldwyn in the mid-1930s had only mediocre box-office performances.[58] Even when Goldwyn lent Hopkins out to RKO in to make *Wise Girl* (Leigh Jason, 1937) and *The Woman I Love* (Anatole Litvak, 1937), both lost money for the studio.[59] Hopkins's box-office appeal was on the wane, as the exhibitor journal *The Motion Picture Herald* revealed in its 1937 poll of the top moneymaking stars (tallied theater manager reports from across the country). She ranked in the "Group III" level and was not among the top ten or the second tier.[60] While independent stardom had strengthened Dunne's career and recuperated Bow's standing in the industry, for Hopkins it came at the expense of less screen exposure and reduced market appeal.

Hopkins's diminished box-office appeal impacted her freelance options and explains her next career move in 1938, when she exchanged her high salary for more creative control over a film's production at Warner Bros. This contract mandated her approval over costar, script, and director in two "A-class" motion pictures in exchange for a reduced salary, from her usual $300,000 for four pictures to $150,000 for the right to do two pictures of "extraordinary" quality and have increased creative control.[61] Hopkins decreased her price in order to help stage a comeback after being off-screen for all of 1938, and used her star-commodity value to secure artistic control over her two-picture deal at Warner Bros. Her special provisions included fixed working hours of no more than eight a day, and greater prominence in advertising (meaning the star's name had to be placed in letters larger than any other cast member's).[62] This bargaining move baffled studio executives at Warner Bros., who surmised that it did not seem logical that an artist would sacrifice $200,000. Studio legal adviser Roy Obringer rationalized that she did it solely to win "the right to appear in two good pictures."[63] Given the lackluster reception of Hopkins's RKO films, the actress's salary reduction in exchange for artistic control made clear sense. In order to preserve her freelance status, Hopkins needed to revive her career (and attempt to ensure future job offers) with good-quality films.

But Hopkins's proactive measures to salvage her independent stardom were not enough to win her the compelling roles promised to her contractually at Warner Bros. She languished at the studio and remained off-screen until 1939, while she clashed with Jack Warner over potential assignments. Many of the films that Hopkins wanted had already been promised to the studio's top contract female star, her rival Bette Davis, including *Dark Victory* (Edmund Goulding, 1939) and *All This and Heaven Too* (Anatole Litvak, 1940). Hopkins even requested to play the more sympathetic role of Charlotte in *The Old Maid* (Edmund Goulding, 1939). Nevertheless, all of these roles went to Davis, despite Hopkins's contractual discretion to approve stories.[64] This point highlights the irony in Hopkins's independent stardom compared to Davis's dependent stardom at Warner Bros. By the late 1930s, Davis had finally gained considerably more leverage over her career. With two Best Actress Oscars in hand, she reigned as the top female star at Warner Bros., leaving few plum parts for other actresses. It was also in Warner Bros.' long-term interest to bolster the careers of their contract talent rather than freelancers who came and went on short-term deals. Thus, Hopkins's experience after she left Paramount demonstrates how professional independence and a non-exclusive affiliation with a major studio sometimes came at the expense of stardom, especially when faced with competition from long-term contract stars with the full support and resources of a studio at their disposal.

INCARNATIONS OF [SEMI] INDEPENDENT STARDOM: ANN HARDING, KATHARINE HEPBURN, CLAUDETTE COLBERT, AND JANET GAYNOR

As we have seen with the women discussed in the preceding sections, freelancing in Hollywood could be a very lucrative and savvy career move, allowing stars not only higher salaries but increased control over their screen image. At the same time, freelancing amplified career risks since these women were bereft of studio support if the films failed to deliver at the box office. However, even those stars, including Ann Harding and Katharine Hepburn (both at RKO) and Claudette Colbert (at Paramount), who were too risk-averse to give up stable employment at a studio, could negotiate for a supplemental percentage deal from their films' profits, renegotiate for more creative discretion, or arrange for outside deals at other studios. If dissatisfied with their experience as an exclusive long-term contract star, as Janet Gaynor was at Fox in 1936, they could terminate the relationship and move elsewhere, leveraging their established market value for a better deal. These women can be understood as semi-independent stars who maintained largely exclusive affiliations with studios that sheltered them from the risks of freelancing but still granted a considerable level of professional agency as their star value grew, and as they renegotiated their contracts.

Ann Harding was a respected Broadway actress in the 1920s until Hollywood wooed her to the screen. Pathé Studios developed sophisticated melodramas like *Holiday* (Edward H. Griffith, 1930) in upper-class settings, hoping that the cultured Harding would broaden the studio's appeal beyond male action-driven films.[65] After RKO purchased Pathé in 1931, Harding was the new studio's most valuable actress under contract, and she was marketed as RKO Pathé's answer to MGM superstar Norma Shearer.[66]

The contract battle that ensued in 1931 between Harding and RKO Pathé reflected both her professional agency and commercial value. With slightly more than a year left before her initial Pathé contract would expire in early February 1931, Harding received counteroffers from both MGM and Paramount. That motivated Pathé's head of production, Hiram Brown, who viewed her as one of the studio's "assets," to renegotiate her current contract.[67] Harding, however, turned down Pathé's offer of an $840,000 salary for a three-year period, paying $240,000 for four pictures in the first year and $400,000 by the third year, which equates to a range of "$65,000 to $100,000 per picture."[68] The actress preferred to retain the creative provisions specified in her current $2,000 weekly salary, which guaranteed her final say on stories and directors. The proposed new RKO Pathé contract would eliminate those assurances, thus thwarting her star agency. To keep the actress on their roster, RKO Pathé worked to address Harding's grievances, and she stayed on at the studio until the mid-1930s, eventually earning a salary of $60,000 per picture. She was also supposed to receive a 15 percent cut of the gross receipts on the World War I love-triangle film *The Fountain* (John Cromwell, 1934), but the picture resulted in a loss of $150,000 for the studio.[69]

Harding's stardom was relatively short lived. The popularity (and profits) of her sophisticated urban films adapted from Broadway plays had waned by the late 1930s. Though she retired from the screen in 1937 after her marriage to conductor Werner Janssen, Harding resurfaced in Holly-

Ann Harding reviewing costumes with RKO head designer Walter Plunkett circa early 1930s. She chose to retain creative control rather than receive a higher salary. Courtesy of the Margaret Herrick Library, the Academy of Motion Picture Arts and Sciences; copyright holder unknown.

wood as a freelance character actress in the 1940s and 1950s. Nevertheless, her negotiations with Pathé and RKO in the 1930s set a precedent for transitioning from exclusive studio association to a semi-independent relationship with an employer.

Katharine Hepburn arrived in Hollywood in 1932 and soon eclipsed Harding's star status at RKO. Her experience demonstrates how a long-term option contract agreement evolved into a semi-independent relationship.

She signed with RKO in the wake of her stunning screen debut with acting legend John Barrymore in *A Bill of Divorcement* (George Cukor, 1932), in which the actress played a young woman who discovers, and confronts, her family's hidden history of mental illness. Hepburn then became their most prominent star after the box-office success of *Little Women* (1933), in which she played Louisa May Alcott's famous literary heroine Jo March, and an Academy Award for Best Actress for her turn as a struggling stage actress in *Morning Glory* (Lowell Sherman, 1933). These successes enabled her to renegotiate percentage deals. With the help of her agent, Leland Hayward (who ran Myron Selznick's New York office), Hepburn mobilized her star value to supplement her $2,000 weekly salary with a percentage deal for her films beginning in 1933.[70] She was to receive 12.5 percent of the pictures' gross, but only after they had earned back twice their base production cost, which RKO estimated at $175,000.[71] However, the two films released under this agreement were box-office disappointments, particularly *Spitfire* (John Cromwell, 1934), so Hepburn's percentage did not kick in.[72] She had personally campaigned for the lead in *Spitfire*, a poor, uneducated mountain girl in the American South, but the educated New Englander was terribly miscast in the role. Although the film grossed $113,000 profit, it spawned what Richard Jewell calls a "public disenchantment" with the actress at the box office that continued to grow for most of the decade, undermining her professional agency.

Nevertheless, Hepburn remained an important asset to RKO, which had few stars on its roster. The studio was willing to renegotiate her contract yet again on June 1, 1934, giving Hepburn $50,000 per film (with a total of six films in two years), and a percentage of the profits, but only after a film grossed $600,000.[73] Her first two films under this agreement—romantic dramas *Alice Adams* (George Stevens, 1935) and *Break of Hearts* (Philip Moeller, 1935)—did generate some profits ($164,000 and $16,000, respectively), but not enough for Hepburn to collect any percentage earnings.

Although RKO increased Hepburn's salary again in 1936, to $60,000 per picture with the same percentage-deal terms, her films failed to perform at the box office, and her standing at RKO became much more precarious. As Jewell explains, "[B]eginning with *Sylvia Scarlet*, the studio's first release of 1936," Hepburn appeared in "one flop after another, thereby diminishing her standing on RKO's star roster."[74] This was distressing for both the actress and the studio. For Hepburn, it endangered her ability to negotiate advantageous contracts and capitalize on her percentage deals. For RKO, a waning Hepburn translated to fewer profits, since it sold its films in blocks, "largely by promising to deliver a certain number of films

Semi-independent stardom in action: Katharine Hepburn with director George Stevens on the set of *Alice Adams*. Courtesy of the Margaret Herrick Library, the Academy of Motion Picture Arts and Sciences; copyright 1935, RKO Radio Pictures.

featuring public favorites."[75] As such, it was "imperative to boost Hepburn back to the lofty position she had once occupied in the show business hierarchy."[76] Despite both the actress and RKO having high hopes for her 1937 films, they failed to meet box-office expectations due to their high production costs.[77]

The confluence of these events led Hepburn and RKO to mutually terminate their agreement in 1938, with the actress agreeing to repay the

$22,740 advance she had received on anticipated percentage earnings.[78] Hepburn appeared to be washed up, but as we know now, the intrepid actress would have one of the most astonishing comebacks in Hollywood history. In fact, Hepburn's experience at RKO emboldened the actress to seek creative control over future projects, both in film and on the stage. This was the case with *The Philadelphia Story* (George Cukor, 1940), in which she retained the screen rights (which she then sold to MGM while safeguarding her right to star in the film).[79]

Claudette Colbert achieved semi-independent stardom at Paramount Pictures in the 1930s with far more success than Hepburn or Harding. Her contractual renegotiations included creative provisions, the right to do outside pictures, and percentage deals. She began in Hollywood as a long-term option contract actress in 1932, earning $2,500 a week for five pictures a year.[80] She soon emerged as one of the studio's most profitable leading ladies, appearing in box-office hit historical epics such as Cecil B. DeMille's *Sign of the Cross* (1932) and *Cleopatra* (1934). Colbert crystallized her star agency in 1934 when she won the Best Actress Academy Award for Frank Capra's surprise hit comedy, *It Happened One Night*, an outside film deal that she had negotiated as part of her Paramount contract.[81] At this point, she and agent Charles Feldman renegotiated her contract to reflect her new market value in Hollywood. In a six-picture agreement signed in 1934, Paramount agreed to pay Colbert $100,000 per picture for a two-year period.[82] Moreover, her new deal worked around her films at other studios (one for Columbia, two for producer-director John Stahl at Universal, and another for Warner Bros.) and stipulated that she would only work with directors in the highest salary brackets, which nearly guaranteed casting her in prestige productions.[83]

The Stahl-Universal collaboration also included her first percentage deal, a 2 percent share of the film's gross receipts, and produced *Imitation of Life* (1934), an adaptation of Fannie Hurst's popular (and controversial) novel about motherhood and race—another solid critical and commercial success for Colbert. Feldman's hand substantially bolstered her professional agency as a semi-independent star, just as it had for Irene Dunne. Likewise, he advocated for better creative incentives, winning Colbert the right to approve stories in all of her outside agreements. Kemper contends that these deals gave Colbert the "autonomy in developing her range as an actress"; thus, her semi-independent stardom facilitated her ability to mold her onscreen persona by letting her choose the stories and directors for these productions.[84] Her newfound role versatility included the Walter Wanger-produced *Private Worlds* (Gregory La Cava, 1935), which cast her

Colbert's 1934 contract with Paramount granted her creative discretion in her loan-out deals. She chose John Stahl to direct *Imitation of Life* at Universal, seen with her on set here. Courtesy of the Margaret Herrick Library, the Academy of Motion Picture Arts and Sciences; copyright 1934, Universal Pictures Corp.

as a doctor making great strides in treating the mentally ill; more screwball comedies, such as Columbia's *She Married Her Boss* (Gregory La Cava, 1935), in which she played an executive secretary secretly in love with her boss; and the off-beat political satire *Tovarich,* directed in 1937 by Anatole Litvak at Warner Bros. that featured Colbert as a cunning Russian duchess in Paris seeking funds to start a counter-revolution.

In 1936, Colbert renegotiated yet again with Paramount and amended her percentage deal. In addition to her $100,000 salary per film, Colbert would earn a 10 percent share (approximately $10,000) after the film recovered its production cost.[85] Furthermore, the actress retained her approval of stories and directors, resulting in collaborations with the studio's top directors, including Ernst Lubitsch (*Bluebeard's Eighth Wife,* 1938) and Mitchell Leisen (*Midnight,* 1939). By the end of the decade, these savvy deals had made Colbert one of the highest paid and most highly praised actors in Hollywood.[86]

Similarly, while Janet Gaynor maintained an exclusive professional affiliation with Fox Studios for a decade as one of their leading female stars, she found her star power significantly diminished after the 1935 merger with Twentieth Century. Her subsequent decision to freelance helped her regain the creative and professional agency that she had previously had at Fox. Gaynor had signed a five-year, long-term option contract with Fox in 1926 and soon achieved widespread acclaim for her work with the most prominent directors on the lot: Frank Borzage on *Street Angel* and *Seventh Heaven,* and the German émigré F. W. Murnau on *Sunrise* (1927). These three performances culminated in her winning the first Best Actress Academy Award in 1927.[87] Even so, Gaynor's Fox contract paid her only $300 a week, gave her no casting or story approval, and included no special provisions regarding work hours, cameramen, and so on.[88] In short, the actress had retained little control over her career or screen image in her Fox contract. Nonetheless, the young actress learned from this experience and applied it in her subsequent contract negotiations at Fox.

Gaynor's stardom continued to flourish after a successful transition to sound, with her voice complimenting her innocent waif persona in musicals, many costarring Charles Farrell. Billed as "America's favorite lovebirds," she and Farrell were a popular team who made twelve films between 1927 and 1934, and she was also cast alongside superstar Will Rogers in *State Fair* (Henry King, 1933).[89] Indeed, her films helped sustain the financially troubled Fox Studios in the early 1930s, which went into receivership after its founder, William Fox, was forced out of the company in 1930.[90] Gaynor consistently ranked as one of the top five moneymaking stars in the *Motion Picture Herald* poll from 1930 to 1935, and five of her films were top-grossing pictures of the first half of the decade.[91]

Realizing her importance, Fox renewed Gaynor's contract option in 1933, giving her a higher salary and granting certain creative provisions that reflected both her commercial value to the studio and her empowered agency as a bankable star. Her new contract called for six films total, with her salary increasing on a film-to-film basis, beginning at $100,000 and culminating at $115,000. After exercising little creative control over her career up to that point, Gaynor now had the right to approve the story and script for each of her films.[92] She renegotiated again with Fox in 1935 to make only two films a year for $115,000 each. She retained story and script approval, and her contract stipulated that Fox producer Winfield Sheehan would produce her films.[93] What's more, Gaynor had the final say as to whether Fox could loan her services.[94]

After Fox Film Corporation merged with Joe Schenck and Darryl F. Zanuck's Twentieth Century Pictures in the summer of 1935 to create Twentieth Century-Fox, Gaynor found her status as the studio's most valued star in question, even though her newly negotiated contract preceded the merger by more than three months. The new studio's general sales manager had conducted an exhibitor survey that revealed a public preference for all-star-cast films, which led Twentieth Century-Fox to enact a policy of casting two or more stars per film. However, this contradicted Gaynor's earlier deal, which awarded her sole star billing for her films and in studio publicity.[95] A front-page *Variety* story in September 1936 titled "Fox Skeds Co-Star Policy for Gaynor" noted that the actress would star alongside artists of equal talent, as exemplified in the film *Ladies in Love* (Edward H. Griffith, 1936), in which she costarred with Constance Bennett, Loretta Young, and Simone Simon, and that plans to produce a series of pictures starring Gaynor had been "abandoned."[96] The actress, a long-time asset to the company, viewed this new policy as detrimental to her career, and she retaliated with her own press release: "My contract with Twentieth Century-Fox ended with the completion of *Ladies in Love*. I was asked to make a new term contract with that company, but several days ago, and before the announcement appearing in Saturday's trade papers, I notified Mr. Zanuck I would not make a new contract."[97] Gaynor effectively dissolved her exclusive association with Twentieth Century-Fox after ten years and twenty films. Her swift exit continued to draw speculation from *Variety*, which noted, "There was a good deal of speculation of whether Miss Gaynor would freelance as a star, or make a limited picture arrangement with one of the major studios."[98]

Janet Gaynor accepting her fictional Best Actress Oscar for her performance as Vicki Lester in David O. Selznick's independent production *A Star Is Born*, her first freelance venture. Courtesy of Cinematic Arts Library, University of Southern California; copyright 1937, Selznick International Pictures, Inc.

Indeed, the actress signed a freelance deal for one film with David O. Selznick's SIP in the fall of 1936, playing the sole female lead in the Technicolor *A Star Is Born* (William Wellman, 1937).[99] Gaynor's contract with SIP retained her star status (guaranteeing her first billing) and a no-loan-out clause; it also included several new provisions, such as male costar and story approval.[100] Gaynor had abandoned the security and stability of the major studio for professional independence as a freelance artist. Furthermore, she and Selznick later renegotiated her SIP contract to include a percentage deal on *A Star Is Born*, reducing her $137,000 per film salary to $100,000 in exchange for a 10 percent cut of the net distribution profits.[101] It was a smart career move, as the film was a critical and commercial success, and brought her a second Academy Award nomination for Best Actress. *A Star is Born* was ranked as one of *Variety*'s top grossing films as well as one of *Film Daily*'s ten best films of the year, and Gaynor's new "color" persona was extolled by critics and the industry trades. Gaynor's performance as Vicki Lester, the struggling actress turned Hollywood star, earned this praise from *Variety*: "Miss Gaynor gives to her role, the small town girl who makes good, a characterization of sustained loveliness which will arouse generous sympathy. . . . She is equally good in the comedy passages and probably has not given a more satisfactory performance in her career."[102] Subsequently, the actress extended her agreement with Selznick to include two additional films.

The examples of Harding, Hepburn, Colbert, and Gaynor reveal how even stars who were exclusively associated with a major studio could cultivate a semi-independent stardom by renegotiating their contracts. They bargained for special creative and financial provisions that allowed them to be more dynamically involved in their films' production processes, albeit with different results. In the case of Harding, even increased creative discretion and the percentage deal guaranteed by her RKO contract were not enough to counter changing audience tastes and her films' dwindling box-office profits. Likewise, Hepburn's experience at RKO shows the potential downside of profit sharing, as her forays into semi-independent stardom were hindered by her films' soaring budget costs and her faltering popularity with audiences and critics. Although the actress still made money because her contract guaranteed her a weekly salary, she had to return her advance on projected earnings after the cancellation of her RKO contract. By contrast, Colbert's career demonstrates how contract renegotiation furnished star agency even in an exclusive studio relationship. As her stardom remained secure and her films popular at the box office, so did her bargaining power and her ability to negotiate percentage deals and creative guarantees at her home studio, Paramount remain strong. Gaynor's career shows an evolutionary independent stardom, from an exclusive affiliation with a major studio to freelancing, a move that enabled her to regain professional agency and better creative and working conditions at SIP after losing them at Twentieth Century-Fox.

A CONTRACT LIKE NO OTHER: CAROLE LOMBARD

Of all the freelance stars in the 1930s, Carole Lombard was the savviest in terms of maintaining her independent stardom through the complex power of an advantageous Hollywood contract. Her astute wheeling and dealing over the course of the decade remade her career, allowing her to transcend her clotheshorse, long-term contract-player image at Paramount to emerge as Hollywood's most important freelance actress and highest paid A-list star. As such, her career illuminates the full potential of independent stardom in the studio system.

Lombard proved to be an equally adept negotiator in her freelance contracts and collaborations with creative producers (again with David O. Selznick) after the conclusion of her long-term option contract at Paramount in 1936. Her attention to legal nuance traced back to her frustration with Paramount's mismanagement of her career; fed up with being a second-tier leading lady in the early 1930s, she decided to off-cast herself in loan-outs to Columbia (*Twentieth Century*, 1934) and Universal (*My Man Godfrey*, 1936) to develop her talent as a budding screwball comedienne persona that blended sex appeal with zany wit. Receiving the A-list star treatment from Paramount in *Hands Across the Table* (Mitchell Leisen, 1935), which featured her comedic talents as Wanda Nash of Brooklyn masquerading as "Princess Olga of Sweden" to win a movie contract, left her craving more discretion in her career beyond what the studio offered. Lombard's agent, Myron Selznick, was key to achieving what she wanted. After she hired him in 1933, he propelled her to independent stardom and helped the actress capitalize on her successes. For example, he immediately negotiated to raise her salary from $750 to $1,000 a week, and then to $3,000 a week the following year. By the expiration of her exclusive seven-year contract with Paramount in 1936, Lombard was ready to take control of her career. In fact, Myron Selznick was already shopping Lombard around as a freelance artist at SIP and Warner Bros.

Lombard's tentative contract negotiations piqued the interest of the industry trades, as exemplified by the *Hollywood Reporter* headline in July 1936 that read "Carole Lombard Asks Para for Freedom or Boost."[103] Myron also made sure to include Paramount in his client's new matrix of contracts: a new limited, non-exclusive contract for three pictures for one year at $150,000 each, making her the highest paid star in the industry for 1937, with an annual income of slightly under half a million dollars.[104] Lombard's one-picture deal with Warner Bros. for the comedy *Fools for Scandal* (Mervyn LeRoy, 1938) typified the freelance contract that she and Myron lobbied for in that it contained several special provisions that directly shaped the presentation of her onscreen image. These included employing her personal costume designer of choice (Travis Banton) and her preferred cinematographer, Teddy Tetzloff, A.S.C., as well as specifying her star-billing font and type size, and limiting her shooting schedule to an eight-hour day.[105]

Carole Lombard, early 1930s, during her Paramount years as clothes-horse glamour girl. Courtesy of the Margaret Herrick Library, the Academy of Motion Picture Arts and Sciences; copyright holder unknown.

The new Carole Lombard in 1937: freelance career woman. Courtesy of the Margaret Herrick Library, the Academy of Motion Picture Arts and Sciences; copyright holder unknown.

Carole Lombard with David O. Selznick in a publicity still for *Nothing Sacred*. Courtesy of the Margaret Herrick Library, the Academy of Motion Picture Arts and Sciences; copyright 1937, Selznick International Pictures, Inc.

Meanwhile, Lombard's SIP deal maintained her $150,000 salary for the Technicolor screwball comedy *Nothing Sacred* (1937).[106] David O. Selznick first became enamored with the idea of signing Lombard after his brother Myron let him know her freelance intentions. (Myron earned a 10 percent cut of Lombard's salary from all of her deals, a profitable deal in its own right.) Selznick's memo to SIP partner Jock Whitney underscores the actress's popularity, as well as his eagerness to strike a deal: "Lombard will have four outside pictures in either two or three years under the terms of her Paramount deal which calls for one hundred fifty thousand per picture. As you know I regard this figure fantastic but apparently the sky the limit [*sic*] on personality salaries and there is terrific demand for these outside Lombard pictures."[107] Selznick's memo attests to the actress's market value in the latter half of the 1930s, as well as the industry's willingness to compensate her with a hefty salary. She also successfully lobbied SIP for the hiring of Travis Banton as her personal designer, the managing of her fan mail, and the personal crafting of her press campaigns with publicity director Russell Birdwell.[108]

Lombard's interest in the behind-the-scenes production process led to her taking the profit-sharing deal one step further by forming an independent production company in 1938 with Myron Selznick, fellow actor (and ex-husband) William Powell, and director/producer Ernst Lubitsch. The *Hollywood Reporter* noted that Lombard and Powell would be "the first thesps to gamble on profits in the New Myron Selznick production set-up. Pair will co-star in the second film by recently formed Ernst Lubitsch Productions, Inc., with Lubitsch directing."[109] Acting as production partners, the principals would forgo their up-front salaries in exchange for a share of the films' distribution profits. Lombard extolled the idea as a pioneering endeavor and argued that it was a long-overdue strategy for Hollywood talent. In an interview with gossip columnist Gladys Hall, the actress revealed her keen understanding of the future of talent negotiations in the film industry:

> It's what should have been done from the beginning. For the Lubitsch Company is the first of a series of units to be formed by Selznick in partnership with stars, directors, writers, all of the creative talent forming units. And all of us will be done [*sic*] on a profit-sharing basis, accepting no salaries. We'll be in partnership with our producer. If any one of us falls down, the job will fall down on us too. That's the way it should be. We'll get ours for what we do now, not for what we may have done seven years ago.[110]

Even Myron's brother David contemplated emulating the Lubitsch Company's financial structure because of the low overhead resulting from the A-list stars' deferral of their salary. He discussed this structure for a deal with Lombard (and William Powell) in a memo to his associate Dan O'Shea:

> I know that Myron is proceeding with plans to make a picture with Powell and Lombard on a percentage basis. I know further, that Carole would be very excited about working up a proposition, whereby Bill and she would do a percentage picture with us, as co-stars. . . . [W]e could work out a deal whereby neither Powell nor Lombard received any salary whatsoever and simply took a percentage of the net, and offhand it is my belief that we could afford to give the pair of them 50 per-

cent of the net, with perhaps Powell receiving 30 percent and Lombard 20 percent.[111]

Despite this proposed SIP deal, Lombard's enthusiasm for the company, and the positive coverage in the industry trades, the Lubitsch Company never materialized (likely due to Myron Selznick's inability to secure production funding and a distribution outlet).[112] Even still, Lombard's aspirations to become an independent producer revived the precedent established by the UA founders, especially Mary Pickford, and foreshadowed the postwar move by talent to independently finance and release films through a major studio.

Following the failed aspirations of the Lubitsch Company and the financial disappointment of Warner Bros.' *Fools for Scandal* (whose budget swelled to over $1,000,000 yet generated only $585,000 in profits), Lombard was back on the freelance market and looking to recast her image in Hollywood as a serious dramatic actress after four straight years of screwball comedy.[113] She found such an opportunity in a two-picture deal at RKO in 1939 in which she maintained her standard creative provisions and control of her publicity campaigns (which she hired publicist Russell Birdwell to handle, with her approval).[114] Although she dropped her price to $100,000 per film, her salary was supplemented by 50 percent of the film's distribution gross after it recouped 1.7 times its total production cost, until she collected $50,000.[115] This total would not only match her asking price of $150,000, but would also give the actress more take-home pay since these distribution earnings would be taxed at the lower capital gains rate. However, Lombard's percentage receipts for this deal amounted to only $4,519 from *In Name Only* (John Cromwell, 1939), a love-triangle melodrama that costarred Cary Grant, while *Vigil in the Night* (1940), directed by George Stevens, did not gross back its production costs, despite her moving performance as a noble nurse determined to uphold the ideals of the medical profession.[116] Although these dramatic roles reflected Lombard's desire to establish her acting versatility, the films did not appear to resonate with audiences.

Undaunted, Lombard and Myron Selznick renegotiated a "contract like no other" in 1940 with RKO president George Schaefer. It called for Lombard to make six films in three years; retained her approval of costar, director, and story; and significantly enhanced her percentage deal. The actress relinquished an up-front salary in order to participate directly in the distributor's gross as soon as the film was released, earning 10 percent of the profits until it reached $1.5 million, and 5 percent thereafter.[117] This

Carole Lombard conspiring in a story conference with director Ernst Lubitsch (her would-be production partner of the proposed Lubitsch Company), costar Jack Benny, and other talent for the film *To Be or Not To Be* (1942). Courtesy of the Cinematic Arts Library, University of Southern California; copyright 1942, Romaine Film Corp.

contract better delineated the terms of her percentage, specifying a cut of foreign box-office receipts and arbitrated those from block-booking exhibition deals.[118] The second film made under this agreement was *Mr. and Mrs. Smith* (1941), for which Lombard personally requested Alfred Hitchcock as director, and it marked her return to screwball comedy. In this case, the new percentage terms were much more profitable. The film was a box-office success, with total domestic and foreign gross amounting to $1,311,855, thus bringing in $582,000 in total profits for RKO, with Lombard's percentage totaling $131,185.[119] Furthermore, under the terms of this deal, she would participate in the gross even when her films did not turn a profit. For instance, RKO eventually lost $291,000 on *They Knew What They Wanted* (1940), but the actress collected receipts totaling $91,074.05.[120] As Tom Kemper observes, obtaining a piece of the distributor's gross, as opposed to the overall gross, "became the high prize in [Myron] Selznick's negotiations of percentage deals" by the early 1940s for his star clients.[121]

In response to Lombard's initial RKO deal, David O. Selznick was eager to convert his own contract with Lombard to a percentage deal, as he expressed in a memo to one of his SIP associates: "Would you please inject yourself into the Lombard proposition? She had expressed to me repeatedly in the last few days her willingness and even desire that we translate her deal into a percentage one. She is willing to gamble in large part, and I think is even willing to gamble in entirety."[122]

Accordingly, Lombard and David Selznick converted her SIP contract from one that guaranteed her salary up front to one that emulated her percentage deal at RKO, since he surmised that "any Lombard picture would do at least $1,500,000" in box-office profits.[123] This deal was never finalized because Selznick subsequently bought Lombard out of her contract in 1940 for $25,000 after the disappointing box-office returns on her SIP films *Nothing Sacred* (a $350,000 loss) and *Made for Each Other* (John Cromwell, 1939, which grossed a modest $200,000).[124]

After the dissolution of her SIP contract and the lukewarm box-office receipts for her first three dramatic films for RKO, Lombard's high salary and her ability to maintain her freelance career by sealing future studio deals were in jeopardy. She attributed these shortcomings to Myron Selznick—her agent and the chief architect of her freelance contracts—and his apparent loss of interest in her career. In 1941 the actress joined a sea of displeased clients leaving the agent due to Myron's ailing health and the deterioration of his talent agency.[125] Lombard fired Selznick and sued for an early release from her contract with him (slated to expire in 1943) and to stop any future 10 percent payments based on her percentage earnings from her RKO deals negotiated in 1939 and 1940. Her argument was complex; while she did not wish to nullify the lucrative deals that Selznick had struck, she argued instead that it was his behavior and personal life (mainly alcoholism and an increasing personal and professional apathy) that justified nullifying their agreement.

Although Lombard won the release from her contract with Selznick, the verdict also ruled that the agent had inflicted no professional fraud or harm on Lombard or any other clients; therefore, the actress could not invalidate their agreement simply because she disapproved of the agent's lifestyle.[126] The arbitrators also noted that Selznick had bolstered her professional standing and raised her salary, and thus she was still contractually obligated to pay him nearly $30,000 based on the estimated commissions and percentages of her projected income.[127] As the Lombard–Myron Selznick experience demonstrates, the star-agent relationship was a profitable yet at times contentious one. Although Selznick had helped Lombard achieve independent stardom and dramatically improve her standing as a top freelance actress, professional setbacks in the early 1940s led her to dissolve their nearly ten-year relationship.

MINIMUM INDEPENDENCE: ANNA MAY WONG AND LUPE VÉLEZ

For Lombard and the other independent female stars discussed thus far, freelancing provided a means to attain creative control, more jurisdiction over their screen image, higher salaries, and increased visibility in the industry. These female stars rejected long-term option studio contract offers because they limited their career choices. Yet for other working talent in Hollywood, such binding contracts—providing secure, stable employment—were a coveted commodity. This was especially true in the 1930s for minority actresses hoping to ascend to stardom; because they were not offered lucrative long-term studio contracts, freelancing represented their only option for participating in the film industry.

The careers of Anna May Wong and Lupe Vélez offer several insights into Hollywood's institutionalized and discriminatory business practices.[128] Their freelance status and the level of celebrity that they achieved in Hollywood as B-movie stars and as featured players in A-class pictures (as well as their international stardom in Europe and Mexico, respectively) provide a striking juxtaposition that reveals how free agency in 1930s Hollywood differed according to race.[129] The major and minor studios did not offer either actress exclusive long-term contracts. Compelled to work at an array of studios as jobs became available, Vélez and Wong were not freelancers by choice; rather, freelancing represented their sole option for steady employment in Hollywood. Furthermore, their freelance contracts were often devoid of the lucrative financial incentives and creative-control provisions that were standard for leading white female freelancers. Wong typically signed SAG's "minimum contract," which employed her only "for a specified picture and with a specified commencement date."[130]

This *minimum independence* that Anna May Wong and Lupe Vélez experienced relegated them to lead roles in B movies, and as such, their films received less attention and financing. When they did appear in A-level productions, they were cast in supporting roles or character parts. Wong and Vélez were both notable feature players in 1930s Hollywood, yet they never achieved Hollywood A-list stardom despite breakout performances, critical acclaim, and rival offers to work abroad. It is useful to refer to Richard Caves's theory of creative contracts in order to understand how Hollywood industry practices ultimately shaped these two women's careers. He maintains that one reason why the "creative industry" contracts of Hollywood produced unequal terms has to do with the hierarchies of star labor.[131] An A-list star (such as Lombard) may have cost a studio more in salary and contractual provisions, but her films tended to generate more box-office revenue because studios could charge more in rental costs than for a B film starring a second-tier actress such as Wong or Vélez. Caves contends that star rank mattered because of the money at stake for the studios, and this notion is particularly illuminating in regard to how the studio system's industrial practice sustained a form of forced freelancing:

> The relevant economic concept is the differential rent—the extra total amount that people will pay to see a movie with an A-list star over the same film with a B-list star. That differential rent limits the maximum pay that an A-list star can demand. To ask less is to leave money on the table. The rent concept also explains why the B-list artist might find it difficult to sell her services at any price. No matter how cheaply she works, the resulting film revenue might not cover its other costs. Or, given *infinite variety*, she may face long waits between films in which her services can be a cost-effective substitute for an A-list artist.[132]

Whereas A-list stars such as Constance Bennett, Irene Dunne, Janet Gaynor, Carole Lombard, and Barbara Stanwyck were all distinct star commodities who distinguished their careers and public personae as freelance artists, Wong and Vélez were still regarded as B-list actresses whose images relied on playing different ethnic "types" that exploited stereotypes (the vamp, the exotic, etc.). Yiman Wang explains that despite Wong's screen popularity in the United States and Europe, her stardom remained marginalized because her acting was continually defined as "Chinese" in the off-screen discourses surrounding her stardom. According to Wang, "Throughout her life, she was defined by her Chinese 'genes,' a racializing discourse that further justified the essentializing of her acting."[133] Likewise, Victoria Sturtevant contends that Vélez's stardom was marked by "Otherness," fitting into the Latina stereotype of exotic sex object or ignorant comic.[134] Both actresses sought out opportunities to escape Hollywood's stereotyped casting by working abroad or, in Vélez's case, on the New York stage. Both actresses had talent representation as well; in the early 1930s Vélez even had the power of Myron Selznick's Agency behind her. But their agents' influence seems to have had little lasting impact on these actresses' contractual labor negotiations and their careers as a whole.[135]

Another industry policy that impacted the careers of Wong and Vélez was Hollywood's self-enforced censorship doctrine, the Motion Picture Production Code, and the office responsible for its implementation, the Production Code Administration (PCA), led by Joseph Breen. The code declared that "miscegenation is forbidden," especially between white and black races.[136] Upon its inception in 1930, producers did not strictly adhere to the code, engendering what has been called the "Pre-Code" Hollywood era due to its more liberal depiction of sex, eroticism, and violence on screen.[137] Correspondingly, Wong and Vélez were most consistently employed by major Hollywood studios in A-class productions during those years. This changed after the code's enforcement in 1934 due to the threat of a national boycott of Hollywood films by religious groups and women's and civic organizations, as well as possible government censorship of films. Thereafter, PCA policy barred interracial love stories in major films, which influenced casting choices for the major studios and limited starring roles for ethnic actors such as Wong and Vélez. As Thomas Doherty explains, by the late 1930s, Breen and the PCA "smoothed out the multicolored rawness of Pre-Code Hollywood into a monochromatic monotony" that equated to "ignoring" people of color onscreen.[138] The consequence, according to Ruth Vasey, was that "both male and female leads of patently foreign origin became more scarce" in Hollywood as the 1930s wore on, "in line with the general effacement of ethnic difference onscreen."[139] Hence, Hollywood's industry regulations regarding the Production Code also provide insight into why the types of roles available to Wong and Vélez were vastly reduced, which in turn meant that they had to find work in B movies in the latter part of the decade.

A Los Angeles native, Anna May Wong first began acting as a movie extra in the early 1920s. At the age of seventeen, she made an indelible impression in her major screen debut in the two-color Technicolor production *Toll of the Sea* (Chester M. Franklin, 1922), a modern adaptation of *Madame Butterfly* relocated from Japan to China. Despite the film's success and the critical praise for her lead performance, Wong did not receive any long-term offers from Hollywood studios and continued to play bit parts in an array of genre films. These roles (as well as her standout performances) reinforced the racist Other stereotype associated with her ethnic Chinese heritage. For example, her next important roles were with Douglas Fairbanks' *The Thief of Bagdad* (Raoul Walsh, 1924), playing a Mongolian slave girl, and Princess Tiger Lily in *Peter Pan* (Herbert

Anna May Wong early in her Hollywood career, circa 1920s. Note how her costuming reinforces an exotic "Other" stereotype. Courtesy of the Cinematic Arts Library, University of Southern California; copyright holder unknown.

Brenon, 1924). But despite her noteworthy turn in these films, Wong did not attain major stardom. Consider her 1927 Warner Bros. "engagement agreement" for *A Million Bid* (released as *Old San Francisco*, directed by Alan Crosland); it details her lack of ascendancy in terms of salary and star profile, as well as indicating the low commodity value of her image.[140] To play a "Chinese" character in the film (Wong was twelfth billed), she received $300 for seven days of work, and her contract contained no special provisions, creative control, billing specification, or options for renewal.[141]

Dissatisfied with her plight in Hollywood, Wong left for Europe in the spring of 1928 to star in several British-German coproductions. Among these were some of the best films of her career, notably *Piccadilly* (Ewald André Dupont, 1929), which cast her as a lead dancer in a London nightclub, and *Pavement Butterfly* (Richard Eichberg, 1928), which gave her the multifaceted role of a carnival performer-turned-mistress of a wealthy man who becomes a bohemian muse. Hollywood finally seemed to take notice of Wong's talent when Paramount offered her a contract for $1,500 a week in 1931.[142] Nonetheless, she was again cast in stereotyped Orientalist roles such as the daughter of Dr. Fu Manchu in *Daughter of the Dragon* (Lloyd Corrigan, 1931).[143] Her most noteworthy film during this time was Josef von Sternberg's *Shanghai Express* (1932), which cast her alongside Marlene Dietrich as "coasters" living by their feminine wits along the China coast. Consequently, in 1934 the actress again abandoned Hollywood to make three films in Britain. This time, however, Wong's experience did not differ significantly from her trajectory in Hollywood; the low production values and colonialist attitudes in films such as *Chu Chin Chow* (Walter Forde, 1934) and *Java Head* (Thorold Dickinson and J. Walter Ruben, 1934) echoed her Hollywood roles and no longer offered a real alternative.[144]

Wong's Hollywood contracts throughout the 1930s contained virtually none of the special provisions or lucrative financial opportunities that freelance A-list stars received. Her 1938 Warner Bros. SAG basic agreement minimum contract for *When You Were Born* stipulated $1,750 for three weeks ($5,250 total). Although the studio did imply the option to renew her employment for two additional years, her salary would rise to only $2,000 a week to make three films total (whereas an A-list star like Lombard would make only one film in this period).[145] The only special rider in the contract that denoted her freelance status is Warner's agreement to schedule her film around her concurrent contract with Paramount.[146] In sum, freelancing did not give Wong the freedom to shape her star image, only the ability to find work. And if she wanted to work, she had to play roles that continued to stereotype her and limit her creative opportunities.[147]

At the same time, Wong's career did receive noteworthy attention in Hollywood, especially after she left for Europe. The industry took note of Wong's return to the Hollywood screen in the mid-1930s, and her starring film deals at Paramount and Warner Bros. were covered in the trade press. The *Hollywood Reporter* noted that Wong's new deal in Harold Hurley's B-unit at Paramount would cast her as woman detective and doctor, and that the studio hoped to lure former Japanese silent star Sessue Hayakawa back to Hollywood from France to costar with Wong in a film series.[148] Even though her films at Paramount and Warner Bros. in the late 1930s were B movies with cheaper production values—for instance, *When You Were Born* (William C. McGann, 1938) had a low budget of $131,000 and was made in three weeks—Wong received star billing and a production unit to design and produce her films.[149]

Lupe Vélez experienced a similar trajectory in Hollywood and was also subject, as a Latina actress, to being typecast as an exotic Other.

She began acting in her native Mexico, where she appeared in numerous stage productions before coming to California at the request of renowned stage actor Richard Bennett (father of actresses Constance and Joan) to play the female lead in his film *The Dove* (Roland West, 1927), though he eventually deemed her too young for the part at age seventeen. Nonetheless, Vélez quickly broke into Hollywood films by working for a variety of studios and with important stars such as Douglas Fairbanks and leading directors, including D. W. Griffith and Cecil B. DeMille. Despite this promising beginning, Vélez did not land a long-term contract and instead hopped from studio to studio for film work. Although she earned $2,500 a week for her work in several RKO films in 1932, this came in the form of freelance employment for three- to four-week periods with no creative control and no percentage deals.[150] In fact, her salary peaked at only $3,000 a week for three weeks of work ($9,000 total) in June 1942.[151] And like Wong, Vélez was employed at only three-week intervals by RKO from March 1939 to April 1943, when she made a series of B films.[152] Also, because she never ranked among the top fifty box-office stars, her stardom was of less value overall in the industry, as reflected in her salary and short-term employment terms.

Like Wong, Vélez was cast in foreign roles that heightened racially sexualized stereotypes and either highlighted her Latina ethnicity or conflated it with a range of non-white, "exotic" characters. Indeed, typecast as Hollywood's sexualized Other, Vélez played everything from a Cuban dancer (*The Cuban Love Song*, W. S. Van Dyke, 1931) to a Russian peasant girl (*Resurrection*, Edwin Carewe, 1931) to a Chinese immigrant (*East Is West*, Tod Browning, 1930). Furthermore, as her career continued throughout the 1930s in tandem with the enforcement of the Production Code, Vélez's persona evolved from the "sex object" into the "ignorant comic," as embodied in her RKO B-movie series *The Mexican Spitfire* (1939–1943).[153] This series initially revived Vélez's career after an eighteen-month absence and was successful for RKO (the first two films, *The Girl From Mexico* and *The Mexican Spitfire*, generated $40,000 and $102,000 in profits, respectively). However, profits were uneven for the remaining films in the series (*Mexican Spitfire Sees a Ghost* brought in a scant $1,000) leading RKO to conclude the series after the eighth film, *Mexican Spitfire's Blessed Event* (1943).[154] Because she made this series film by film in three-week increments, Vélez was effectively without either a long-term studio contract or steady employment. What is more, this lack of choice with regard to roles meant that the actress could not off-cast herself to revamp her image (as Bennett, Lombard, and Stanwyck did).

The freelance experience of fellow Latina actress Dolores del Río, who achieved Hollywood stardom in the silent era with Fox's *What Price Glory* (Raoul Walsh, 1926) and made a successful transition to sound, provides an interesting comparison to that of Vélez. Although del Río also hailed from Mexico, she was often characterized as an elegant "visitor" of "Spanish" or "Latin" heritage with an upper-class European pedigree that implicitly erased any explicit mestizo Mexican identity.[155] Conversely, as Victoria Sturtevant argues, Vélez was from "a much more nationally specific Mexican class of immigrants," and thus subject to the United States' negative and stereotyped conceptions of its southern neighbors.[156]

Del Río's freelance contracts contained special provisions that protected her against the stereotyped casting that haunted Vélez and guaranteed her a much higher salary. The two actresses briefly earned the same salary while they both worked at RKO; however, del Río was paid $2,000 a week for a total of thirty weeks between 1931–1933 ($60,000 a year), meaning that she maintained more stable employment at the studio.[157] Del Río left RKO in 1934 for an "exclusive" one-year, three-picture deal at Warner Bros., earning an impressive salary of $25,000 for the first film and $35,000 for the next two.[158] Her contract also stipulated casting rights. The actress was aware that her Mexican ancestry had prompted studios to typecast her in exotic roles and market her as the "female Valentino" in the 1920s and early 1930s. After the controversy engendered by *Bird of Paradise* (King Vidor, 1932), a South Seas adventure film that cast del Río as a Polynesian princess in love with a white sailor (played by Joel McCrea), the actress used her contract to circumvent this image, and Warner Bros. agreed not to cast the Latina star in "any native girl or south seas island type of picture without her approval."[159] She also approved the stories for her first two films at Warner Bros.: *Madame Du Barry* (William Dieterle, 1934)—in which she played the title French heroine—and *Wonder Bar* (Lloyd Bacon, 1934). She made three more films at Warner Bros. that performed fairly well at the box office; nevertheless, she and the studio did not come to terms to renew her contract.[160] After making one film at Columbia in 1937, she moved to Twentieth Century-Fox for a three-picture deal. Although the actress's first films were A-class productions (including the World War I film *Lancer Spy* [Gregory Ratoff, 1937], in which she played a dancer), she was relegated to the B-movie unit for her last Fox film, *International Settlement* (Eugene Forde, 1938).

Ultimately, del Río's freelance agency was short-lived, and despite her off-screen persona as a Spanish aristocrat, she was unable to avoid stereo-

Lupe Vélez in Hollywood circa late 1930s, around the time of her *Mexican Spitfire* series. Courtesy of the Cinematic Arts Library, University of Southern California; copyright holder unknown.

typed Latina roles. Consider her roles as the Mexican dancer La Españita in *In Caliente* (Lloyd Bacon, 1935) and the duplicitous Mexican dancer Carmen in *Devil's Playground* (Erle C. Kenton, 1937) at Columbia. In her insightful study of del Río, Joanne Hershfeld explains, "While for almost twenty years Hollywood had worked to promote del Río as an 'acceptable' ethnic 'other,'" her visible onscreen presence as a "foreign body reminded the public and the industry that the 'problem' of race" could not

Dolores del Río in the mid-1930s. To a certain extent, she avoided Hollywood's "exotic Latina" stereotyping through her contract at Warner Bros. Courtesy of the Margaret Herrick Library, the Academy of Motion Picture Arts and Sciences; copyright holder unknown.

be avoided.[161] When leading Hollywood roles dried up, del Río returned to Mexico in 1942 to star in a series of acclaimed films directed by Emilio Fernández.

Despite being subject to stereotyped casting, Vélez and del Río were exemplary as leading Latina actresses who achieved stardom in 1930s Hollywood. As such they prove to be the best case studies for a different type of independent stardom because they were anomalies. A comparable Latina actress who transcended the Other stereotype to become empowered, savvy stars came later, in the 1940s. Born Margarita Carmen Cansino to a Spanish father and American mother of English-Irish heritage, Rita Hayworth was trained as a dancer and caught the attention of Fox executive Winfield Sheehan in 1935 during a performance in Los Angeles. As Rita Cansino, she was cast as the exotic foreigner in B movies, appearing in *Charlie Chan in Egypt* (Louis King, 1935) and as a Russian in *Paddy O'Day* (Lewis Seiler, 1935), among others. After Fox did not renew her six-month contract, she signed a long-term contract at Columbia, where studio head Harry Cohn advised her to shed her Latina image in order to expand her range of roles. She subsequently changed her name to Rita Hayworth and drastically altered her physical appearance in order to achieve mainstream stardom.[162] Adrienne McLean describes Rita Hayworth's anglicization as a sort of "erasure," citing studio motivations for her transformation from Rita Cansino to the "more marketable, and more desirable Rita Hayworth."[163] While McLean contends that Hayworth was able to maintain her cultural identity for much of her Hollywood career in off-screen publicity, she was ultimately marketed as "white" on screen. By contrast, the Hispanic names of Lupe Vélez and Dolores del Río marked them as ethnic, which in turn impacted the types of deals they were able to negotiate in Hollywood.

After ascending to superstardom at Columbia in the 1940s, Hayworth's "white" star agency enabled her to bargain for greater creative control and input in her films' production. In fact, the actress became the protégé of Columbia's lone female producer, Virginia Van Upp, who helped develop *Gilda* (Charles Vidor, 1946) for Hayworth.[164] The actress then used her star power to create her own production company in 1947, the Beckworth Corporation—named after her daughter, Rebecca, and herself—which gave her script approval and a share in the distribution profits of her films at Columbia. What's more, the Beckworth Corporation enabled Hayworth to expand her role from actress-producer to choreographer by incorporating her dancing expertise into her films.

One option for actresses of color who wanted to secure a long-term studio contract was to specialize as a character actor, although this often involved accepting Hollywood's stereotyped casting. In this instance, African American actress Hattie McDaniel's move from freelancer to contract player at a major studio after her Best Supporting Actress Oscar in 1939 provides a striking exception. McDaniel was a free agent when David O. Selznick signed her to play Mammy in *Gone with the Wind* (Victor Fleming, 1939) at a salary of $450 a week (even lower than Wong's and Vélez's

Rita Hayworth's agency in practice: the actress on the set of *Affair in Trinidad* (1950) with director Vincent Sherman, Victor Scheurich, and Joseph Walker. Her company Beckworth produced the film, and Hayworth choreographed the dance routines. Courtesy of the Margaret Herrick Library, the Academy of Motion Picture Arts and Sciences; copyright holder unknown.

weekly rates). Winning the Oscar increased her market value as a featured character actress in the studio system. In fact, Selznick sold her contract to Warner Bros. in 1940 for $9,460, and her long-term option contract there guaranteed first-feature billing on all screen credits, advertising, and publicity, meaning that she would have lead billing of the supporting cast.[165] McDaniel remained employed for much of the 1940s as a stock character actor, yet like Wong and Vélez, McDaniel's race led to perpetual typecasting as the actress's long-term security at Warner Bros. depended on her reprising her "Mammy" domestic servant character. She replayed this role in *Since You Went Away* (John Cromwell, 1944) on loan-out back to David O. Selznick (but for his new production company, Vanguard) and *In This Our Life* (John Huston, 1942) and *They Died with Their Boots On* (Raoul Walsh, 1942) for Warner Bros., among others. Thus, while McDaniel found stable employment at major studios by the end of the 1930s and escaped the minimum freelance "options" that other actresses of color experienced, she lacked the contractual agency to choose her roles and avoid stereotyped casting.

CONTRACTUAL REVISIONS

In the late 1930s, David O. Selznick realized he had a problem; SIP did not have enough reputable male stars to team up with the freelance women he had under contract. "We are going to need men for these women," the producer declared to his associates.[166] Selznick's male talent shortage highlights the power dynamics of Hollywood stardom at play in the 1930s, when female stars ruled the box office in projects marketed for the presumed female audience. Collectively, women achieved freelance edge in the industry more than male stars. Given these numerous examples of female stars who established some incarnation of independent stardom, why do histories of studio-era Hollywood tend to attribute the achievement of professional agency and savvy contracts more often to men than to women?[167]

We can investigate this historical mishap through the case study of the frequent costar and freelance collaborator of these women in the 1930s, Fredric March. Indeed he worked with Constance Bennett, Katharine Hepburn, Janet Gaynor, and Carole Lombard, earned a similar salary per film ($100,000–$125,000), and was also represented by top agent Myron Selznick. Although March was not alone among the A-list male freelancers, he is a demonstrative case study for independent stardom because his contemporaries, mainly Ronald Colman, did not costar with the leading freelance female stars discussed here, while Cary Grant's independent career did not truly pick up until the 1940s.[168] After leaving Paramount in 1933, March split his time between an array of major studios for the remainder of the decade, including Twentieth Century, RKO, MGM, and Warner Bros., appearing primarily in swashbuckler or historical pictures such as *Anthony Adverse* (Mervyn Leroy, 1936) and *Anna Karenina* (1935). He also worked for independent producer Walter Wanger and David O. Selznick's SIP, which gave him the opportunity to return to the modern, urban roles that initiated his screen career.

Selznick cast March opposite his two leading freelance ladies of 1937, Gaynor and Lombard, in *A Star Is Born* to play washed-up film star Norman Maine, and in *Nothing Sacred* as ace reporter Wally Cook. A juxtaposition of their deals underscores the disparity between male and female freelance star contracts in the 1930s. March's contract stipulations at SIP suggest that the actor was more concerned with salary, billing, and work schedule (i.e., "that he not be required to work on Sunday") than with having more creative input in the production process or more control over his screen image.[169] Although March finally jumped on the percentage-deal bandwagon for his next freelance agreement with Walter Wanger to make the film *Trade Winds* (Tay Garnett, 1938), he mostly returned to flat-rate salaries in future freelance contracts and preferred not to gamble directly with his salary.[170]

In essence, March was more concerned with the "perks" of independent stardom rather than with the artistic, creative, and financial incentives that motivated female freelancers. This attitude is epitomized by his typical "special deal contract" to make Warner's *One Foot in Heaven* (Irving Rapper, 1941): "Jimmy Townsend [a Myron Selznick agent] of that office pointed out that there are certain minor conditions contained in all of March's contracts, covering such things as dressing room, stand in, wardrobe, etc., etc. and that Townsend will bring over Monday one of March's old executed contracts, which you can use as a basis for drawing up our agreement."[171] Why was there such disparity between March and his female costars in their freelance dealings? It appears that March was not as preoccupied with having creative input in his pictures, nor was he as bankable at the box office and in a position to make such demands.[172] Put simply, due to their popularity, which increased their market appeal to producers, the women had more contractual muscle to flex than the men. Moreover, freelance female stars asserted their self-interest and as a result attained more agency in their careers than their male counterparts.

Hence, by examining the contractual nuances of independent stardom, this chapter has revised the historical record to underscore how female agency prospered in 1930s Hollywood. In addition to impressive salaries, freelance female stars' contractual provisions included costar, director, and story approval; advertising campaign input; work-hour limits; and the right to choose their own designers and/or cameramen. The creative agency that these provisions provided enabled these women to choose their professional collaborators and projects, which was instrumental in shaping their screen personae. These artistic stipulations also gave them a professional advantage over male stars of equal caliber, as illustrated by the case of Fredric March. Many of these freelance actresses had a keen business sense that compelled them to hire excellent agents to negotiate with executives and producers in the studio system on their behalf. Bennett, Dunne, Gaynor, Hopkins, and Lombard used their contracts to engineer profit-sharing agreements that effectively aligned them with the producers and studio executives who employed them. These women stood to gain or lose from the film's fate with audiences, and thus they took a personal interest in the distribution and exhibition components of the studio system. Their use of the percentage deal to earn additional income by securing a portion of their films' box-office receipts was a pioneering business tactic that became standard practice for Hollywood talent in the 1950s.

Actresses of color, however, for whom freelancing was the only viable form of empowerment in the studio system, often experienced the adverse effects of independence. White actresses were able to maintain a more multidimensional star persona than actresses of color, thanks in large part to their ability to off-cast themselves in challenging roles and control their off-screen image through publicity. By contrast, actresses of color found their personal lives welded to their screen personae with remarkable fidelity. Take the case of Lupe Vélez, whose tumultuous marriage to Johnny Weissmuller (star of MGM's *Tarzan* series) often made headlines in the fan press, which exploited her "spitfire" persona in their coverage. This disparity speaks to the very different contractual terms available to white and minority actresses, but also points to another important dimension of 1930s independent stardom: the role of studio publicity and the press. How did these stars' freelance status influence their off-screen personae as modern career women? Why did fan magazines and the press report the details of these women's studio contracts, and why might women readers be interested in such details? These sorts of questions, which suggest the need to reconsider the relationship between Hollywood and shifting gender roles in the 1930s, are explored in the following chapter.

THREE

Labor and Lipstick

PROMOTING THE INDEPENDENT STAR PERSONA

In October 1931, the fan magazine *Movie Classic* highlighted Barbara Stanwyck's contractual dispute with Columbia and Warner Bros. This indicates the degree to which the actress's legal battles and her possible screen retirement made headlines not only in the film-industry trade and fan magazines, but also in the national press. *Movie Classic*'s coverage of Stanwyck's negotiations highlighted the actress's unconventional freelance labor practice and, by doing so, simultaneously underscored her independent stardom:

> It is said that Barbara has not been satisfied with her salary arrangement with the two studios. She did not want to do *Forbidden* scheduled as her next picture for Columbia. She did not like the story and in view of the success of her three last pictures, she felt she rated a decided increase in salary in keeping with her box-office draw. She was also anxious for a new salary agreement with Warner Brothers.[1]

Why, the article asked, would Stanwyck contemplate turning her back on Hollywood at the age of twenty-five after her successful performance in *Illicit* (Archie Mayo, 1931)? The actress had "stepped right up to take her place among the best box-office stars of them all," and her services were in such demand that two studios—Columbia and Warner Bros.—offered her contracts. "Hollywood was just about Barbara's oyster—yet she is refusing to open it . . . she says she is quitting . . . why?"[2]

Speculation in the press was rampant. Some thought the actress did not want her career to eclipse that of her husband, actor Frank Fay; others thought she wanted to follow her husband back to New York, or that she simply wanted return to the Broadway stage. *Movie Classic*, however, remained skeptical of these presumed explanations, insinuating that Stanwyck's announcement of her retirement was more of a "business tactic": "If things were not as Barbara wanted them—what could be a better time than the present lull in picture production to step out of the picture temporarily to go to New York and indulge a little process known as 'smoking them out' until things are brought about to her satisfaction?"[3] While the *Los Angles Times* and the *Hollywood Reporter* also covered her studio-contract jumping, *Movie Classic* did so for a different audience: movie fans and consumers of film culture.[4] Its observation of Stanwyck's contract disputes became representative of how 1930s fan magazine discourse informed fans about stars' careers. Strikingly, *Movie Classic*'s discussion of her contractual bargaining presumed that readers took as much interest in the legal aspects of Stanwyck's career as they did in her screen roles, movie-star image, and personal life.

One obvious reason for all the press coverage of independent stardom was the Hollywood publicity machine. Studio publicists, the press, and major fan magazines all called attention to the freelance film stars such as Stanwyck, reporting on their career moves alongside more typical "feminine" topics such as consumerism, glamour, and romance. Highlighting independent stardom as a defining characteristic of a star's persona was in the best interest of both the stars and the studios that employed them; it served as a marketing tactic to "sell" these stars and their films to the public, and to women audiences in particular.

By the 1930s, fan magazines were highly popular with film audiences, maintaining monthly circulations of nearly a half million copies each.[5] They provided a reflexive space in which A-list stars and their representatives spoke to fans about their careers and place in the film industry. Fan magazines such as *Photoplay*, *Modern Screen*, *Motion Picture*, *Movie Classic*, *Movie Mirror*, *Screenland*, *Screenplay*, and *Silver Screen* did not distinguish between the on- and off-screen personae of freelance stars, thereby raising key questions about labor and gender roles. Why would the predominantly female fan magazine readers *care* about the contract negotiations and freelance labor practices of stars? Why was the discourse on star careers presented to fans in such laudatory terms?

This chapter examines the popular construction of independent stardom in fan magazines, the press, studio publicity announcements, and marketing campaigns. Analyzing fan magazine discourse and studio publicity together shows not only how these actresses' freelance practices were understood within the industry and presented to fans, but also how their business acumen and career independence became a significant characteristic of their star personae. These women's star agency also enabled direct involvement in choosing their onscreen roles as well as shaping their public personae in fan magazines, thereby challenging the assumption that the so-called Hollywood machine solely objectified their images for its own material gain.[6]

Each of the stars profiled in this chapter—Constance Bennett, Barbara Stanwyck, Miriam Hopkins, and Carole Lombard—connected their freelance careers to professional and lifestyle opportunities for women that were unorthodox at the time. From Bennett's touting of Hollywood as an equal-opportunity employer in *Modern Screen*'s "In Hollywood Women Maintain Equality with Men," to Lombard's promotion of a "male code" for female success in business and in love for *Photoplay*, to Hopkins's critique of the patriarchal business structure of the studio system, these stars mobilized their publicity as a self-referential space through which to negotiate their freelance careers in relation to their celebrity images.

Bennett, Stanwyck, Hopkins, and Lombard—along with their publicists, fan-press reporters, and the studio publicity engines—all appropriated their independent stardom to inform their public personae. Thus we can see that *independent stardom* refers not only to these stars' freelance contractual labor, but also to their hybrid public celebrity as independent, working, "modern" women. The press coverage of these four women provides the most illuminating case studies from my corpus of freelance stars because all four worked consistently throughout the decade but experienced different levels of success with independent stardom. Additionally, the Hollywood freelance-career discourse was predominantly a female-star-driven phenomenon; articles on equivalent male stars focused more on their acting craft or love life.[7]

HOLLYWOOD PUBLICITY AND FEMALE AUDIENCES IN THE 1930S

As the Hollywood film industry matured, stars became the currency through which to sell and market films to the public. As such, studio press releases and publicity campaigns, as well as fan magazine coverage, played a substantial role in promoting the star system and the careers of individual actors. The chief architects behind all of this industry wheeling and dealing were the studio publicists and their staffs. Publicity departments were organized much like a newspaper office and were run by a director: Howard Strickling at MGM, Edward Selzer at Warner Bros., Tom Bailey at

Paramount, Harry Brand at Twentieth Century-Fox, and Russell Birdwell at Selznick International Pictures (SIP) were the key publicity directors in the 1930s.[8] For freelance stars, publicity was essential; it generated public and industry interest not only in their upcoming films, but also their star personae, as a well-timed press release could increase the value of their image. At the same time, bad press could tarnish a star forever. As Carole Lombard herself observed, stars would be wise to make it their "business to know publicity from the ground up" in Hollywood.[9] It was especially important for a freelance star to nurture a personal as well as professional working relationship with publicists and journalists to ensure favorable press and broader coverage that could enhance box-office popularity and, thus, sustain an independent career. In this regard, independent publicists such as Helen Ferguson were a vital resource for freelance talent and other stars interested in career promotion.[10]

Fan magazines provided some of the earliest publicity for stars in the burgeoning film culture. They had begun circulating nearly two decades earlier, in the 1910s, in tandem with the emerging star system and in response to audience demand for information about their favorite screen personalities. The first fan magazine, *Motion Picture Story Magazine*, began in 1910, and rival magazines soon followed, the most noteworthy being *Photoplay*. Established in 1912 in Chicago, *Photoplay* really took off in 1917 when it started targeting a more middle-class, gentrified readership.[11] Demographically, women came to be seen as key players in the new culture of consumption that crystallized during the economic boom in the United States during the 1920s.[12] In order to cater to this target audience, the Hollywood press envisioned the movie fan as what film historian Shelley Stamp has called the "star-struck girl," infatuated with the spectacle of cinema and the star system.[13] Yet by the 1930s, these female readers had more sophisticated knowledge about the institutional operations of Hollywood.[14] Although article topics ranged from stars' shopping habits to keeping up with the latest fashions and balancing motherhood with work, they also included frank discussions of business negotiations, financial maneuvering with producers, and film industry practices. Consequently, female fans better understood what film industry terms such as "option contract" and "freelancing" meant. Fan magazines thus functioned much as DVD extras, fan Internet websites, and social media sites do today for contemporary Hollywood stars.

These industry publicity tactics not only represented Hollywood's marketing efforts to target female audiences, but also corresponded with the growing presence of women in the US workforce during the 1930s.

This rise can be attributed to three key factors: industrialization and the growth of consumerism; increased labor demand in cities as rural farmwork declined; and the relatively large population of young, single American women.[15] With the passing of the Nineteenth Amendment and the shifting social mores of the Jazz Age, the 1920s saw women's continued expansion into the workplace. By the 1930s, women made up nearly a quarter of the US workforce, reaching 25.1 percent in 1940—all despite the widespread unemployment and economic turmoil caused by the Depression.[16]

The American women who went to work during the Depression were usually married, slightly older, and better educated than the wage-earning women of the 1920s; they also tended to have fewer children, live in shared households, and enter the labor market at twice the rate of men.[17] Professional women in high-profile fields also made noteworthy inroads as government officials, an achievement symbolized most prominently by President Roosevelt's appointment of Frances Perkins as labor secretary in 1933.[18] Thus, the 1930s represented a period in which working women emerged both in the film industry and in the general population; as historian Alice Kessler-Harris notes, "The Depression that should have driven women back to the home instead solidified their positions as workers."[19] The sustained visibility of professional women in the 1930s helps to explain why female independent stardom was such a focus in popular discourses of the period.

Of course, the careers of female freelance stars were exceptional compared to those of most working women in America, especially in terms of salary. While the average earnings for working women were only $20 a week in the 1930s, in stark contrast, female stars—both freelancers and those on long-term contracts—earned exponentially more. For example, consider Carole Lombard's $16,000 a week payment from SIP in 1937.[20] The economic independence of independent female stars was, for the most part, uncommon in the US workforce at the time, making for exciting copy in publicity and trade magazines, despite the class and salary disparities between stars and their fans.

Given their high profile in the press and the growth of female employment in the 1930s, the freelance careers of Stanwyck, Bennett, Hopkins, and Lombard became the defining aspect of their star personae.[21] A gloss of the 1930s fan magazines frequently reveals distinct variations in the trope of "independence" attached to each of these stars: Stanwyck's is "honest," Bennett's is "cunning," Hopkins's is "intelligent," and Lombard's is "witty." By examining excerpts from fan magazine articles and interviews, we can determine how stars' freelance business practices informed and shaped their public images during the mid-1930s to early 1940s, while also endearing them to a Depression-era female fan base.[22]

HOLLYWOOD'S BELOVED TROUPER: BARBARA STANWYCK

As the *Movie Classic* profile on her "studio jumping" suggests, Stanwyck had nurtured a reputation for independence from the very beginning of her screen career. She supported her independent stardom in both her contract negotiations and in fan magazine discourse by developing a public persona as a consummate professional. This off-screen image worked to enhance her reputation with her colleagues (costars, directors, writers, and below-the-line workers on the set) as well as with Depression-era audiences, thus bolstering her opportunities for continued freelance employment in Hollywood.

It is difficult to discern the level of control that Stanwyck had over publicity campaigns in the early phase of her career; nevertheless, the actress generally received positive press coverage of her seemingly impulsive studio-jumping deals.[23] For instance, in 1932, on the heels of Stanwyck's Columbia-Warner Bros. contract dispute, *Modern Screen* interpreted her off-screen labor negotiations as indicating a "challenging spirit of independence" and praised her dedication to her craft.[24] What's more, Stanwyck described her independent stardom as an occupation, stressing her role as a *worker* who had little patience with Hollywood elitism and snobbery. She explained to *Modern Screen*, "If I am not going to be happy here [in Hollywood], if I am not going to make good pictures, I may as well quit!"[25] The magazine expressed admiration for Stanwyck's humility as a rare quality among stars: "Successful people, not only in Hollywood but the world over, are supposed to shed humble pasts the way a snake sheds its skin."[26] Here *Modern Screen* insinuates that although Stanwyck's independence at times clashed with studio policy, fans should not assume that she was the "temperamental kind who holds up productions and makes things difficult for the studios," as she was "too good a trouper for that."[27] To underscore their characterization of her "trouper" persona, the magazine cited Stanwyck's insistence on finishing the day's work even after she fell off a horse while filming *Forbidden* (1932) for Columbia.[28] In this way, fan publicity amalgamated Stanwyck's headstrong acting onscreen with her behind-the-scenes professional business decisions. What we see here is a self-reflexive co-opting of her independent stardom—from the actress

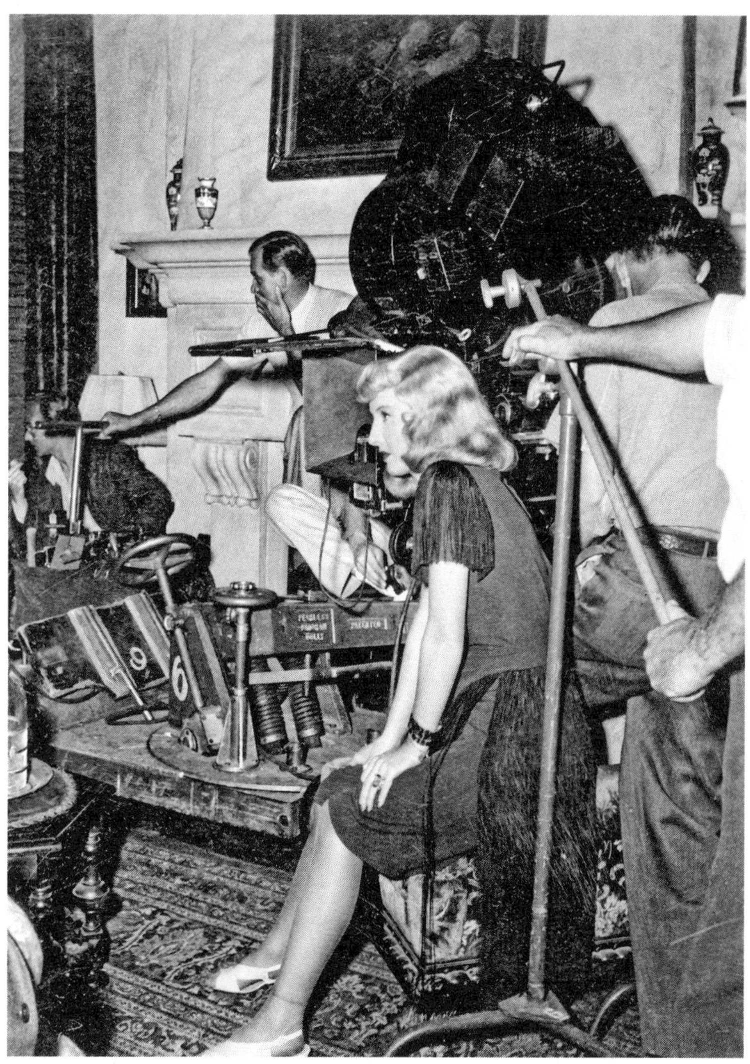

Barbara Stanwyck, known as a consummate professional, on the set of *Double Indemnity* (Billy Wilder, 1944), looking on with the crew. Courtesy of the Margaret Herrick Library, the Academy of Motion Picture Arts and Sciences; copyright 1944, Paramount Pictures, Inc.

herself (who discussed her professional convictions openly with reporters) to publicists (who circulated her interviews) and the studios that simultaneously employed her.

Stanwyck's synthesis of freelance labor with her trouper persona in interviews and publicity continued to strengthen both her creative agency and control over her screen image. In 1936, Stanwyck spoke to *Modern Screen* about the personal satisfaction she had found in her career: "I don't honestly think I could be called temperamental. Not about my work anyway. I take [work] far too seriously to have tantrums about it, I want to work. . . . It brings me more peace than anything I do."[29] Although Stanwyck was as hard a bargainer as some of her freelance peers, she capitalized on her freelance status to construe herself as an actress committed to her profession instead of money and respected by her peers. In response to the question "What one adjective would you use to describe yourself?" Stanwyck said, "We'll call it honesty, and I suppose it is the most adequate description of me, both personally and in my work . . . it's a good thing I can get across." This was particularly the case for her most recent films, including the Western biopic *Annie Oakley* (George Stevens, 1935) and *Banjo on My Knee* (John Cromwell, 1936), which profiled riverboat communities along the Mississippi.[30] These roles illustrated a shift from her earlier roles as sexually liberated women in Pre-Code sensational films such as *Baby Face* (1933) and *Ladies of Leisure* (Frank Capra, 1930).

The trope of upward class mobility was also exploited in press coverage on the actress. Readers were often reminded that Stanwyck started life as Ruby Stevens from Brooklyn, the orphan turned Broadway chorus girl now film star who had achieved the American dream through perseverance and hard work.[31] This alignment generated a good public relations strategy and simultaneously depicted her as an attractive investment to the studios that sought out her services. Providing an explanation for Stanwyck's "famous personal popularity" in Hollywood, *Modern Screen*, in concert with major industry trade journals such as *Variety* and the *Hollywood Reporter*, highlighted her unique freelance contracts with three major Hollywood studios in 1937: "She's under contract there [RKO] for a certain number of pictures a year, just as she has a similar contract arrangement with Twentieth Century-Fox and Paramount."[32] Comments like this represent industry-reflexive promotion not only for the actress but for the film industry as well, particularly when *Modern Screen* recounted numerous laudatory anecdotes about the actress from those in the film community: "Everyone who has ever worked with her, or who has ever met her, always has a similar eulogy to tell. To prop boys and stars alike, she is Hollywood's 'Beloved

Trouper.'"[33] Stanwyck's trouper persona translated to freelancing at multiple studios, working incessantly, and being respected professionally—all key to maintaining independent stardom in Hollywood.

Stanwyck's freelance experience also began to influence the advice she gave to female fans. In a 1936 interview with fan magazine writer Gladys Hall, she declared, "Independent, strong-minded women go down like blades of grass in a storm when they are in love."[34] Drawing on personal experience, she urged "girls to have their own lives" before "losing their wits" in love."[35] After her divorce from Fay in 1935, Stanwyck explained, she was now "living dangerously" on her own terms, outside the constraints of marriage. "I am free. I am my own man. And it's dangerous because no woman can live in marriage this way"; instead, she preferred "the romance of living."[36] Notably, Stanwyck described her off-screen autonomy from marriage as masculine, which also correlated to her independence from major studios as a freelance artist who undermined the patriarchal and paternal structure of Hollywood. The actress had no behind-the-scenes man shaping her career, either personally or professionally.

The star discourse on Stanwyck continued to focus on her new single life as well as the satisfaction she felt from her burgeoning freelance career. A 1936 article from *Silver Screen* titled "Everything Under Control But Love" notes the astounding success of Hollywood women, profiling Stanwyck, Kay Francis, Joan Blondell, and Virginia Bruce. Nevertheless, as the magazine observes, these actresses are "sitting on top of the world until love comes along."[37] The article features Stanwyck in a still from a recent film, *Message to Garcia* (George Marshall, 1935), in which she plays a Cuban woman assisting the US Army during the Spanish-American War. *Silver Screen* explains that Stanwyck is "the most outstanding current example" of this romance-career dilemma for Hollywood women:

> Barbara had gotten a flourishing start on a promising career when she began to be harassed by marriage difficulties with Frank Fay. The career practically faded away and disappeared when she was trying to cope with those difficulties. . . . [S]he emerged suddenly to make one of the finest come-backs seen in many a moon. Her splendid performance in *Annie Oakley* led to the coveted role in *A Message to Garcia*.[38]

Hence, coverage of Stanwyck's stunning freelance "come-back" in these two films (at RKO and Twentieth Century-Fox, respectively) lauded her individuality and achievement in Hollywood apart from personal entanglements. *Silver Screen* contends that the actress "has won her way

Barbara Stanwyck with hairstylist Marion Barnes, whom she personally selected, during the making of *Union Pacific* for Paramount in 1939. Courtesy of the Margaret Herrick Library, the Academy of Motion Picture Arts and Sciences; copyright holder unknown.

alone, has fought for her own chance in this fantastic profession," while "love seems merely to hamper her, restrain her, constrict her."[39]

This positive tone about Stanwyck's freelance career prevailed, as evidenced by the 1939 *Modern Screen* article "Sunny Side Up," which profiled the upswing in her career. The actress had recently received her first Best Actress Academy Award nomination for her freelance performance in *Stella Dallas* (1937). In the article Stanwyck reflected on her recent critical achievement in the context of discussing her suspension from RKO in 1937: "Last year I wasn't feeling well. I was suspended from RKO because I wouldn't make a picture they wanted me to make for them. . . . Last year everything was upside down. I was upset and unhappy about everything. This year everything is right side up. Now I feel well. I am free of my RKO contract. Now I am free-lancing."[40]

Once again, Stanwyck tied her newfound professional and personal happiness specifically to her freelance career. About her current projects, the actress noted that she was "terribly happy about *Union Pacific*. I love my part in *Golden Boy*. I like the script of my next picture at Paramount."[41] Stanwyck realized the potential of favorable publicity to both safeguard a freelance career and bolster a trouper persona that emphasized her humble past and current success. In this she was unique, as the contrary experiences of Constance Bennett and Miriam Hopkins will illustrate.

HOLLYWOOD'S MOST INTELLIGENT STAR: CONSTANCE BENNETT

From the beginning, Bennett's career tactics (and, consequently, her public persona) were scrutinized by the press, which paid particular attention to her $30,000 a week salary from Warner Bros. in 1931. The intrepid actress saw film acting as a business that afforded her financial security and an independent lifestyle; she was not in it for artistic ambition or because she was infatuated with fame. In the early 1930s, she told reporters that her sole goal was "to earn a million dollars by my own efforts. I want to be rich not for luxury that wealth brings but for the independence it affords. . . . I give [acting] my best efforts, but I don't want to give it my entire life."[42] In contrast to "trouper Stanwyck," Bennett did not feel a kinship with film crews, nor did she credit the collaborative filmmaking process, feeling that she alone was responsible for her success. Even though she negotiated concurrent contracts with Pathé-RKO and Warner Bros. in 1931, her creative provisions did not extend to control over her publicity campaigns or the right to sanction the use of her image in marketing campaigns. Coupled with her uncooperative attitude about working with the press, this lack of creative autonomy undermined Bennett's professional agency in fan magazine discourse and, consequently, tarnished her public image.

Bennett's unapologetic stance toward her high salary ambitions was profiled by *Movie Classic* in a 1931 article, "Constance Bennett Huge Salary Spells Trouble." The article first notes how the "unemployed resent her weekly wage of $30,000" at the height of the Depression, prompting "dangerous and desperate letters" from the public; even her younger sister, Joan, "received poison-pen letters" from disdainful fans.[43] *Movie Classic* lucidly details Bennett's shrewd negotiations between Warner Bros. and her home studio, RKO. Underscoring how she was paid a five-figure weekly salary during her twelve-week vacation from RKO, the magazine explains how Warner Bros. "argued that box-office returns had justified the investment in Connie's blondeness," insisting further that "she would have been a good rental proposition at $50,000 a week"—this at the same time other studio producers were complaining that her grandiose earnings would rally their own stars to make comparable demands.[44] While *Movie Classic* delineated the contractual market terms of Bennett's joint agreements, their negative spin on her "money publicity" undermined the actress's image with a Depression-weary public, so much so that "she was deluged with nearly a hundred thousand letters of protest and indignation."[45]

The popular fixation on Bennett's lavish salary continued with the publication of "How Constance Really Spends her Money" in the August 1931 issue of *Modern Screen*, which also showcased her independent stardom in its explanation of the freelance dual contract and the terms of her steep salary: "Besides her amazing ten week Warner Brothers' contract which pays her the $30,000 every seven days, she also holds a Pathé contract said to net her several thousands more weekly. . . . [I]t makes you stop and wonder what this twenty-four year old girl does with so much money."[46] The actress agreed to outline her budget and spending habits for the magazine in order to recuperate her supposed "extravagant" image with the press.[47] Nonetheless, her persona as a self-centered, privileged movie star pervaded much of the text. For example, despite Bennett's rationalization that only one-fourth of her income went for "luxuries and expenses," she still maintained two homes (in Malibu and Beverly Hills), employed servants at a cost of $6,000 a year, took a ten-week, $10,000 vacation in Europe, and spent only $100 a week for personal needs.[48] While *Modern Screen* succeeded in producing an itemized list of how this well-compensated actress spent her money, this did little to rehabilitate Bennett's public persona.

The negative press continued in regard to Bennett's obstinate behavior on the set, particularly her aversion to studio publicity campaigns (which she was contractually obligated to participate in). This provides further explanation as to why Bennett was portrayed as "unpopular in Hollywood."[49] In 1932, *Photoplay* stressed the importance of "stills" as the "photographs by which studios advertise pictures," and clearly disapproved of the star's refusal to pose for stills in lingerie.[50] For all the money that MGM paid Bennett for the risqué fallen-woman film *The Easiest Way* (1931), the publicity department (and *Photoplay*) expected the actress to pose undressed, but she refused. Even though producers backed up her intransigence, *Photoplay* continued to characterize Bennett's self-respecting behavior as "difficult." They reported that when one of her employers, Warner Bros., requested Bennett's presence for an entire day to shoot publicity stills, the actress agreed to only three hours. When the cameraman objected and conveyed his concern to production chief Darryl Zanuck (a personal friend of the actress), Zanuck stood by Bennett. As he and Jack Warner had learned by allegedly "being forced to pay her income tax on top of her salary when they first demurred at the figure," they knew that it was in their best interest not to argue with the headstrong actress.[51] At the same time, *Photoplay*'s critical stance toward Bennett's attitude about publicity also revealed her cunning contractual lobbying and characterized her as a hard bargainer with the major studios.

Initially, from 1930 to 1932, Bennett's films were quite profitable for RKO and Warner Bros. The actress's specialty was the fallen-woman genre, which showcased her petite figure in glamorous clothing on stylized art deco sets in films such as *The Common Law* and *Born to Love* (both directed by Paul L. Stein in 1931), and *Two Against the World* (Archie Mayo, 1932).[52] However, by 1933, her films were no longer turning a profit for RKO. The romantic melodramas *Rockabye* (1932) and *Our Betters* (1933), both directed by George Cukor, were $100,000 losers, while the Hollywood exposé *What Price Hollywood?* (also directed by Cukor in 1932) and the pre-code love triangle *Bed of Roses* (1933) lost $50,000.[53] Bennett's high price tag did not equate to high profits for RKO, and this sheds light on her subsequent move to freelancing in 1934. Indeed, as Bennett gained more control over her career, she became more cooperative with the press, perhaps realizing how essential good public relations were to a freelance artist.

The press attitude toward the actress shifted gradually to a more positive tone. The Hollywood studios that employed Bennett effectively appropriated her clever business expertise as part of their publicity campaigns for her films, all in the hope of generating more box-office returns. The following excerpt from a Twentieth Century press release for Bennett's first free-lance film, *Moulin Rouge* (Sidney Lanfield, 1934), indicates this change in tone as it lauds the actress for her business savvy: "Constance was not designed by nature for business detail, but her record proves that she can take this work in full stride. Among the great women of the screen she is second only to Mary Pickford as driver of hard bargains. She sees acting as a business—a service which one places on the market at one's own price. Either you pay the figure demanded or there's no soap."[54] By 1934, it was also in Bennett's best interest to generate more positive press because her agreement with Twentieth Century gave her a direct cut of each film's distribution profits. As a good businesswoman, Bennett took a more active approach in cooperating with the studio, and, in turn, the studio used its star's business prowess to their advantage. Considering her cutthroat contractual negotiations, it comes as no surprise that she was one of the few women among Hollywood's poker-playing elite: a male-dominated group that included studio moguls and producers Sid Grauman, David O. Selznick, Darryl Zanuck, Samuel Goldwyn, and Jack Warner.[55] As she sought to sustain independent stardom in the mid-1930s, Bennett (and the studios that employed her) strove to counter her earlier aloof, negative attitude toward the press and maintain a vibrant market for her films.

A more positive spin on Bennett's "money publicity" was also evident in the 1934 *Silver Screen* article titled "In Hollywood Women Maintain Equality with Men." Praising Bennett as the industry's "most intelligent star," the magazine emphasized her autonomous career choices and asked the actress to comment on the professional opportunities that motion pictures gave to women. Bennett enthusiastically responded, "Acting in pictures is the most fascinating career in the world for women. It's the only one where they are on an absolute equality with men."[56] She also referred to the collaborative work ethic of the film industry, which aligned actors with producers, noting that the two shared "equally in the business sense" when it came to supplying the public with quality pictures. Here Bennett connected her professional agency to her ability to make good films, explaining that most actresses have "absolutely nothing" to say about the films in which they appear since they are under contract to a studio.[57] Moreover, Bennett explained, if the picture receives poor reviews, "so many times the blame is laid on an actress," even though she likely lacked creative control, and that "All she can do is play the parts they assign her, and if she balks, stories immediately go the rounds that she is becoming temperamental."[58] Bennett noted how she, in comparison, was fortunate enough to be part of an elite group of actresses who maintained some creative control over their careers: "I *am* permitted to select the unit with which I want to work and I select men in whose judgment I have confidence."[59] Bennett was now using publicity to parlay her persona as a hard-bargaining businesswoman with contractual power, spinning career independence as a virtuous attribute.

This theme continued in subsequent publicity, as evidenced by a 1936 *Motion Picture* article on Bennett. Titled "Why Hollywood Fears Constance Bennett," it too extolled her business acumen as "one of Hollywood's most level headed bargain drivers."[60] The magazine explained that the entire industry "fears and respects her," especially producers who "tremble when they sit down to talk contracts . . . [as] the only arguments she considers are her own," and "despite her demands, she's a moneymaker for them."[61] The actress also reflected on her "declarations" of independence in Hollywood, particularly on the importance of safeguarding her personal rights in studio contracts.

> I am what I learned to be. Hollywood taught me to fight for my rights. . . . When I first came to Hollywood, inexperienced in Hollywood's methods, I'd much to learn. In Paris, I had been urged to sign a contract offered to me by Pathé Studios. I was on the verge of an operation for appendicitis and so, almost without realizing what I was doing, I signed. Pathé put me in one picture. Then they began lending me out at a huge profit to the studios. I thought I should share in that profit and demanded a bonus whenever they "loaned" me at more than they were paying me. They refused and I signed my first declaration of independence in Hollywood.[62]

Here Bennett clarified that it was her personal rights (and not excess money, as depicted by prior publicity) that motivated her prior bargaining at RKO and Warner Bros., as well as her burgeoning freelance career and the founding of her own corporation. These latter two career moves ensured that the actress did indeed share in the profits that she earned for Hollywood.

Even so, Bennett never truly overcame her public reputation as an indulged, overcompensated film star. The actress worked consistently through the mid-1930s as a freelancer in projects such as MGM's *After Office Hours* (Robert Z. Leonard, 1935, in which she costarred with box-office king Clark Gable) and Twentieth Century-Fox's *Ladies in Love* (1936), and she received some of the best critical reviews of her career for her comedic turn in *Topper* (1937). Nevertheless, by the end of the decade

Bennett was finding fewer starring roles; she was passed over as the lead in Twentieth Century-Fox's *The Rains Came* (Clarence Brown, 1939) and received second billing after Alice Faye in *Tail Spin* (Roy Del Ruth, 1939). Bennett was then relegated to secondary leads or supporting roles in the early 1940s, as in Warner Bros.' *Law of the Tropics* (Ray Enright, 1941).

These professional setbacks aside, Bennett's independent stardom remained a topic of interest in fan magazine press, which began characterizing the actress as a survivor. In the 1939 article "The Indestructible Miss Bennett," *Modern Screen* commended her longevity in the film industry in the face of "interruptions, criticism, and setbacks," and attributed her achievements to her "unorthodox methods," meaning her freelancing.[63] The intractable actress detailed her professional convictions to the magazine, particularly when it came to choosing the right screen parts: "'Hollywood is full of politics and yes-men. . . . I never 'yes' to anybody. . . . I take pride in sticking to it and proving that it's right for me. When I'm given a story and I think it's bad, I say so."[64] Noting her affinity for certain film producers, Bennett explained her friendship with Darryl Zanuck and his forthright explanation of his decision not to cast her in *The Rains Came*:

> The English people overwhelmingly voted for me to play Lady Esketh. . . . Zanuck won't let me play it. He tells me frankly I haven't a certain exotic glamour that Lady Esketh should have and he prefers Myrna Loy. . . . That would have killed a lot of women. But it doesn't kill me, because I know Myrna Loy is bigger box-office than I am, and I don't blame him. It's a fact, and I can accept it.[65]

Recognizing her capacity for Hollywood business, Bennett sought out opportunities beyond the screen as the 1930s came to a close. *Modern Screen* explained that she is "really happiest in business, where she can meet men on their own footing," and they unveiled the actress's plan to expand her role in the film industry as a film producer, explaining that both her industry experience as an independent actress and her successful company Constance Bennett Cosmetics had prepared her well for the transition.[66] A few years later, Bennett did produce two films through her own company: *Paris Underground* (Gregory Ratoff, 1945), released through United Artists, for which she received producer credit, and *Smart Woman* (Edward A. Blatt, 1948), released through Allied Artists.[67] Although her early publicity permanently impacted her reputation in the film industry, Bennett managed to revitalize her public persona in the fan press in the late 1930s, even with her diminished star status. She was intelligent enough to realize that she needed to remain in good standing with the public to continue her freelance career.

MIRIAM HOPKINS: A MODERN BECKY SHARP

Throughout her tenure at Paramount in the early 1930s, Miriam Hopkins played cunning and overtly sexual young women in successful films such as *Trouble in Paradise* (Ernst Lubitsch, 1932), *Dr. Jekyll and Mr. Hyde* (Rouben Mamoulian, 1932), and *Design for Living* (1933). Many of her films generated controversy with the Production Code Administration (PCA), best personified by her portrayal of a rebellious Southern belle in *The Story of Temple Drake* (Stephen Roberts, 1933). As the screen adaptation of William Faulkner's sensational novel *Sanctuary*, the film violated the Production Code's prohibitions of the onscreen depiction of prostitution and rape.[68] After the threat of a national boycott, the film industry strictly adhered to its self-censorship organ.[69]

The publicity surrounding *Temple Drake* showcased Hopkins's vivacious off-screen personality, especially her willingness to take on challenging roles, regardless of their "moral" implications. In a 1933 *Movie Classic* interview titled "My Movie Moral Code," which presumed that readers were aware of the institutional practice of Hollywood self censorship, Hopkins critiqued the Production Code. The magazine reminded readers of the actress's standing in the film industry as "mentally the most daring woman in Hollywood," with her own take on motion picture censorship and an "enlightened moral code" that she adhered to both on and off the screen.[70] This interview was particularly striking in that Hopkins criticized the Production Code, which substantially affected her own star image, calling for motion pictures "with no regard for censorship" that "show life truthfully with artistic realism."[71] And, she added, "The censors' decision on whether this picture was morally good or bad, clean or unclean, depended on the flip of a coin—obviously the censors are to blame here; the producers have to do the stories that will *get by* the censors."[72] Hopkins encouraged fans to trust the film industry more than the moral watchdog groups. *Movie Classic* reaffirmed Hopkins's code as "the logical, more wholesome one. . . . She doesn't believe, like our official guardians of morals, that marriage is a miracle-worker that can instantly change black sin to pearly virtue!"[73]

After her departure from Paramount, Hopkins embarked on an independent career by signing with Samuel Goldwyn as his lead actress, wooed by the promise of greater creative autonomy and more challenging film

Miriam Hopkins's freelance debut as *Becky Sharp*. Courtesy of the Cinematic Arts Library, University of Southern California; copyright 1935, Pioneer Pictures, Inc.

roles. This deal also allowed her to take extended leaves of absence from Hollywood to do Broadway plays in New York.[74] In a 1935 *Screenland* interview, the actress remarked on her decision, emphasizing that she had never worked under such happy and pleasant conditions: "With Goldwyn's undivided personal attention, I feel like an individual, never part of a great machine. For instance, he even looks at tests of coiffures and costumes. He will rush up and say 'Honey, your hair is lovely that way' or 'Let's try it again, a little smoother.'"[75] However, prior to starting at Goldwyn, Hopkins first signed for the coveted role of the Technicolor *Becky Sharp* (1935), one of the most publicized films of the decade and the high point of her film career.

Despite Hopkins's initial reluctance to promote *Becky Sharp*, once she realized that her cooperation was imperative for a successful publicity campaign, she acquiesced and delivered interviews in conjunction with the film's release. A 1935 *Motion Picture* interview with Hopkins synthesized her new freelance status and vivacious screen image, fusing her on- and off-screen public personae into the very character of *Becky Sharp*. Here Hopkins maintained that even "ultra-modern women" like herself had to resort to the same methods of "feminine flattery" used by nineteenth-century women.[76] *Motion Picture* also posed a compelling question that underscored how Hopkins's newly established freelance career influenced her screen image:

> You are the most independent actress in Hollywood. You turn down long-term contracts, rush away to New York, leaving picture roles which other stars would give their teeth to get. You turn your back on enormous Hollywood paychecks to do plays on Broadway. You come nearer to living as you please than any other girl I know. How can an ultra-modern like you understand poor Victorian Becky Sharp whose whole plan of life depended on winning the help and protection of some man?[77]

In her response, Hopkins emphasized how Becky's flirtatious tactics could also work to modern women's advantage and applied this nascent theory to the patriarchal business structure of Hollywood. She explained that even she, a successful film and stage actress, still answered to the male executives and producers who ran the film industry:

> Women today might be able to support themselves, and to earn big salaries and hold high positions. But they are paid by men, and given positions by men, and it is to men that they have to look for everything just

> as it has always been men who owned and run the world! It is said that this is a "woman's town" but it isn't! Men own the picture business, men produce the pictures, give our contracts. It is a man who hires the biggest woman star and a man who directs her work. The same thing holds true in all professions. . . . To get ahead in the world, modern, emancipated, independent women have to know how to get along with men. . . . It brings out the Becky Sharp in them all![78]

Hopkins's frank critique of male hegemony in Hollywood noted that women in Hollywood must know the system and work alongside men in order to achieve professional agency, as she herself had done.

Indeed, Hopkins appeared to be a real-life Becky Sharp in her disdain for Hollywood publicity and her proclivity for the Broadway stage (which she believed was superior to film), both of which eventually undermined her independent stardom and ability to freelance. After the lackluster box office performance of her films *The Woman I Love* (1937) and *Wise Girl* (1937), she found her star power (and her freelance offers) waning.[79] She left Goldwyn's company in 1938 and returned to work for a major studio, negotiating directly with Warner Bros. in the hopes of reviving her floundering career. Although she and the studio eventually came to terms on a film project, Hopkins initially struggled to find a comeback vehicle and remained off-screen for all of 1938, not returning until 1939, when she costarred with Bette Davis in *The Old Maid* (1939). The publicity industry attributed her absence to her high salary demands. *Modern Screen* observed that fans had not seen her in a picture "for quite some time," but rationalized that it was *not* her recent marriage to director Anatole Litvak that had kept her from working. Rather, as the magazine commented, while producers "like her," she "likes money."[80] And yet, as already noted, behind the scenes Hopkins was negotiating a comeback deal at Warner Bros. for a substantial salary cut in exchange for increased creative control.[81] Much like Constance Bennett, Hopkins's aversion to publicity ended up having a negative effect on her freelance career. Mirroring her character Becky Sharp, Hopkins's penchant for money led the public to label her "greedy," thereby wedding her on- and off-screen image. Although she could (and did at times) negotiate to be contractually free of interviews and press campaigns, such publicity was necessary to market her films and bolster box-office attendance, which, in turn, would keep Hopkins employed.

It seems that in 1939, after her year-long absence from the screen, Hopkins finally realized the importance of publicity. The actress publicly attributed the hiatus to her desire to make films of artistic merit. A *Mod-*

ern Screen article praised her dedication to quality films and upheld her high artistic standards: "If that is a fault, it is perhaps a wise one. For many stars have suffered because they have been forced to take mediocre parts. Miss Hopkins, consequently, has waited for what she considered something really worthwhile."[82] Nonetheless, Hopkins's stardom never fully rebounded, despite attempts to maintain her independent public persona in her contracts and in the press. Like Bennett's, her freelance career did not necessarily translate to favorable press or strong box-office profits, which left her with limited options in Hollywood by the end of the 1930s.[83]

THE ULTIMATE PUBLICITY HOUND: CAROLE LOMBARD

For several reasons, Carole Lombard is the most revealing example of how freelance work could substantially remake a star's image and public persona. Of all four actresses discussed in this chapter, Lombard made the most drastic image transformation in that she waited until the completion of her long-term, seven-year contract with Paramount in the late 1930s to freelance, subsequently revamping her image from second-tier leading lady to A-list star. Furthermore, she actively courted various studio publicists to keep her name constantly appearing in fan discourse and the press. Known as the "ultimate publicity hound" of the 1930s, the actress appeared in more fan magazines than any other star, posed often for cameras, granted numerous interviews, and issued frequent press releases.[84]

Coupled with her status as the highest-paid Hollywood star of 1937, Lombard's freelance career became a popular topic in fan discourse and studio publicity with the release of her films at Paramount (*True Confession*) and SIP (*Nothing Sacred*). Lombard was a rare exception in the studio era, a star who actively courted the press, noting herself that "publicity and exploitation are as important to a star" as any other facet of motion pictures.[85] Lombard's prime incentive for doing publicity was not personal vanity, but career advancement. The actress realized that her continued success in the film industry, especially as a freelance star without the ongoing support of a major studio, depended on favorable press as well as box-office success. She knew it was in her best interest to win the public's favor through good public relations and to "sell" herself.

Accordingly, then, Lombard retained publicity rights in her freelance deals with SIP in 1937 and again with RKO in 1940 (as discussed in the previous chapter).[86] This resulted in an enthusiastic collaboration with SIP publicity director Russell Birdwell (who became her personal publicist after he founded his own firm in 1940), and plenty of successful press stories that kept Lombard's name in the headlines before and after her films' releases. Lombard even took over Birdwell's job at SIP for a week, a publicity stunt documented by the *Hollywood Reporter* in October 1938. In "Every Actor Should Take At Least One Week's Whirl at Publicity," Lombard described the "young modern press agents" of Hollywood as first-rate journalists who make news happen, and reaffirmed her own "personal and necessary" stake in the press in order to maintain her box-office popularity with film audiences.[87]

Of particular interest are two key campaigns that Lombard and Birdwell created, both of which illuminate the actress's independent stardom in studio-era Hollywood. The first was featured in a June 1937 *Photoplay* interview titled "How I Live by a Man's Code," which provides a compelling example of how Lombard used her publicity autonomy to help sell her revamped "career woman" image. In this first collaborative press campaign with Birdwell, she created solidarity between women readers and female stars by offering advice on how to have a feminine career with a *masculine* twist. Lombard's code offered ten rules for women to follow: (1) Play Fair; (2) Don't Brag; (3) Obey the Boss; (4) Take Criticism; (5) Love is Private; (6) Work—and Like It!; (7) Pay Your Share; (8) The Cardinal Value; (9) Be Consistent; and (10) Be Feminine.[88] Under the heading "Work—and Like It!," Lombard warned against women becoming idle, asserting, "Working women are interesting women, they're easier to live with precisely because they keep busy."[89] Under "Pay Your Share," Lombard disputed the assumption that men should take care of all financial matters: "You don't have to surrender your femininity if you pay your share of the bills," she explained, noting that the custom of "Dutch treat" was quite in vogue.[90]

As a glamorous career woman with a "male" business sense, Lombard urged women to "be feminine," remarking that a male work ethic did not prevent women from preserving their feminine side: "You can still be insane about what kind of perfume you wear . . . but play fair and be reasonable. When a woman can do that, she'll . . . wind up running a whole department store!"[91] Like Hopkins, Lombard utilized "all her feminine prerogatives" as a career woman.[92] Although she construed her freelance professionalism as masculine, noting how she organized all her affairs, lived by a code designed to fit a man's world, and handled her business affairs with "devastating serenity," at the same time she retained her feminine Hollywood glamour and asserted that "a woman's first job is to choose the right shade of lipstick."[93] This line illustrates how Lombard attempted to

"HOW I LIVE BY A MAN'S CODE"

SHE'S as delectably feminine as Eve, but watch out! That's no apple in her hand; it's a blackjack!

Because that apparently soft and defenseless girl curled up in the pillows is completely deceiving, and if you think you, most lordly Male, can deal with her in the time-honored manner of the dominant sex, then you don't know Carole Lombard.

Having found herself plumped down into a world where men are supposed to be masters of all creation, Carole has simply adapted herself to her surroundings.

She lives her life on the logical premise that she has equal rights with the male of the species, but she also (wise girl) preserves all her feminine prerogatives

She organizes her affairs, lives by a code designed to fit a man's world, and handles her business affairs with devastating serenity; yet she never forgets that a woman's first job is to choose the right shade of lipstick.

She competes in sports and plays tennis better than most men, but she doesn't let her nose get shiny doing it.

All of which makes "Missy" Lombard the perfect example of the modern Career Girl.

So you girls who live alone and still don't like it, take a leaf from the private notebook of that ultra feminine success-in-life, Carole Lombard What one woman has done, others can do.

Of course you need a few of the more essential elements, such as a pair of eyes that can open wide in bland innocence or give off sparks that can shock and numb; a figure that looks so luscious in an evening gown that it wouldn't seem possible that it could look even better in riding dungarees—

"... DON'T KISS AND TALK ABOUT IT—MEN DON'T..."

"... DON'T BURN UP OVER CRITICISM—STAND UP TO IT LIKE A MAN..."

"... BE EFFICIENT—DON'T MEN MARRY THEIR SECRETARIES?..."

12

In *Photoplay*'s June 1937 feature, Carole Lombard explained, "How I Live by a Man's Code." Courtesy of the Media History Project.

streamline the disjuncture between her on- and off-screen images. Known in Hollywood as the "profane angel," Lombard was also often characterized as a tomboy "shooting it with the boys" off-screen.[94] Her male code thus downplayed her masculine traits by underscoring the more glamorous, feminine attributes that her film roles showcased.

Citing Mary Pickford as an example, Lombard also construed the film industry as a place in which women could succeed professionally and develop business skills. As an "excellent example of success in business," the interview also showcased Lombard's new contract agreements as ones that "many a big star would give his eye teeth to own, plus the right to do an outside film at another studio. She has already negotiated for that extra film."[95] The contracts in question were Lombard's 1937 Paramount and SIP freelance agreements, which made her the highest-paid star of that year. Yet Lombard realized the importance of relating to her fans so as not to alienate the public by appearing to be an overpaid and ungrateful film star (as was the case with Bennett and Hopkins). This imagined alliance was necessary to maintain the success of the star system overall.[96] The actress cultivated this empathy by delineating the challenges that an independent star faced when she did not have the stable support of a "parent" studio. *Photoplay* explained:

> She has to talk business with dozens of producers scrambling to sign her up to their advantage, not hers. . . . Carole must have every wit sharpened to be on guard against a bad contract or even worse a script. . . . [S]he has counsel, as all good business men should. She has a capable agent, plus the advice of a most capable associate—who happens to be another woman, her secretary [Madeleine Fields].[97]

Here Lombard clearly detailed the added responsibilities that came with her freelance career. This self-promotion as "the modern Career Girl" of 1937 vividly demonstrates Lombard's active negotiation of the image her freelance agency engendered.

The second campaign of interest is one that Lombard and Birdwell invented to publicize her status as Hollywood's highest-paid star of 1937 (with an annual income of approximately $500,000) but at the same time humanize her as an ordinary, hard-working American through an unusual subject: income tax. Similar to Twentieth Century's earlier publicity campaign on Bennett's business sense, Birdwell and Lombard issued a "Four-Part Biography" press release on the actress's career, announcing that she was a "freelance star" who would make at least one picture a year at SIP, which left her "free for outside pictures of her own choosing."[98] The biography goes on to highlight how, despite her impressive income, "by the time she had paid federal taxes, business and personal expenses, she had $20,000 of this sum left for herself."[99] Yet Lombard was "far from complaining," and enthusiastically explained, "I'm glad to pay my country's taxes. For all the things this country has done for me, for the things that it has made possible, for the things it's doing for its citizens, the price is not too high."[100]

This scheme proved to be a publicity goldmine, prompting not only favorable press but also President Roosevelt's personal thanks for her devoted citizenship and patriotism. This story also purportedly produced the "largest and most intelligent" amount of fan mail for Paramount in fifteen years (the actress was concurrently filming *True Confession* in a separate freelance deal for the studio and also received fan mail there).[101] This campaign also appeared in fan magazines, including a *Motion Picture* article in November 1938 in which the star explained her take-home salary after all the various deductions. Again this feature put a down-to-earth spin on Lombard's A-list stardom by underscoring her commonsense approach to her lofty salary. The magazine explained, "For Carole is one of the few actors who doesn't figure her income in terms of what you may read she gets paid for a picture. She figures her earnings in terms of *what she has left over* after she has deducted her income tax, her living expenses, the amount she sets aside and labels 'savings.' She is an excellent business-woman."[102]

Lombard's publicity stories stressed dedication to her work as a defining characteristic of her off-screen persona to demonstrate that there was "no better craftswoman" in all of Hollywood.[103] The discourse surrounding Lombard emphasized her congeniality and professionalism. For instance, *Modern Screen* stated that every "director, cameraman, actor, actress, or extra" who had worked with Lombard witnessed her devotion to her craft, adding, "She studies a script until the ink is absorbed right off the page. She knows good writing. She has a critical faculty second to none when it comes to detecting weaknesses or appreciating [the] strength of fine characterization in a script. . . . She knows her business."[104]

Lombard's outreach to the movie-going public worked to ameliorate any resentment. By presenting herself as an enthusiastic citizen eager to do her part for the country, she spun her freelance film-star career as more of a public service than an abused privilege. At the same time, Lombard's patriotism served her well by quelling the rumors circulating about her ongoing love affair with the then-married Clark Gable. By emphasizing her freelance career, publicity about the actress attempted to counter any extratextual gossip about her illicit romance and protect her reputation, which was particularly vulnerable as a free agent. By contrast, as a long-term contract star, Gable had the stalwart protection of the powerful studio MGM and its resourceful publicity director, Howard Strickling.

The income-tax storyline eventually made the headlines of popular middle-class American magazines. The October 1938 *Life* cover story on Lombard, "A Loud Cheer for the Screwball Girl," provided a fruitful opportunity for both the star and her employer, SIP. The article again extolled Lombard's good-Samaritan tax approach, the fact she was "glad to give the Government $285,000" and "$54,000 to the State" of California from her salary.[105] More important, *Life* explained that Lombard was perfectly happy to pay her agent, Myron Selznick, a $45,000 cut of her salary, a decision championed by the magazine as part of her sharp understanding of Hollywood business.[106] This coverage pleased David O. Selznick immensely, as it emphasized her overall market value in Hollywood and reinforced his confidence in signing the star: "I think a note might go out to the exchanges concerning the terrific break in *Life* on Carole Lombard, using this [to] point out what a tremendous swing in public favor there has been toward her in recent months and since her last picture—and stressing what an important star she is today."[107] *Life* noted that "unlike most movie stars," Lombard "discovered early in her career that the primary requisite for acting in the movies is not talent for mimicry but talent for fighting with producers."[108] In fact, the majority of the *Life* cover story focused on Lombard's Hollywood career and business skills instead of her personal life, which again showcased the trope of independence to avert possible scandal over her affair with the married Gable.

Lombard's freelance career as an actress and self-serving publicist prevailed until her death in a plane crash at Potosi Mountain, thirty-two miles southwest of Las Vegas, Nevada, on her return to Los Angeles from a war-bond tour in 1942. Even her obituaries highlighted her business acumen over her marital status or memorable film performances. The *Los Angeles Times* obituary, titled "Tomboy Lombard Earned $2,000,000," accentuated her "sure pay climb" as "the highest of any woman in motion pictures," noting Lombard's career as a trendsetting freelance actress.[109] The *Saturday Evening Post* also posthumously profiled Lombard's cutting-edge business erudition in its story on talent agents titled "Hollywood's Ten Percenters," published in August 1942. The magazine lauded Lombard's reputation as a behind-the-scenes trickster with a penchant for practical jokes, one in particular relating to business at the expense of her agent, Myron Selznick.

The article recalled an incident from the summer of 1938 when Myron

Selznick sent Lombard a renewal contract based on their prior agreement. The magazine explained that the prevalent belief in Hollywood is that "artists never read contracts," while their agents and lawyers memorize legal discourse "by heart."[110] Lombard decided to test this theory and see if her long-time agent had actually read the agreements: she rewrote the contract to say that *he* should pay her 10 percent of his salary as opposed to the reverse, signed it, and sent it back to Selznick's office. After a month, Lombard's lawyers called the agent to inquire about the payment owed to the actress. A confounded Selznick finally read the contract and discovered Lombard's covert alteration. "Neither the Selznick lawyers nor the Selznick executives had read it with sufficient attention to notice that the wrong party was getting the 10 percent."[111] Of course, the stunt was all in jest for Lombard, who sent over a signed copy of the authentic contract soon thereafter. The *Saturday Evening Post*'s coverage of her playful scheme again highlighted the actress's uncanny comprehension of contracts and industry know-how, along with her madcap on- and off-screen personae. Lombard's experience demonstrates a direct correlation between her professional agency and her publicity autonomy, both of which helped the actress navigate the film industry as a freelance actress. As we shall see, her name was even more omnipresent in the press after her marriage in 1939 to the top box-office star Clark Gable, which also shaped her independent stardom public persona.

A LABOR OF LOVE: INDEPENDENT STARDOM AND HOLLYWOOD MARRIAGE

Bennett, Hopkins, Lombard, and Stanwyck were all married at various times during the 1930s, and fan magazines took note of their romantic affairs and correlated them with their freelance careers. How did fan magazine discourse, studio publicity, and, in some cases, the stars themselves reconcile these women's independent public personae with their status as married women? These off-screen, extratextual aspects of independent stardom illuminate shifting gender power dynamics and modern romantic coupling in regard to life-work balance in 1930s Hollywood. Several scholars have underscored the conflicting interpretations of fan magazines from the 1920s to 1940s, which steered female readers toward the traditional path of marriage, motherhood, and consumption while simultaneously undermining this message in their laudatory representation of female stars' careers as routes to social mobility and monetary success.[112]

As Adrienne McLean contends, "[T]he labor of star work was essentially incompatible with Hollywood's own valorization of domesticity in its films and its mediated representations of star life."[113] Stardom trumped being a wife in Hollywood.[114] In the context of independent stardom, we can interpret the publicity emphasis on freelance stars' career choices and the satisfaction they gained from them as a way to mitigate negative scrutiny of their unsuccessful domestic and romantic pursuits. Hence, the fan magazine press sanctioned female star labor outside the home and endorsed fulfillment based on individual achievement as part of the fantasy of stardom for consumers of cinema.

The discourses on Barbara Stanwyck and Carole Lombard—and their "modern marriages" in particular—equally emphasized their love lives and freelance careers. More specifically, the fan press distinguished these stars from their husbands in the Hollywood star hierarchy in terms of autonomy, public persona, gender, and marriage dynamics. They endorsed the ideal, balanced union between these freelance, *independent* women and their long-term-contract, studio-*dependent* husbands (Robert Taylor and Clark Gable, respectively, both on long-term contracts at MGM), which provided for compelling publicity that promoted Stanwyck and Lombard as freelance career women.[115]

Both women tied the knot with their matinee-idol husbands in 1939 after being previously married to (and subsequently divorced from) actors earlier on in their careers. The press spotlighted these former unions and attributed their failures to the couples' differing levels of success in the star system. In Lombard's case, the Hollywood press speculated that her two-year marriage to the established star William Powell, sixteen years her senior, ended because their careers had led to irreconcilable differences in 1933. As a 1935 *Screenland* article titled "Carole's Colorful Career" indicates, the fan press correlated the actress's revitalized career with her divorce, which they explained as a "successful failure" because it bestowed upon Lombard "a sense of responsibility, for now she had her own home and her own affairs to run," along with a budding career after her star-making turn in *Twentieth Century* (1934).[116] *Screenland* implied that Lombard's career could only thrive outside of her marriage to Powell, since it was "an unwritten law in Hollywood that no woman can be both a successful wife and a successful actress."[117]

Similar to the representation of Lombard's failed union, fan magazine discourse blamed the demise of Stanwyck's earlier marriage on conflicting career aspirations and star ranking. This resonated with her public persona as a dedicated trouper, particularly after her much-publicized, bitter divorce from Frank Fay and the ensuing custody battle over their adopted son, Dion. This opinion is apparent in *Photoplay*'s 1936 "The Story Behind the Stanwyck-Fay Break-Up," which recounted a saga that supposedly "Hollywood didn't know," unveiling the darker side of Stanwyck's apparent Cinderella rags-to-riches story.[118] They reported that at the age of nineteen she married successful Broadway comedian Fay, who took her to Hollywood in 1929 after he signed a contract with Warner Bros. While his film career fizzled and (as a result) his alcoholism worsened, Stanwyck's star soared; their marital troubles really began as her career eclipsed Fay's. The couple adopted a son (Dion Anthony Fay) in 1932 in an attempt to salvage their marriage, but by 1935, Stanwyck had filed for divorce, and Fay had returned to New York. Their tribulations made such an impression on the film community that they were rumored to have inspired the reflexive Hollywood melodramas *What Price Hollywood?* and *A Star Is Born* (1937).[119]

Photoplay not only provided readers with a detailed history of Stanwyck's stardom; it also demystified the allure and glamour of Hollywood fantasy to explain how the actress's ultimate success as a film star undermined her off-screen role as a wife. The magazine explained her failing marriage in melodramatic terms: "With her bleeding hands she was trying to restore the balance of power that Hollywood had destroyed," and now Stanwyck was "alone with her fame."[120] As with Lombard and Powell's failed union, *Photoplay* insinuated that the power imbalance resulting from Stanwyck's thriving career was to blame for her troubled marriage. Nonetheless, the magazine also reassured readers not to despair, as the actress would "survive it . . . in her work," implying that if Stanwyck did not find success in love off-screen, she could still attain satisfaction in her Hollywood career.[121] This public relations strategy began to blend Stanwyck's private life more with her professional reputation as a "trouper."

Influenced by her anguished divorce and subsequent career success, Stanwyck chose to cohabitate with Robert Taylor clandestinely after they began a romantic relationship in 1936. For Lombard, the major obstacle in her relationship with Clark Gable was his wife, Rhea Langham, who refused to grant him a divorce. This resulted in their covert cohabitation as well in the late 1930s. Both Stanwyck's and Lombard's off-screen liaisons eventually made headlines, as evidenced by *Photoplay*'s sensational story "Hollywood's Unmarried Husbands and Wives," which made the romantic live-in relationships of some of Hollywood's top stars public knowledge. The couples disclosed included Lombard and Gable, Stanwyck and Taylor, Constance Bennett and Gilbert Roland, as well as Charlie Chaplin and Paulette Goddard, among others. The magazine explained that the stars were "'Just friends' to the world at large—yet nowhere has domesticity taken on so unique a character as in this unconventional fold."[122]

Although *Photoplay* did not specifically connect these stars' unorthodox relations to their equally unconventional freelance careers, readers could make the association themselves from previous articles that had framed the off-screen public personae of Stanwyck, Lombard, and Bennett. Certainly, fans could choose to believe the article's conclusion that upheld the sanctity of marriage literally: "The best way to hunt happiness is with a preacher, a marriage license, and a bagful of rice," since "not even Hollywood's miracle men, [have] ever improved on the good old-fashioned, satisfying institution of holy matrimony."[123] However, the fact that all of the aforementioned stars had already been divorced (Stanwyck, Lombard, Chaplin) or were currently still married to other people (Bennett, Gable) suggests, as *Photoplay* also hinted, that living together might be a more attractive alternative to marriage. The article painted a sharp contrast to the onscreen narratives of Hollywood films that adhered to the film industry's Production Code, which upheld the sanctity of marriage, and this troubled Will Hays, head of the Motion Picture Producers and Directors Association (MPPDA). After the article caused a public sensation, MGM head Louis B. Mayer insisted Gable and Taylor marry..[124] The other star couples named by *Photoplay* also married shortly after these revelations, only to once again divorce in subsequent years.[125] The article's ambiguous tone seems to anticipate these outcomes and invites readers to draw their own opinions about the integrity of marriage.

Correspondingly, fan magazines began to link the success of Stanwyck's freelance career to her marriage to Taylor in 1939, focusing on the harmonious balance between work and private life that the two enjoyed.[126] In contrast to its depiction of her first marriage, *Modern Screen* noted the positive change in Stanwyck after her marriage to Taylor; the actress also told them directly that these personal changes had bolstered her career. Stanwyck commented that she and her husband were "keen" about their work, which accentuated her personal enthusiasm: "You know how crazy I am about mine. Talk about our work at home? Of course we do. Why not? Next to each other, next to Dion [her adopted son], it's the main interest in our lives. I'm interested in everything Bob does as he is interested in about everything I'm doing."[127] The continued focus on Stanwyck's work ethic and her marriage to Taylor also diverted attention from any anomalies that did not align with her trouper persona (such as her turbulent first marriage and the at-times tenuous relationship with her son).

Husband and wife working the publicity circuit: Barbara Stanwyck and Robert Taylor around the time of their marriage. Courtesy of the Margaret Herrick Library, the Academy of Motion Picture Arts and Sciences; copyright holder unknown.

A 1940 article in *Modern Screen* also upheld Stanwyck's career-woman image, reassuring fans that the actress's marriage had not compromised her work in any way: "Barbara is always called Miss Stanwyck, for instance, never Mrs. Taylor. . . . For Barbara being called Miss Stanwyck means that marriage hasn't submerged the 'selfness' of the Stanwyck self."[128] According to the fan magazine discourse, the career-versus-marriage dilemma did not preoccupy the actress; in fact, she explained that the idea of "giving up" her career had never arisen with her husband. This sentiment aligned with her independent persona, as it continued to underscore her work ethic alongside her domestic happiness. Furthermore, on the subject of retiring, Stanwyck confessed: "I break out in a cold sweat. Why, there's nothing I could do, I tell you, *nothing*. I never want to stop working, there's no stopping me!"[129] Moreover, the fan magazines hailed her marriage to Taylor as an ideal partnership based on their mutual respect for the other's career.

The press's juxtaposition of Stanwyck's freelance status with Taylor's as an MGM contractee suggests how their star marriage presented a balanced union that was not subject to competing ambitions. Taylor began his career opposite veteran actresses (Irene Dunne, Greta Garbo) or glamour queens (Joan Crawford, Jean Harlow) and quickly became known as a romantic screen lover. In response, MGM released publicity to emphasize his masculine qualities, featuring him as a ranch owner, hunter, and athlete. In contrast to his wife, his off-screen bargaining and contracts are never mentioned, likely because of Taylor's long-term studio contract. *Screenland* explained in 1940 that the former "Pretty boy" has "squared his jaw" by focusing on his acting craft and doing his "own brainwork now" and making "no more silly pictures":

> From now on the idol of American womanhood intends to be an actor, but a *good* actor. . . . Bob is determined to be Hollywood's number one actor, he'll stop at nothing until he's just that. And fortunately for Bob, he has a wife who believes in him, who is always ready to work with him, and who never fails to encourage him when he needs it.[130]

Here the magazine extolled Taylor's transition from screen lover to actor and acknowledged Stanwyck's wifely support. This is an important discrepancy in the press discourse on the two stars. Much of the MGM-controlled publicity on Taylor fixated on his masculinity and the remaking of his image to mirror that of their top male star, Clark Gable, who had also married a top freelancer in 1939, Carole Lombard.[131]

After the *Photoplay* tell-all, Gable divorced his wife and married Lombard, and the union received a great deal of positive press. As Hollywood's most vibrant and zany hostess, Lombard was an extrovert who played as hard off-screen as she worked on-screen. Her second marriage called for a new framing of the actress's image, amending her free-spirited party girl persona to that of a devoted wife who enthusiastically embraced Gable's interests, including camping, fishing, and hunting. *Modern Screen* quoted Gable to describe the actress's metamorphosis:

> I like the kind of girl who has a grasp of masculine feelings. The girl who, when a man comes home tired on a Friday night and says, "Listen, honey, I don't feel up to going to the Jones' shindig. Let's grab a few old clothes and dig out for the weekend," will say, "It's okay with me" and mean it. Carole is that sort of girl.[132]

Carole Lombard and Clark Gable in 1939, soon after their marriage, at home on their Encino ranch. Courtesy of the Margaret Herrick Library, the Academy of Motion Picture Arts and Sciences; copyright holder unknown.

The new "rustic" Carole Lombard as Mrs. Gable: outdoorswoman, hunter, and domestic companion. Courtesy of the Margaret Herrick Library, the Academy of Motion Picture Arts and Sciences; copyright holder unknown.

To accentuate their point, *Modern Screen* reminded readers how Lombard "used to be Hollywood's most amusing hostess," but now "Carole rarely gives or goes out to parties anymore. She knows Clark does not care for them."[133] Like Stanwyck's second union with Taylor, the public spin on Lombard's marriage also emphasized domestic bliss, perhaps to smooth over any leftover public disapproval of their illicit affair.

Lombard's new role as Mrs. Clark Gable suited her sophisticated career-woman persona, and Gable's praise of his wife's comprehension of masculine sentiment resonated with her male code of business sense and freelance initiatives. What's more, it also complemented the image of Gable's male bravado that MGM had cultivated. Like Taylor's, Gable's press was managed by MGM and fixated on his masculine hobbies, which ranged from hunting and camping to fixing cars and painting houses, as well as his "sensible" work ethic. In sharp contrast to Lombard, who monitored her publicity campaigns and was praised for her acumen and career discretion, Gable had famously told *Photoplay* in 1932, "I just work here. I try to work well and hard. . . . After all, they [MGM] have an investment in me. They spent money on me. It's my business to work; not to think. I do my work without talking."[134] This "company man" theme remained consistent in Gable's publicity copy throughout the decade, even after his marriage to Lombard and her efforts to win him more professional agency at MGM. For example, she pressed her husband to sign with Myron Selznick, claiming that he was the only agent "with enough guts to fight producers," and that Gable's current agent, Phil Berg, was a puppet of MGM executive Eddie Mannix.[135] Thus, the humble "company man" Gable contrasted sharply with the savvy freelancer Lombard, highlighting the distinction between dependent male stars with less input in studio-sanctioned publicity and independent female stars with more control over their careers and public images.

SUMMING UP SELF-PROMOTION

Over the course of the 1930s, fan magazines and studio press publicized the unorthodox freelance career decisions of Bennett, Stanwyck, Hopkins, and Lombard, which then became integral to their public images as both Hollywood stars and working women. In Bennett's case, her initially aloof relations with the press undermined her professional agency; compared to other elite freelancers, she was slower to utilize public relations to maintain her independence in the studio system. However, once she engaged with studio publicity, the actress took an active role in touting her business integrity as a way to sell her freelance films. Miriam Hopkins's story emulates Bennett's in this regard, as her independent stardom also negatively impacted her public persona due to her aversion to publicity. This reluctance to use the press to optimal effect ultimately cast a shadow over both of their careers and led to their inability to maintain A-list stardom by the 1940s.

In contrast, Stanwyck's and Lombard's professional autonomy accentuated their off-screen personae as modern working women with an independent "spirit" that endeared them to movie fans. They mobilized the press to bolster their career agency; indeed, both were among the first Hollywood stars to hire personal publicists (Helen Ferguson and Russell Birdwell, respectively). Furthermore, their independent stardom affected the representation of their personal relationships, as demonstrated by the many articles that highlighted the balance of power in their marriages to stars Robert Taylor and Clark Gable. Ultimately, this fan magazine marital discourse became another way for these women to "spin" their public personae as modern career women trying to handle both work and marriage. In this way, these stars negotiated with the press over their public personae just as they did with agents and studio executives over their contractual agreements.

Lombard most keenly understood the appeal of her independent stardom and no doubt framed her financial success in positive terms to the public, the film industry, and even to the federal government. Her incessant reflection in the press on her freelance career represents what John Caldwell has defined as "industrial reflexivity," in which film industry workers "reflect obsessively back upon themselves and invest considerable energy in over-producing and distributing industrial self-analysis to the public."[136]

The press discourse analyzed in this chapter provided a forum for that self-reflection, and now it also broadens our understanding of the industrial nature of female stardom in the Hollywood studio era. This history underscores the varying levels of professional agency that women could achieve by using the press as a tool to manage their off-screen images. Taken together with legal contracts, trade magazines, and studio memos, this fan magazine discourse suggests a nuanced and richer view of female stardom in the 1930s, revealing that independent stardom in Hollywood was a female-driven, trendsetting alternative to studio-controlled and -managed stardom.

FOUR

Independent Stardom Goes Mainstream

The freelance labor practices of independent stardom became an increasingly alluring alternative for A-list stars who sought greater creative freedom in Hollywood during the 1940s. As Thomas Schatz observes, this was an obvious career choice for stars who had "reached maturity in the early 1940s and exercised a considerable leverage over their careers," with many of them "deserting the studios for freelance status in 1939–40."[1] The high demand for quality pictures compelled the studios to be more receptive to making deals with independent talent and producers, often with unprecedented terms.[2] Moreover, new regulatory conditions enforced by the 1940 Paramount consent decree, negotiated between the US Justice Department and the Big Five studios, now limited block-booking exhibition packages to no more than five films. This forced the studios to have their A-class features ready well in advance of their scheduled release dates. These new industry conditions gave leverage to independents and affected long-term contract talent as well. The studios were forced to grant creative and administrative authority to above-the-line personnel—stars, top directors, and writers—as well as staff producers (who developed their own production units within a studio) in order to keep them "in house."[3]

Nonetheless, as this book has demonstrated, freelancing among A-list talent in Hollywood was by no means a new trend in the 1940s. Although previous film historians have recognized how artists transitioned to independence in the studio system, they have generally limited their focus to directors-turned-producers such as Frank Capra, John Ford, Ernst Lubitsch, Leo McCarey, and Cecil B. DeMille, all of whom were "top-level talent" that successfully transitioned to independent status in the 1940s.[4] As we have seen, several A-list female stars worked independently alongside these directors. Many of these women began freelancing in the 1930s, thereby setting a precedent for independence among above-the-line talent. By choosing to take an independent path in studio-era Hollywood, they clearly took ownership of their careers as top leading ladies a full decade before their male counterparts joined their ranks in significant numbers.

This chapter considers how these innovators of independent stardom fared in the 1940s as freelancing became more widespread. Claudette Colbert, Irene Dunne, Carole Lombard, and Barbara Stanwyck successfully continued their freelance careers, while other actresses—notably, Constance Bennett, Clara Bow, Janet Gaynor, Ann Harding, and Miriam Hopkins—were unable to do so for a variety of reasons. Former top stars of the silent and early sound era, Bow and Gaynor had retired by the end of the 1930s, and Lombard's untimely death in 1942 brought her vibrant freelance career to an end. Harding returned to the Broadway stage when film offers began to dwindle, as did Hopkins after the poor box-office performance of her films in the latter part of the 1930s.[5] Additionally, the founding of the Production Code Administration (PCA) in 1934 and its enforcement of self-censorship in Hollywood likely contributed to Bennett's and Hopkins's fading fortunes, as the once-popular fallen woman and sex-comedy genres that had prominently featured these two actresses were in decline by 1940.[6]

Ageism also remains a viable explanation as to why many popular 1930s actresses (many of whom were approaching their mid-thirties or early forties by the early 1940s) were not working as prolifically in the new decade.[7] Nevertheless, this did not inhibit Dunne (b. 1898), Colbert (b. 1903), and Stanwyck (b. 1907) from enjoying continued critical and commercial success as free agents. Indeed, these three actresses delivered some of their most memorable screen performances as they approached (and entered) their forties, and they received well-deserved laurels from the film industry in return. Irene Dunne appeared in two box-office successes during World War II, *A Guy Named Joe* (1943) and *The White Cliffs of Dover* (1944), and in 1948, at the age of fifty, she delivered an Oscar-nominated performance in George Stevens's *I Remember Mama*. Claudette Colbert appeared in the popular *The Palm Beach Story* (Preston Sturges, 1942) and received a Best Actress Oscar nomination for her performance in David O. Selznick's World War II homefront production, *Since You Went Away* (John Cromwell, 1944). Stanwyck reached the pinnacle of her career in this decade, receiving three Best Actress nominations for her roles in *Ball of Fire* (Howard Hawks, 1941), *Double Indemnity* (1944), and *Sorry, Wrong Number* (Anatole Litvak, 1948).

Irene Dunne consulting with director George Stevens on the set of *I Remember Mama* (1948). She was the lead star at age fifty, and this was one of her most successful films, resulting in her fifth Best Actress Academy Award nomination. Courtesy of the Cinematic Arts Library, University of Southern California; copyright holder unknown.

Perhaps, then, the most plausible rationale for the contradictory experiences of independent stardom for the 1930s female stars in the wartime and postwar years was a shift in marketing tactics from a focus on what was presumed to be a primarily female audience in the 1930s to that of a male and more youth-oriented one by the mid-1940s. This altered perception can be attributed to the advent in the late 1930s of "scientific" audience research used to anticipate box-office success. Engineered by George Gallup (founder of Audience Research Institute) and Leo Handel (of the Motion Picture Research Bureau), these polls set out to challenge the "myth" of the female-dominant motion picture audience in the late 1930s. A survey by ARI for RKO in 1937–1939 indicated that women made up *only* 51 percent of the film audience, while Handel insisted in 1942 that women and men attended the movies in equal numbers.[8] Foreshadowed by the numerous male-bonding films produced during World War II, this change becomes evident through a gloss of key industry trade journals, mainly the annual *Motion Picture Herald*'s exhibitor polls (a regular survey of the nation's theater owners, who ranked stars according to their films' overall box-office performance for the past year) and *Variety*'s top-grossing film lists for the decade. The top stars in the 1930s were consistently female, with Greta Garbo, Shirley Temple, Claudette Colbert, Janet Gaynor, Joan Crawford, Jean Harlow, Norma Shearer, and Mae West all making the list, many of them numerous times. In the 1940s, however, male stars—mainly Mickey Rooney, Humphrey Bogart, James Cagney, Bing Crosby, Clark Gable, Gary Cooper, Bob Hope, and Spencer Tracy—supplanted them in exhibitor polls.[9] What is more, the films in which they starred—*Boom Town* (Jack Conway, 1940), *Sergeant York* (Howard Hawks, 1941), *Honky Tonk* (Jack Conway, 1941), *This Is the Army* (Michael Curtiz, 1943), and a host of other action, Western, or war films—began to dominate the domestic box office.[10] By comparison, veteran freelance female stars such as Dunne, Lombard, and Stanwyck dropped off these exhibition star polls largely because their professional independence guaranteed them a limited number of pictures per deal, which resulted in their making fewer films than their studio counterparts (who were often compelled to meet an annual quota of films as studio contract employees).

Two male stars who began their careers in the 1930s and made *Motion Picture Herald*'s top twenty-five in the 1940s were Gary Cooper and Cary Grant.[11] Like Carole Lombard, both men abandoned long-term contract employment at Paramount to freelance by the late 1930s. Their deals emulated those of their female costars, stipulating casting and director approval as well as permitting work at multiple studios simultaneously.[12] In 1946, both men negotiated for percentage deals in which they relinquished an upfront salary in exchange for a cut of their films' box-office gross. Despite being late to jump on the freelance, percentage-deal bandwagon (recall Lombard's "contract like no other" at RKO six years earlier, in which she also wagered her salary entirely on the film's gross) by the mid- to late 1940s, male stars had attained similar creative and financial provisions in their freelance contracts. However, unlike some of the female pioneers of independent stardom, aging male stars like Grant and Cooper remained in demand due to the preponderance of male-driven films produced in postwar Hollywood.

Even as men ascended the freelance ladder in Hollywood stardom, the female stars of the 1930s did not completely disappear from the exhibitor polls in the new decade, nor were they denied professional independence. Bette Davis and Ginger Rogers continued to be top audience attractions as they attained more independence in their careers. In 1943, Davis's agency, MCA, established an independent production company, B.D., Inc., for Davis at Warner Bros., which would give her 35 percent of the net earnings from her pictures.[13] However, the company folded after one picture, because, as Schatz surmises, Davis ultimately showed "little interest in becoming her own producer."[14] By 1940, Ginger Rogers was RKO's only major star under long-term contract. Following Rogers's Best Actress win at the 1940 Oscars for *Kitty Foyle* (Sam Wood, 1940), the studio was eager to keep the actress on an exclusive contract. Rogers, however, chose to go freelance in 1941, arranging for the same kind of limited, non-exclusive deal at RKO that Dunne and Lombard had negotiated four years earlier.[15] Davis's and Rogers's career decisions continued the trajectory initiated by their female star colleagues earlier in the 1930s, and they were not alone.

Actress Olivia de Havilland was eager to freelance following the expiration in 1943 of her seven-year contract with Warner Bros., but the studio attempted to thwart her independence by extending her contract to account for the cumulative time that she had been put on suspension for refusing film assignments. In response, de Havilland brought suit against the studio in what became a landmark legal precedent known as the "De Havilland Law,"[16] which formally recognized the right of screen actors to be free agents.[17] Although film historians have noted the importance of de Havilland's case, the key details and events leading up to the suit and its ramifications for postwar Hollywood talent negotiations merit further consideration, especially in the context of independent stardom.[18] Furthermore, de Havilland's quest to achieve independent stardom through a freelance career demonstrates how stars turned to the courts when bargaining and contractual negotiations failed in Hollywood.

FROM THE POINT OF VIEW OF THE LAW

Like Carole Lombard and Janet Gaynor before her, Olivia de Havilland completed a seven-year contract before embarking on a freelance career. She first entered into a long-term contract with Warner Bros. in 1936 after appearing in their film production of Shakespeare's *A Midsummer Night's Dream* (Max Reinhardt, 1935).[19] Her weekly salary was set at $250, which rose in increments to $2,500 by 1943, but her contract gave her no creative discretion over her roles. Consequently, she found herself typecast by the studio as the brunette ingénue, appearing often as Errol Flynn's love interest in the Michael Curtiz directed films *Captain Blood* (1935), *The Adventures of Robin Hood* (1938), and *Dodge City* (1939), among others. The actress finally received a career-changing opportunity when she convinced Jack Warner to loan her out for the plum part of Melanie Hamilton Wilkes in David O. Selznick's blockbuster *Gone With the Wind* (1939), for which she received an Academy Award nomination for Best Supporting Actress. She followed up this success with another Oscar nomination, this time for Best Actress, for her performance in *Hold Back the Dawn* (Mitchell Leisen, 1941), this time on loan-out to Paramount. Back at her home studio, de Havilland kept receiving lackluster film assignments, even though she had proven her talent and market value. She found herself in precisely the same situation as Carole Lombard had been in in 1936: she was only being cast in important roles on loan-out to other studios. As the actress recalled:

> I finally began to do interesting work like Melanie, but always on loan out to another studio. I was nominated for *Gone With the Wind*, and then two years later, I was loaned to Paramount for *Hold Back the Dawn* and was nominated again. So I realized that at Warners I was never going to have the work that I so much wanted to have. I knew that I had an audience, that people really were interested in my work, and they would go to see a film because I was in it, and I had a responsibility toward them, among other things. I couldn't bear to disappoint them by doing indifferent work on an indifferent film.[20]

In 1939–1940, the emboldened actress began declining assigned film roles (taking a cue from her fellow Warner Bros. actress, Bette Davis), and by 1943 she had been suspended five times.[21] Despite her frustrations, de Havilland entered into negotiations with Warner Bros. to renew her agreement, but not as an exclusive long-term contractee.

Instead, the actress asked for a non-exclusive, freelance three-picture deal at a salary of $75,000 per film, with the right to do one outside picture. The following memo to Jack Warner from studio executive Steve Trilling elaborates on de Havilland's rationale for making such a deal:

At Warner Bros., Olivia de Havilland played supporting love interest to Errol Flynn in several films, including *The Adventures of Robin Hood* (1938). Courtesy of the Margaret Herrick Library, the Academy of Motion Picture Arts and Sciences; copyright 1938, Warner Bros. Pictures, Inc.

> She originally preferred to be free at the end of her present contract, but realizes Warner Bros. have been very good for her and probably in some respects it would be best to be tied up with us. But she wants to reserve the right to do at least one outside picture each year, so that when a *Hold Back the Dawn* . . . role does come along she would be in a position to accept.[22]

Trilling concluded the memo by asking his boss whether he had any interest in pursuing this offer; Warner did not, even though he had sanctioned similar deals with free-agent directors and other stars at the studio. He reasoned that de Havilland still owed the studio many months of work from her original long-term contract signed in 1935 due to all the times she had been suspended (without pay), which was approximately nine months total. As a result, the studio boss elected to extend the duration of her seven-year contract by adding this cumulative sum of her suspension time. But when the standard wheeling and dealing between the star, her agents, and the studio failed to garner de Havilland independent stardom, she turned to the courts to achieve freelance status.

De Havilland took the advice of her agents, Phil Berg and Bert Allenberg, and sued to have her prior contract declared unenforceable because it violated California Labor Code 2855, which limited personal-service contracts to no more than seven years. Warner Bros. countered that de Havilland had "effectively waived the protection of section 2855 by her breaches of the contract and was thus stopped from disputing the validity of the contract extensions."[23] She expected to lose in Superior Court and planned to appeal, but to her surprise, the court ruled in her favor, thereby guaranteeing the rights of the employee over the corporation. Warner Bros. immediately appealed to the Appellate Court, which upheld the Superior Court ruling and sided with de Havilland. The court argued:

> Seven years of time is fixed as the maximum time for which they may contract for their services without the right to change employers. . . . [T]hereafter they may make a change if they deem it necessary. . . . As one grows more experienced and skillful there should be a reasonable opportunity to move upward and employ his abilities to the best advantage and for the highest obtainable compensation.[24]

The court's ruling underscored an actor's right to the highest salary possible contingent upon his or her market value. However, this ruling did not eliminate the seven-year personal-service contractual norm; in fact, the court reaffirmed the legality of it in its interpretation of Section 2855, in that an employment contract could not extend beyond the calendar time of seven years.[25] So the "De Havilland Law" upheld the right of Hollywood talent to freelance, but only after they had completed prior contractual obligations. This was the major legal obstacle that had complicated and derailed the suit Bette Davis had brought against Warner Bros. in the 1930s because the actress had signed a legal, long-term option contract.

In sum, de Havilland's legal victory represents the delayed culmination of the quest for independent stardom in studio-era Hollywood. By the time she won her suit against Warner Bros. at the Los Angeles Superior Court in March 1944, a substantial number of freelance women were already working in the studio system. Her case and its legal precedent underscore the pivotal role that she, as well as the 1930s female stars who preceded her in their freelance paths, played in establishing the right of free agency in Hollywood, past and present.[26]

After her court battles concluded, de Havilland received multiple freelance offers, despite having been off the screen for nearly three years due to Warner's successful efforts to bar other major studios and producers from hiring her.[27] The first of these offers was Paramount's *To Each His Own* (Mitchell Leisen, 1946), followed by Universal's *The Dark Mirror* (Robert Siodmak, 1946)—both of which won her critical praise and her first Best Actress Oscar (for *To Each His Own*). Indeed, de Havilland was among many independent artists in Hollywood honored at the nineteenth Academy Awards in 1946; Fredric March (a veteran freelancer since 1933) won the Oscar for Best Actor for his work in *The Best Years of Our Lives*, a Samuel Goldwyn independent production directed by William Wyler and distributed by RKO that also garnered the Best Picture award.[28] It makes sense that freelance talent and independent productions made an impression at the 1946 Academy Awards, considering that nomination voting privileges had been extended to members of the Directors, Screen Actors, and Writers Guilds, many of whom had often been at odds with the major studios over their long-term contract policies since their inception in the 1930s in pursuit of greater creative autonomy.[29] Within this context, de Havilland's Oscar win also signifies an acknowledgment from her peers not only of her acting talent, but also her legal victory.

Other former long-term contract stars from the 1930s also remade their image in the new decade, but not always in the mold of independent stardom or through the legal system. For example, consider how de Havilland's case differs from that of Joan Crawford, another former 1930s studio

De Havilland victorious as a freelance star in her Oscar-winning role of Jody Norris in *To Each His Own*. Courtesy of the Margaret Herrick Library, the Academy of Motion Picture Arts and Sciences; copyright 1946, Paramount Pictures, Inc.

star who revitalized her career in the subsequent decade and won a Best Actress Oscar for *Mildred Pierce* (Michael Curtiz, 1945). Crawford found herself without major studio support after she and MGM mutually agreed to dissolve their nearly twenty-year affiliation in 1943. Later that year, Crawford signed a two-year contract with Warner Bros., but it was still an option contract, renewable at the studio's behest, and lacked any creative control (such as director, costar, or story approval) or financial incentives (such as profit sharing).[30] Essentially, Crawford's Warner Bros. contract was a condensed version of her prior long-term agreements with MGM. Nevertheless, Crawford did decline her first assignment at Warner Bros. and went on suspension for a few months, which ironically made her available a year later for *Mildred Pierce* (1945), her Oscar-winning comeback. The role resonated with the persona she had developed at MGM—that of an ambitious, working-class woman with aspirations for a better life for herself and her family.[31] At the same time, Crawford's glamorous sex-symbol image had to be "restyled" with a new "maturity" for the urban and hard-boiled Warner Bros. house style.[32] Producer Jerry Wald molded Crawford's new persona in *Mildred Pierce* and subsequent pictures such as *Humoresque* (Jean Negulesco, 1946) and *Possessed* (Curtis Bernhardt, 1947).

Crawford's case deviates strikingly from de Havilland's, as well as from the experiences of the other freelance stars profiled in this book. Her revitalized career and screen image were still very strongly associated with a major studio and its brand. Nevertheless, she and de Havilland achieved the same goal: freedom from long-term exclusive contracts and a revived career with Academy Award wins.

Certainly, de Havilland's court case remains a milestone in both Hollywood legal and labor history. However, her breakthrough should be analyzed alongside the other avenues of contractual bargaining through which her fellow actors attained independent stardom—both before and after her case in 1944—and within the broader changes that occurred in the Hollywood film industry in the postwar period. For example, just a few years after de Havilland's legal victory, the major studios began to relinquish their talent contracts, partially due to industry changes brought by the 1948 consent decree *United States v. Paramount Pictures Inc.*, which superseded the previous 1940 decree by divorcing the five major studios' production and distribution operations from their exhibition outlets.[33] The studios transitioned to become producer-distributors, but without guaranteed exhibition for their films, so production declined overall. Thus, it was in the studios' financial interest to hire talent on a freelance basis rather than under costly long-term contracts. The factory-oriented studio system was now impractical in post–Paramount decree Hollywood. While these legal, regulatory, and economic changes led to the end of the vertically integrated studio system, they bolstered the practice of independent stardom and remade the Hollywood hierarchy, with agents and talent gaining substantial power in the postwar American film industry.

INDEPENDENT STARDOM VENTURES INTO PRODUCTION

In the aftermath of the *De Haviland* and *Paramount* rulings, independent production became an attractive and viable option for actors to attain independent stardom in postwar Hollywood. In this regard, another former long-term-contract female star at Warner Bros., Ida Lupino, provides a demonstrative case study. Her decision to form her own production company, The Filmmakers, in 1949, brings the trajectory of independent stardom in Hollywood—starting with Mary Pickford and the founding of United Artists in 1919—full circle and underscores the industrial changes that had occurred over the intervening forty years. Whereas UA was founded in defiance of the nascent vertically integrated studio system, by the late 1940s, the studio system was in decline and not nearly as powerful. Postwar Hollywood called for a different type of niche film product than the A-class, prestige pictures that Pickford made for UA to distribute in the 1920s and '30s. In Lupino's view, the market called for social-problem B films grounded in realism. Like Pickford, as a result of her disappointing experience at a major studio, Lupino became an actress-turned-producer, running her own company with fellow independent-minded artists. By the early 1950s she had become something of a "Pickford plus" as actress, producer, director, and screenwriter of low-budget movies.

Lupino's impulse toward independence evolved over the course of her experience working under the studio contract system of late 1930s and early 1940s Hollywood. The British-born actress arrived in Hollywood at age fourteen when Paramount offered her a contract, but her career did not take off until her breakthrough role in *The Light That Failed* (William Wellman, 1939), which established her film persona as a hard-boiled woman, "outwardly tough and cynical, but a 'marshmallow on the inside'" in Annette Kuhn's words.[34] Her performance attracted the attention of Warner Bros. producer Mark Hellinger, who signed her for the role of the seductive murderess in *They Drive by Night* (Raoul Walsh, 1940). This move marked the inauguration of Lupino's independent stardom, for rather than signing a long-term option contract, the actress instructed her agent, Arthur Lyons, to negotiate for a one-year deal with Warner Bros. that paid her $2,000 a week, the right to do three outside freelance pictures, and make radio appearances free of studio control.[35] In the wake of three more successful films for Warner Bros.—*High Sierra* (Raoul Walsh, 1941), *The Sea Wolf* (Michael Curtiz, 1940), and *Ladies in Retirement* (Charles Vidor, 1941)—Lupino renewed and renegotiated her agreement with Warner Bros. in 1942 to increase her salary to $3,000 a week and extend her freelance agreements to four outside pictures.[36]

Unfortunately, just like fellow Warner Bros. stars Bette Davis and Olivia de Havilland, Lupino did not have story approval. Beginning with her refusal to appear in Sam Wood's *King's Row* in July 1941, the recalcitrant actress repeatedly clashed with Jack Warner over film assignments and found herself on suspension for the latter part of the year. Nevertheless, because Lupino's contract guaranteed her a certain number of outside pictures per year, suspension hardly fazed the actress, who continually stood by her artistically minded convictions to secure good acting roles. Her outside films included *Life Begins at Eight-Thirty* (Irving Pichel, 1942) and *Moontide* (Archie Mayo, 1942), made for Fox, and *Forever and a Day* (René Clair, 1943), made for RKO. Despite critical acclaim in Warner Bros.' *The Hard Way* (Vincent Sherman, 1943)—for which she won the New York Film Critics' Circle Award for Best Actress—Lupino's experience in what she perceived to be second-rate film roles ultimately left her embittered and frustrated. By her own admission, she considered herself a "poor man's Bette Davis." After fulfilling her contract obligations, in 1946 she rejected Warner Bros.' offer of a four-year exclusive contract.[37] Following the "De Havilland Law," Warner Bros. could not use her various suspensions to compel her to keep working for the studio.

Lupino also had ambitions to expand her role behind the camera. She had already penned several screenplays, one of which, *Miss Pennington*, she cowrote with Barbara Reed and optioned to RKO for $5,000.[38] In 1948, she and her second husband, Collier Young (former executive assistant to Columbia head Harry Cohn), went into independent production, joining Anson Bond's fledgling Emerald Productions. She and Young arranged to coproduce their first picture, *Not Wanted* (Ida Lupino, 1949), which dealt with an unplanned pregnancy. Lupino not only collaborated on the screenplay but also cast the lead roles; when director Elmer Clifton had a sudden heart attack at the beginning of shooting, Lupino stepped in to direct and keep the production on schedule. Although produced on a shoestring budget of $153,000, the film ended up grossing over a million dollars by April 1950.[39] Emboldened by their success, Lupino and Young

Ida Lupino—star-turned-director-writer-independent producer—on set with her Filmmakers partners: her husband, Collier Young; and Malvin Wald. Courtesy of the Margaret Herrick Library, the Academy of Motion Picture Arts and Sciences; copyright holder unknown.

then formed their own production company, The Filmmakers, with writer Malvin Wald. As Annette Kuhn explains, Lupino's rationale for turning to independent production and becoming an actress-director-producer-writer was to "make high quality but low-cost films with unorthodox and provocative subject matter—films which, if they delivered a message, did so without being 'preachy'—and to provide opportunities for new acting and technical talent."[40]

Between 1949 and 1954, Emerald Productions and The Filmmakers produced twelve features, six of which Lupino directed and wrote, five of which she produced, and three of which she also acted in. These films included *Not Wanted*; *The Hitch-Hiker*; *Hard, Fast, and Beautiful*; *On the Loose*; *Outrage*; *Never Fear*; *The Bigamist*; and *Private Hell 36*. Hence, Lupino's independent stardom blossomed into a multifaceted, tour de force career that converged with the postwar trend of talent forming their own production companies. Indeed, her versatile achievements in front of and behind the camera distinguished her independent stardom from that of her freelance predecessors and the legacy established by Pickford at UA. Despite the marketing shift to prioritizing a younger, male audience that galvanized male stars (and their films) at the box office, Lupino's career demonstrates how female independent stardom prevailed in postwar Hollywood. That success was especially bolstered by the drop in contract talent at studios, and by the changes resulting from legal rulings such as the "De Havilland Law" and the Paramount decree.

Other actresses also went into independent production in postwar Hollywood. Joan Bennett founded Diana Productions in the latter half of the 1940s with her husband, producer Walter Wanger, and director Fritz Lang. Their company released three films through Universal directed by Lang and starring Bennett: *The Woman in the Window* (1944), *Scarlet Street* (1945), and *Secret Beyond the Door* (1948), all of which contributed to the emerging film noir cycle in postwar Hollywood. Bennett's sister, Constance, a pioneer of independent stardom in the 1930s with Constance Bennett Productions, also produced and released two films through UA, *Paris Underground* (Gregory Ratoff, 1945) and *Smart Woman* (Edward A. Blatt, 1948).[41] As these and other freelance women expanded into independent production, and major studio productions (and power) waned, the phenomenon of independent stardom became mainstream in postwar Hollywood.

Now that we have established in this and previous chapters the full impact of independent stardom from the 1930s into the 1940s, I now return to the initial question proposed by this book: Why have Hollywood histories maintained the "traditional" story that attributes freelance practices to the postwar period?

THE FREELANCE FUTURE

This book has presented several possible explanations for the scholarly neglect of independent stardom, and for the failure of film historians to acknowledge the key role that women played in developing this industrial practice. One reason is historical periodization, which has tended to group events and key trends in Hollywood by decade, thus narrowing the time frame and the ability to trace important trends such as independent stardom across decades. Clearly, although independent stardom became a significant industry practice in the 1930s to early 1940s, it was a cross-decade phenomenon, from the founding of United Artists in 1919 through the Stewart/Wasserman brokered *Winchester '73* deal in 1949. We might better conceive of the changes at work in Hollywood and its star system as a historical continuum that connects industrial practices across decades. This allows us to better identify nascent trends and outline them from their development to their full integration into the film industry. *Independent Stardom* has also underscored the importance of utilizing a spectrum of primary archival sources to gain a broader and more nuanced understanding of the contracts and freelance practices of the star system. Moreover, this book presents a versatile sample of female stars who freelanced at an array of studios, revealing the accomplishments of screen legends such as Katharine Hepburn, Carole Lombard, and Barbara Stanwyck, as well as those of actresses lesser-known today, including Irene Dunne, Janet Gaynor, Constance Bennett, and Miriam Hopkins.

Independent Stardom counters approaches to American film history that negatively emphasize the "capitalist" nature of the studio system, with its patriarchal moguls and their supposed dominion over women. The notion of the oppressive Hollywood "factory" was first propagated by Lewis Jacobs and Benjamin Hampton in their studies of the American film industry published in the 1930s.[42] Addressing this issue, Richard Jewell has recognized the need to comprehend the studio system in more complex ways, contending that the field of film studies has thus far mostly reinforced Jacobs's and Hampton's conceptions that studio-era Hollywood was "bureaucratic, impersonal, conservative, rigidly structured and antagonistic to technical innovation and artistic achievement," and that "men and women of taste, intelligence, and imagination are often portrayed as being destroyed by the system—either squandering their talents by producing the formulaic, escapist entertainment demanded by the system, or rebelling against it, only to be crushed" by its assembly-line production ethic.[43] He aptly concludes that the power and authority of A-level talent during the studio era has been "seriously under-estimated."[44] Echoing Jewell's observations, this book has argued that the perception of an oppressive, factory-oriented Hollywood is only one way to conceptualize this era of American film history. It has also demonstrated the professional agency of women who did indeed prosper as empowered actresses, employing savvy talent agents to engineer an innovative freelance career model that remains in place for top Hollywood talent today.

The Hollywood studio system can and should be reimagined as a production culture in which female stars excelled alongside other creative-minded actors, studio moguls, and producers. This was especially the case for the less financially secure studios, such as RKO, and independent producers (such as David O. Selznick and Samuel Goldwyn), all of whom were very willing to embrace the give-and-take that allowed for the creativity and flexibility that sustained independent stardom, while the major studios like MGM and Warner Bros. were less accommodating (hence the preponderance of lawsuits). The contractual terms of these women's screen careers reveal a quite different experience of stardom in the studio system, in which female stars held powerful roles both in front of and behind the camera. Their endeavors prefigured what Denise Mann calls the "postwar talent takeover" in the 1950s, when Hollywood stars not only began to share in their films' profits but also expanded their roles into the producer realm, actively developing creative projects and distributing them through the major studios.[45] By tracing the crystallization of independent stardom, this book makes clear that this talent-turned-producer model, so strongly associated with postwar Hollywood, in fact emerged twenty years earlier, in the 1930s, as the careers of Constance Bennett and Carole Lombard attest in particular.

Freelance female stars of the 1930s studio era also anticipated current modes of stardom in conglomerate Hollywood. The crucial characteristics of independent stardom in the studio era included representation (talent agents, entertainment lawyers); image management (personal publicists, makeup artists, hairdressers, etc.); key contractual provisions that secured the creative team of choice, as well as story approval; and freelance agreements for a limited number of films for an array of producers/studios. These all remain key aspects of post-studio stardom. As Paul McDonald asserts, "In many respects, post-studio stardom did not replace the vertically integrated system but rather unlocked and regularized opportunities for creative and managerial independence."[46]

What McDonald classifies as the "sindie"—the star-led independent production company—has become an industry fixture today.[47] Much like the independent production company that Carole Lombard proposed along with agent Myron Selznick, director Ernst Lubitsch, and fellow actor William Powell in 1938, contemporary sindies enable stars-turned-producers to develop their own projects while being involved in the business end and raising financing, usually with a partner with experienced business acumen. Examples include Tom Cruise, who linked up with his former agent Paula Wagner to form Cruise-Wagner, Reese Witherspoon's Type A Films and Pacific Standard with Debra Siegel, and George Clooney and director Steven Soderbergh establishing Section

Eight. After that company closed, Clooney launched Smokehouse Pictures with producer Grant Heslov.[48] Since the 1980s, sindies have taken advantage of "first-look deals" with the studios, which has become an increasingly sought-out arrangement for A-list talent in which they negotiate for a two- or three-picture deal for financing and distribution by one of the six conglomerate-owned major studios: Twentieth Century-Fox (part of News Corporation), Paramount (owned by Viacom), Sony Pictures Entertainment (a division of the Sony Corporation), Universal (part of NBC-Universal-Comcast), the Walt Disney Company, and Warner Bros. (a division of Time Warner). This trend mirrors many of the industrial labor practices of independent stardom in the 1930s and 1940s, when the limited-picture deal between top talent and major studios first appeared as a semi-independent production venture.

Furthermore, sindie first-look deals offer the same financial benefits to stars as freelancing did in the old studio system, with the income generated from these deals taxed at the lower capital gains rate as opposed to the higher rate for personal income. And just as freelance stars in the 1930s and 1940s depended on independent producers and the major studios for employment, percentage deals, and other benefits, contemporary stars rely on studios in similar ways to sustain their careers. In essence, all the key attributes of independent stardom in the studio system have carried over to contemporary conglomerate Hollywood: freelance employment, negotiating power, inflated salaries, independent companies, creative autonomy, and a viable interdependence with a major studio oligopoly.[49] At the same time, while freelance labor was initially an empowering contractual bargaining tool and career option for A-list Hollywood talent (and still is), its contemporary equivalent lacks an alternative form of long-standing, stable employment in the film industry (which the old studio system's long-term contracts did provide). Perhaps this is why contemporary Hollywood stardom relies on what McDonald calls "dependent independence," whereby actors are independent of the studios but still rely on them for employment.[50] The studios need top stars as much as the stars need them. This "dependent independence" in present-day Hollywood is essentially an updated version of the independent stardom forged by female stars in the studio era.

In sum, *Independent Stardom* has not only assessed the careers of professional women working in the American film industry, but has also suggested an alternative historical framework that allows us to fully comprehend the importance of female stars in 1930s Hollywood and their trendsetting pursuit of freelance work, which prefigured the employment future for Hollywood talent. The women discussed in this book all attained their power through the star system—which at the time catered more to female audiences—by negotiating various contracts at an array of studios, working closely with independent producers, and employing agents. They also used the press to construct independent star personae in supporting fan discourses that accompanied their freelance films' release. Moreover, it was not solely publicity that enabled these women to personally shape their image; they directly reinvented their star personae by off-casting themselves in new roles. While one version of film history depicts Hollywood as an industry of monolithic and patriarchal control that left little room for creative ingenuity or economic autonomy, this book reveals how women cultivated and maintained their own independent stardom in American cinema.

APPENDIX ONE

Key Freelance Deals of Independent Stardom *Case Study Stars,* 1930–1945

CONSTANCE BENNETT

Deal Terms	*Studio(s)*	*Year*	*Special Provisions*
Two-picture deal in ten-week period	Warner Bros.	1931	• Salary $30,000 a week (total of $300,000) • Star billing in all films and related advertising, with her name appearing in 50 percent bigger font than the supporting characters • Producer, director, and story approval • Cameraman of choice
Four-picture deal	Twentieth Century Pictures (later merged with Fox)	1934	• For the first film *Moulin Rouge*, percentage deal in which she receives 10 percent of distributors gross, $60,000 advance salary • For second film, *Affairs of Cellini*, $60,000 advance salary per film, plus 5 percent of the gross until total amounts to $1.2 million • If her share of the gross does not amount to $75,000 within nine months of the general release date, the difference ($15,000) is to be paid her at the time • Third film is for MGM, salary of $75,000 plus $10,000 in distribution profits when gross reaches $1,499,000

CLARA BOW

Deal Terms	*Studio(s)*	*Year*	*Special Provisions*
Two-picture deal	Fox	1932	• Salary $75,000 per film, and a $25,000 bonus should the picture gross reach $800,000 • Star billing in all films and related advertising • Approval of director, cast, and story • First story already approved in contract, adaptation of Tiffany Thayer's *Call Her Savage*

RONALD COLMAN

Deal Terms	*Studio(s)*	*Year*	*Special Provisions*
Two-picture deal	Fox	1933, 1935	• Salary $100,000 advance against his projected earnings from his percentage deal (10 percent of the film's gross profits) • Star billing in all films and related advertising, with his name appearing in larger font • Story approval
One-picture deal (for the *Prisoner of Zenda*)	Selznick International Pictures (SIP)	1935	• Salary of $150,000 per film, plus 10 percent of the film's distribution gross after earning $1.25 million • Director and story approval • Sole star billing on screen and in all advertising
One-picture deal	Selznick International Pictures (SIP)	1942	• Approval of story, leading and feature players, director, cameraman • Work day cannot extend beyond 6 p.m. • Sole billing • Control of radio rights • Producer recognizes that "artist does not want to attend formal openings as a personal appearance, and will not request the same" • Works around his prior agreement to make *Random Harvest* for MGM • The right to approve any commercial tie-ups and employ his own publicity representative • Salary paid in four separate installments across two years

CLAUDETTE COLBERT

Deal Terms	*Studio(s)*	*Year*	*Special Provisions*
Six-picture deal over two-year period	Paramount	1934, 1936	• Salary of $100,000 per film • Right to make outside films as part of the six films at different studios: one picture for Warner Bros., two for John Stahl (at Universal), and one for Columbia • "No loan-out" clause • Director and story approval • Percentage deal (beginning in 1936) in addition to her $100,000 salary: 10 percent of first $100,000 of the film's gross, 12 percent on second $100,000, 15 percent on third $100,000, 17.5 percent on fourth $100,000, and 20 percent if over $400,000

IRENE DUNNE

Deal Terms	*Studio(s)*	*Year*	*Special Provisions*
Six-month contract with two-year option	RKO	1930	• Salary of $1,000 a week, then $1,500 in 1931, $2,000 in 1932 • Featured female billing in all pictures, meaning her name would appear in type larger than any other female player and as large as the featured male player, except if prohibited by prior contracts with male featured players • Right to collect half of any earnings received by RKO for loan-out services over and above her weekly salary
One-year contract for four films	RKO	1933	• Gives her 30 days' notice before the production begins • Story approval • Salary of $45,000 per film with a 15 percent cut of the distribution gross receipts
Three-year picture deal, one per year through 1937	Columbia	1935–1937	• Salary of $65,000 for first picture, $75,000 for second, and $85,000 for third • Story approval

IRENE DUNNE (continued)

Deal Terms	*Studio(s)*	*Year*	*Special Provisions*
			• Acknowledgment of concurrent freelance production agreements and a production schedule based on her availability • No commercial advertising tie-ups • Guarantee of "A-class" productions • Columbia cannot loan out Dunne, nor can the contract be sold, assigned or transferred
Two-picture deal	Universal	1935	• Specifies the two properties as *Showboat* and *Magnificent Obsession* • Story approval • Specifies director John Stahl for *Magnificent Obsession* • Agreement to work around other agreements and attempt to schedule starting date based on outside agreements • Films to be produced in one-year period • Salary of $83,333 per week for both films • Artist to be the sole star on screen and in advertising and publicity
Three-picture deal, one film per year	Universal	1937–1940	• Agreement to design production schedule around her agreement with RKO • Salary of $150,000 per picture • Guarantee of star billing; if she is given co-star billing with any male lead, studio will make sure that male artist "shall not have received credit as a star or costar" in her films. • Guarantee not to work past 6 p.m. on weekdays nor on Sundays or holidays • Guarantee of "A-Class quality" films • "No loan-out" clause • Director guarantee: at least two of the films will be directed by John Stahl, and in the event that he is unavailable, she and studio will "mutually" agree on a director, and that director will not have earned less than $50,000 salary • The right to terminate the agreement should Stahl be unavailable

IRENE DUNNE (continued)

Deal Terms	*Studio(s)*	*Year*	*Special Provisions*
			• Story approval, as well as script approval with the right to make any and all suggestions in connection with such first draft and final drafts • Studio will "not require without written consent" to do a musical picture • Salary supplemented by a percentage deal in which actress receives a cut equal to 10 percent of the gross receipts after the film has earned back its production cost, and a cut equal to 30 percent of the gross receipts and proceeds from the distribution of each, over and above the amount equal to the actual cost of producing the film
Three-picture deal, one per year through 1938	Paramount	1936–1938	• Specifies starting date agreement and schedule flexibilities • Approval over her song "takes" that studio may or may not use in films • Salary of $75,000 per film • Studio agrees to furnish wardrobe, stand-in, hairdresser, dressing room • Director salary is $2,000 for fifty-two weeks under contract or guaranteed compensation for last photoplay of $35,000; specifies either Henry Hathaway or Mitchell Leisen as director • Guaranteed leading female role in each film • Guaranteed costarred or starred unless "Gary Cooper shall be co-starred, then his name first" • "No loan-out" clause
One-picture deal	RKO	1937	• Producer approval • Music will be written by either the Gershwins, Irving Berlin, or Cole Porter • Director salary must be at least $50,000 in past year; specified approval to hire Mark Sandrich or George Stevens • Salary of $150,000 per film

IRENE DUNNE (continued)

Deal Terms	*Studio(s)*	*Year*	*Special Provisions*
			• Contractual acknowledgment of her right to make concurrent agreements with other studios • Studio not able to loan her out nor transfer or reassign contract
One-picture deal	RKO	1939	• Salary of $100,000 • Percentage deal: half of the receipts from distribution gross once the film has grossed back 1.7 times the cost of film's production, until $50,000 has been paid to actress
Two-picture deal	MGM	1942	• *The White Cliffs of Dover* and *A Guy Named Joe*
One-picture deal to make *Anna and the King of Siam*	Twentieth Century-Fox	1945	• Salary is a percentage of the "gross receipts" derived from the sale, distribution, and licensing of the film: a sum equal to 10 percent of the first $1 million of said gross receipts; a sum equal to 5 percent of the second $1 million of said gross receipts; a sum of 2 percent of all money in excess of $3 million of said gross receipts • Star billing • Work hours limited to 10 a.m. to 6 p.m. • Guarantee of first-class director from the industry should the chosen director, John Cromwell, not be available to direct
One-picture deal	RKO	1947	• Percentage-deal salary: an advance of $100,000 based on the projected 10 percent cut of gross receipts • Film made: *I Remember Mama*

JANET GAYNOR

Deal Terms	*Studio(s)*	*Year*	*Special Provisions*
Two-picture deal	Twentieth Century-Fox	1935	• Salary of $115,000 per picture, with a $7,000 advance • Story approval • Producer Winfield R. Sheehan will "personally supervise all photoplays in which the artist shall appear" • *Agreement cancelled in 1936*
One-picture deal	Selznick International Pictures (SIP)	1936	• To make *A Star Is Born* • Salary of $125,000 for twelve weeks • Percentage deal (added ex post facto): 10 percent of the distribution gross after film recoups its net production cost, earnings not to exceed $50,000
Two-picture deal	Selznick International Pictures (SIP)	1937	• Salary of $137,750 per picture • Work hours limited to 9:30 a.m. to 5:00 p.m. • Star or costar credit on each film • Story approval • "No loan-out" clause

ANN HARDING

Deal Terms	*Studio(s)*	*Year*	*Special Provisions*
Three-year contract	Pathé	1929–1931	• Salary of $2,000 a week • Director and story approval
Three-year contract	RKO	1931–1934	• Salary of $60,000 per picture • Director and story approval • Percentage deal: 15 percent cut of the distribution profits for *The Fountain* (1934)

CARY GRANT

Deal Terms	*Studio(s)*	*Year*	*Special Provisions*
Four films made between 1940 and 1944	RKO	1940	• Percentage deal: 2.5 percent of the gross receipts • Base salary of $50,000 per film
Two films	RKO	1944	• Salary of $100,000 per film • Percentage deal: 10 percent of the "producer's gross" after film has grossed back $1.5 million

KATHARINE HEPBURN

Deal Terms	*Studio(s)*	*Year*	*Special Provisions*
Two pictures per year	RKO	1933	• Percentage deal for *Spitfire*: 12.5 percent of the film's gross after it had earned twice its production cost ($175,000) in profits • Salary of $2,000 a week
Six pictures for two years	RKO	1934	• Salary of $50,000 per picture • Percentage deal: 5 percent of $600,000 to $750,000 in profits; 7.5 percent of $750,000 to a $1 million profit earnings; 11 percent over a $1 million in distribution profits
Two-picture deal	RKO	1936	• Salary of $60,000 • Same percentage-deal terms as 1934 contract

MIRIAM HOPKINS

Deal Terms	*Studio(s)*	*Year*	*Special Provisions*
One-picture deal	Pioneer Pictures	1934	• Salary of $60,000 for eight weeks; thereafter $10,000 per week (*Becky Sharp*) • Percentage deal: 10 percent of film's distribution gross after it had grossed over $800,000 • Director approval • Right to have her accountants examine the distribution gross reports
Two-year contract	Samuel Goldwyn	1934	• Salary of $6,500 a week for two years • Right to return to Broadway to do plays between her film commitments to Goldwyn
Two-year contract	Samuel Goldwyn	1937	• Revised 1934 agreement: salary of $7,500 a week, total of $525,000 for maximum of seven films • *Agreement cancelled September 2, 1938.*
Two-picture deal	Warner Bros.	1937	• Story, director, and costar approval for two A-class pictures (*The Old Maid* and *Virginia City*) • Salary of $100,000 for a total of two films

CAROLE LOMBARD

Deal Terms	*Studio(s)*	*Year*	*Special Provisions*
Three-picture deal	Paramount	1937	• Salary of $150,000 per picture
One-picture deal	Warner Bros.	1937	• Salary of $150,000 • Right to employ Teddy Tetzloff as her cameraman and Travis Banton to design her wardrobe • Star billing font size • Work schedule limited to eight-hour day
Three-picture deal	Selznick International Pictures (SIP)	1937	• Salary of $150,000 • Costar billing • Work schedule limited to eight-hour day • Right to employ her designer of choice (Travis Banton) • "No loan-out" clause • Publicity campaign approval rights • Right to approve the use of her image in any advertising and marketing campaigns • Percentage deal negotiated for the last two films in agreement in 1938: salary dropped to $100,000 per picture, supplemented by a 20 percent cut of the distributor's gross of $1.6 to $1.7 million; then a 15 percent cut of distributor's gross at $1.7 to $1.9 million; finally 7.5 percent of distributor's gross over $2 million in profits (agreement cancelled in 1940)
Three-picture deal	RKO	1938–1941	• Salary of $75,000 per picture, supplemented by a net percentage deal giving the actress an additional $75,000 in salary from the distribution profits of her films • Right to employ her personal publicist, Russell Birdwell • A percentage of her films' foreign box-office earnings • New percentage deal for second film in contract: 50 percent of the film's gross after it had earned back 1.7 times its production cost • Percentage deal for third film: 10 percent of gross profits until reaching $1.5 million; 5 percent of profits thereafter
One-picture deal	United Artists	1942	• To make *To Be or Not To Be*

FREDRIC MARCH

Deal Terms	*Studio(s)*	*Year*	*Special Provisions*
Two-year contract to make four films	Twentieth Century	1934	• Salary of $7,500 per week first year, $10,000 per week second year • Salary bonus: Upon the completion of four pictures, March to be paid the difference between his salary received and $300,000, and should the actor renew his agreement, he would be paid the difference between what he has received in salary and $800,000 after the completion of eight films • Screen and advertising clause: March will receive star billing and his name will appear in 50 percent larger font
One-picture deal	RKO	1936	• Salary of $125,000 for eight weeks to make *Mary of Scotland*
Two-picture deal	Selznick International Pictures (SIP)	1936	• Salary of $125,000 per film to make *Nothing Sacred* and *A Star Is Born*
One-picture deal	Paramount	1937	• $150,000 to make *The Buccaneer*
One-picture deal	Walter Wanger	1938	• Salary of $75,000 to make *Trade Winds* • Percentage deal: 7.5 percent of the film's gross up to $1 million in profits, and 10 percent of the gross after earning $1 million in profits
One-picture deal	Warner Bros.	1940	• Salary of $100,000

BARBARA STANWYCK

Deal Terms	*Studio(s)*	*Year*	*Special Provisions*
Two-picture deal	United Artists	1929	
Three-picture deal	Columbia	1930	• First film was *Ladies of Leisure* directed by Frank Capra • Completes remaining two films while jointly working at Warner Bros., 1931–1932
One-year contract for three films	Warner Bros.	1930–1934	• Salary of $150,000 for three films • Story approval and right to decline assignments • Sole star billing • Option contract: to renew for another three years, with salary increasing to $175,000 in year 2, and to $275,000 in year 3 • Option renewed for 1931–1934
One-year contract	Dually shared by Twentieth Century-Fox and RKO	1935–1938	• Two pictures per studio (total of four films) • Salary of $40,000 per film in 1935; increased to $50,000 in 1936–1937 and to $60,000 in 1938 • Star or costar billing on screen credits as well as in all advertising and publicity • Right to negotiate outside freelance deals
One-picture deal	Samuel Goldwyn	1937	• To make *Stella Dallas*
One-picture deal	Paramount	1937	• To make *Union Pacific* for Cecil B. DeMille
One-picture deal	MGM	1936	• To make *His Brother's Wife*
One-picture deal	Columbia	1939	• To make *Golden Boy*
One-picture deal	Samuel Goldwyn	1941	• To make *Ball of Fire*
One film per year for a total of five years	Warner Bros.	1944–1948	• Salary of $100,000 • Right to make two freelance pictures a year at other studios • Studio will coordinate with Paramount to hire Edith Head to design her costumes
Multi-picture deal	Paramount	1940–1944	• Paramount legal files not available for research. Stanwyck made the following films at Paramount during these years: *Remember the Night*, *The Lady Eve*, and *Double Indemnity*
One-picture deal	Universal	1943	• To make *Flesh and Fantasy*

BARBARA STANWYCK (continued)

Deal Terms	*Studio(s)*	*Year*	*Special Provisions*
Three-year contract for three films	Hall Wallis	1944–1947	• Salary of $100,000 per film first year • Option renewed and salary increased to $110,000 per film in 1945. Agreement renewed for two more years • Wardrobe and shoes provided by Edith Head, artist's designer of choice • Right to employ her hairdresser of choice (Hollis Barnes) • Approval of the director of photography; specified preference for either Charles Lang or Daniel Fapp • Artist not required to work beyond 6 p.m. • Contractual recognition of her concurrent agreement with Warner Bros.
One-picture deal	Wallis-Hazen-Paramount	1948	• Salary of $125,000 per picture • Option to renew agreement, one film per year, for five additional years, with salary per film increasing to $150,000 for last two films • Percentage deal: 10 percent of the film's gross receipts until the artist has earned an additional $50,000 in income • Designer and hairdresser of choice (Edith Head and Geraldine Cole)

APPENDIX TWO

Motion Picture Archives and Library Materials Consulted

Irene Dunne Collection, School of Cinematic Arts Library Special Collections, University of Southern California, Los Angeles, California.

Charles K. Feldman Papers, Louis B. Mayer Library, American Film Institute Library, Los Angeles, California.

Cary Grant Papers, Academy of Motion Pictures Arts and Sciences, Margaret Herrick Library, Beverly Hills, California.

Gladys Hall Papers, Academy of Motion Pictures Arts and Sciences, Margaret Herrick Library, Beverly Hills, California.

Jack Oakie Collection, School of Cinematic Arts Library Special Collections, University of Southern California, Los Angeles, California.

Paramount Contract Summaries, Academy of Motion Pictures Arts and Sciences, Margaret Herrick Library, Beverly Hills, California.

Production Code Administration Files, Academy of Motion Pictures Arts and Sciences, Margaret Herrick Library, Beverly Hills, California.

RKO Radio Pictures Collection, UCLA Performing Arts Special Collections, University of California, Los Angeles, California.

David O. and Myron Selznick Collections, Harry Ransom Center, the University of Texas, Austin.

Twentieth Century-Fox Legal Files, formerly housed at UCLA Performing Arts Collections, University of California, Los Angeles.

United Artists Collection, Wisconsin Center for Film and Theater Research, State Historical Society, Madison, Wisconsin.

Warner Bros. Archives, School of Cinematic Arts, University of Southern California, Los Angeles.

Jock Whitney Collection, Harry Ransom Center, the University of Texas, Austin.

Notes

INTRODUCTION

1. This growing trend of A-list stars that Lombard belonged to was also noted in "10 Exclusive Stars," *Variety*, July 3, 1935, 2, 23.

2. Faith Baldwin, "Do Hollywood Women Spoil Their Men?," *Photoplay* 53, no. 5 (May 1939): 18.

3. See "Arbitration between Myron Selznick and Company, Inc. and Carole Lombard," January 1941, Myron Selznick Collection (MSC hereafter), Harry Ransom Center (HRC), the University of Texas-Austin (UT-Austin), p. 53.

4. This revision of her salary and percentage deal is illustrated in RKO payroll cards from July 8, 1940, and September 9, 1940.

5. Road-show screenings were a practice in Hollywood in which a film opened in a limited number of theaters in large cities such as Los Angeles, New York, and Chicago for a specific period of time before the nationwide general release. Block-booking was a practice of the Hollywood major studios in which independent theater owners were forced to take large numbers of a studio's pictures sight unseen, including second-rate B movies along with A-class star features. The contractual terms for Lombard's RKO deal are delineated in Selznick's client notebook, MSC, HRC, UT-Austin.

6. These figures are found in the Carole Lombard legal file, DOSC, HRC, UT-Austin.

7. Larry Swindell, *Screwball: The Life of Carole Lombard* (New York: William Morrow and Company, 1975), 273.

8. The court's ruling, California Labor Code Section 2855, is referred to as the "De Havilland Law." (Even though they misspelled the actress's name in the court case and capitalized the "de" in the ruling, it became published as such.)

9. The term "genius of the system" references the title of Schatz's landmark book on studio-era Hollywood, in which he quotes André Bazin's observation that the American cinema up until the 1950s "is a classical art, but why not then admire in it what is most admirable, i.e., not only the talent of this or that filmmaker, but the genius

of the system." Thomas Schatz, *The Genius of the System* (New York: Henry Holt and Company, 1988), 2.

10. Donated to the University of Southern California in 1977 by Warner Communications, the Warner Bros. Archives spans the period between 1917, when the company was founded, to 1967, when Jack Warner sold the studio to the conglomerate Seven Arts. For more on the novelty of the Warner Bros. Archives at USC, see my article "That's Not All Folks: Excavating the Warner Bros. Archives," in *Moving Image* 14, no. 1 (2014): 30-48. Note that Warner Bros. was one of the "Big Five" studios, along with Paramount, MGM, RKO, and Twentieth Century-Fox. It was vertically integrated in that they owned and operated the three major facets of the film industry—production, distribution, and exhibition—whereas the "Little Three" (Columbia, Universal, and United Artists) did not own and operate all three. While the United Artists files are housed at the Wisconsin Center for Film and Theater Research in Madison, they contain only the distribution records, given that the studio's primary function was as a distributor for independent productions.

11. See Tino Balio's investigation of Cagney's and Davis's labor strife with Warner Bros. in the 1930s in *Grand Design: Hollywood as a Modern Business Enterprise, 1930–1939* (Berkeley: University of California Press, 1995), 157–161. Though their studies expand beyond Warner Bros. stars, even more recent star-system books, including Jeanine Basinger's *The Star Machine* (New York: Knopf, 2007) and Jon Lewis's *American Film: A History* (New York: W. W. Norton, 2007), perpetuate the "star serfdom" narrative of 1930s Hollywood. Although "the Warner three" clearly had poor contracts, agents, and bad overall strategies for their careers at the time, all of them learned from their disappointing experiences. Cagney would return to Warner Bros. with one of the best contracts on the lot by 1939. Represented by his brother, he received story approval and a percentage deal, while Davis became a client of Lew Wasserman in the 1940s and the "queen" of the Warner Bros. lot. De Havilland eclipsed them both with her legal victory over Warner Bros. in 1944.

12. These headlines include "De Havilland Sues For Work," *Variety*, July 14, 1944, 1, 4. For Cagney, see "Warners Adamant," *Variety*, April 19, 1932, 3; "James Cagney Called Bad Boy," *Variety*, March 11, 1936, 3; and "WB Statement Characterizes Cagney Decision," *Variety*, March 18, 1936, 3. See also "Bette Davis Salary Tiff with WB," *Variety*, July 8, 1936, 3.

13. Tom Kemper, *Hidden Talent: The Emergence of Hollywood Agents* (Berkeley: University of California Press, 2010), 131. Kemper's important book underscores the key role that agents played in Hollywood, in particular by negotiating vibrant careers for A-list talent.

14. Eric Smoodin, "The History of Film History," in *Looking Past the Screen: Case Studies in American Film History and Method*, edited by John Lewis and Eric Smoodin (Durham, NC: Duke University Press, 2007), 29.

15. The Twentieth Century-Fox Collection (with records ranging from the 1920s to 1980s) was formerly housed at UCLA but has been reclaimed by the studio and is no longer available for research access.

16. There is no fully centralized or comprehensive archive available for MGM, and unfortunately some of the studio's archival records were discarded. For instance, all MGM musical material, including orchestra arrangements and parts, were discarded in the late 1960s. However, some content is available at USC, the Margaret Herrick Library (art and legal documents related to production and wardrobe departments, as well as scripts), UCLA Performing Arts Special Collections (architectural set plans, scripts, in-house research production files from the 1930s and 1940s), and the Frances Howard Goldwyn Hollywood Branch of the Los Angeles Public Library. I have been unable to determine the precise whereabouts of the pre-1948 Paramount legal materials. Likewise, the UA collection at University of Wisconsin–Madison contains the company's corporate records from its founding in 1919 until the early 1950s, yet its files detail the aspects of motion picture sales and distribution. I was unable to locate any individual talent contracts for my freelance case study stars whose films were released by UA. For a complete listing of the archival collections consulted for this book, see Appendix 2.

17. For a complete listing of USC's special collections pertaining to cinema, see http://www.usc.edu/libraries/collections/performing_arts/.

18. While this approach yields a versatile and rich web of research through which to construct revisionist film histories, it also faces material limitations in terms of access, especially when it comes to legal files. For example, the legal materials of RKO and Twentieth Century-Fox are not currently accessible, while only partial legal records are available for Paramount and MGM. The disappearance of these primary sources from public access has created a research challenge for historians, who are forced to rely on secondary sources from scholars who had the fleeting opportunity to consult these collections. In addition to this book, see Janet Bergstrom's work on F. W. Murnau and his tenure at Fox, "Murnau in America: Chronicle of Lost Films," in *Film History* 14, nos. 3/4 (2002): 430–460; Kemper, *Hidden Talent*; and Lea Jacobs, *The Decline of Sentiment: American Films in the 1920s* (Berkeley: University of California Press, 2008). These are among the most recent and potentially last scholarly works to utilize the Fox collection.

19. I will return to this case in further detail in Chapter 4. See also Emily Carman and Philip Drake, "Doing the Deal: Talent Contracts in Hollywood," in *Hollywood and the Law* (BFI/Palgrave, 2016); as well as Schatz, *Genius of the System*, 318; Jonathan Blaufarb, "The Seven Year Itch: California Labor Code Section 2855," *Communications and Entertainment Law Journal* 6, no. 3 (1983–1984): 653–693; and De Haviland v. Warner Bros., 67 Cal. App.2d 225, 228, 153 P.2d 983, 984 (1944).

20. These include Dennis McDougal, *The Last Mogul: Lew Wasserman, MCA, and the Hidden History of Hollywood* (New York: Da Capo Press, 2001), 153–157; Schatz, *Genius of the System*, 470–473; Denise Mann, *Hollywood Independents: The Postwar Hollywood Takeover* (Minneapolis: University of Minnesota Press, 2008), especially chap. 2, "Backstage Dramas," 31–64; and Douglas Gomery, *The Hollywood Studio System: A History* (London: BFI, 2005), 210–220.

21. This deal gave Stewart a sizable amount of the *adjusted* distribution gross once

they deducted the studio's 25 percent distribution fee, recouped its actual cost (approximately $917,374) for producing the film, and accounted for other general studio overhead costs. As burdensome as these expenses might seem, McDougal explains that "they were minimal compared to the net profit definitions before and after *Winchester '73*." See McDougal, *The Last Mogul*, 153. McDougal goes on to acknowledge that "*Winchester '73* was not the first gross profit deal, but it was the biggest," as gross profit sharing was "real money."

22. See Gomery, *Hollywood Studio System*, 205–206, for more on Wasserman's maverick talent brokering with the studios on behalf of his clients.

23. As Tom Kemper explains, the Stewart/Wasserman deal was "not the pivotal moment it often gets painted as in film histories" and was "more or less a singular accomplishment for MCA." See *Hidden Talent*, 236, 273.

24. Tino Balio's *United Artists: The Company Built By the Stars*, vol. 1: 1919–1950 (Madison: University of Wisconsin Press, 2009) documents the UA story of Hollywood independence.

25. Paul McDonald, *The Star System: Hollywood's Production of Popular Identities* (London: Wallflower, 2000), 1, 3.

26. See Dyer, *Film and Theory*, edited by Toby Miller and Robert Stam (New York: Blackwell, 2000), 603–617, and *Stars* (London: BFI, 1998), to name only a couple of his important scholarly works on film and media stardom.

27. Danae Clark, *Negotiating Hollywood: The Cultural Politics of Actors' Labor* (Minneapolis: University of Minnesota Press, 1995).

28. The phrase "grand design" references the title of Balio's book. Other studies include Schatz, *Genius of the System*; Cathy Klaprat, "The Star as Market Strategy: Bette Davis in Another Light," in *The American Film Industry*, edited by Tino Balio (Madison: University of Wisconsin Press, 1976), 351–376; and Robert Allen, "The Role of the Star in Film History [Joan Crawford]," in *Film Theory and Criticism*, 5th ed., edited by Leo Braudy and Marshall Cohen (Oxford: Oxford University Press, 1999), 547–561. These studies tend to focus on the amount of control that the major studios exerted over their contract stars.

29. Karen Ward Mahar's *Women Filmmakers in Early Hollywood* (Baltimore: John Hopkins University Press, 2008); Cari Beauchamp's *Without Lying Down: Frances Marion and the Powerful Women in Early Hollywood* (Berkeley: University of California Press, 1998); and Jennifer M. Bean and Diane Negra, eds., *A Feminist Reader in Early Cinema* (Durham, NC: Duke University Press, 2002) all underscore various women pioneers in Hollywood.

30. Mahar, *Women Filmmakers*, 203. The obvious exceptions to this rule were Mary Pickford (producer and board member at United Artists), the director Dorothy Arzner, editor Margaret Booth, and screenwriters Frances Marion and Anita Loos (although they were substantially outnumbered by their male counterparts).

31. I discuss the importance of female stars and female fans in 1930s Hollywood cinema in Chapter 1.

32. Mahar, *Women Filmmakers*, 203.

33. An "option" contract denoted that the studio had the option to renew or "drop" the contract with the actor, whereas a "non-option" contract signified that the studio must renegotiate directly with the actor to renew or extend the agreement.

CHAPTER ONE

1. Douglas W. Churchill, "Producers Sign All Comers As Cinema Talent Booms," *San Francisco Chronicle*, March 14, 1937. The article also states there were more than 750 performers under contract in Hollywood, up from the 450 reported in 1936.

2. Ibid.

3. Sarah Berry, *Screen Style: Fashion and Femininity in 1930s Hollywood* (Minneapolis: University of Minnesota Press, 2000), xvi.

4. See Ethan Mordden, *Make Believe: The Broadway Musical in the 1920s* (New York: Oxford University Press, 1997), 6, in which he calls the Broadway stage of the 1920s "the age" for heroines.

5. Balio, *Grand Design*, 235.

6. Ibid., Appendixes 1 and 3, 405–406, 411–412. All of these trade journals polled exhibitors on their top box-office attractions (stars' films that made the most money and sold the most tickets).

7. "Fifty Best Draw Names," *Hollywood Reporter*, July 27, 1936, 1–2. Dunne ranks at 13, Lombard at 17, Gaynor at 20, and Stanwyck at 34. The top fifty star rankings broke down to an almost fifty-fifty split, with female stars gaining twenty-three spots on the list and men slightly outnumbering the women with twenty-eight spots.

8. This presumption persisted into the 1930s, until the advent of "scientific" audience research engineered by George Gallup (founder of Audience Research Institute) and Leo Handel (of the Motion Picture Research Bureau) in their polls for RKO. See Melvyn Stokes, "Female Audiences of the 1920s and early 1930s," in *Identifying Hollywood's Audiences*, edited by Richard Maltby and Melvyn Stokes (London: BFI, 1999), 43–44; and Susan Ohmer, *George Gallup in Hollywood* (New York: Columbia University Press, 2006). I also discuss this audience shift further in chap. 4.

9. Stokes, "Female Audiences," 44.

10. See Frederick James Smith, "Does Decency Help or Hinder?," *Photoplay* 26 (November 1924): 36; Beth Brown, "Making Movies for Women," *Moving Picture World*, March 26, 1927, 34. These numbers are also cited in Gaylyn Studlar, "The Perils of Pleasure? Fan Magazine Discourse as Women's Commodified Culture in the 1920s," in *Silent Film*, edited by Richard Abel (New Brunswick, NJ: Rutgers University Press, 1996), 263; and Stokes, "Female Audiences," 43.

11. Stokes, "Female Audiences," 44. While several film historians have underscored how fan magazines in the American silent-film era affirmed the significance of the female audience to Hollywood cinema through its "textually inscribed" address to female readers, the 1930s has largely been neglected as an equally important era in which Hollywood films were marketed largely toward women audiences. Film

historians who have written about female film audiences of the 1910s and 1920s include Miriam Hansen, *Babel and Babylon: Spectatorship and American Silent Film* (Cambridge, MA: Harvard University Press, 1991); Studlar, "The Perils of Pleasure"; Kathryn Fuller, *At the Moving Picture Show: Small Town Audiences and the Creation of Movie Fan Culture* (Charlottesville: University of Virginia Press, 1996); Shelley Stamp, *Movie Struck Girls: Women and Motion Picture Culture After the Nickelodeon* (Princeton, NJ: Princeton University Press, 2000); and Marsha Orgeron, "Making *It* in Hollywood: Clara Bow, Fandom, and Consumer Culture," *Cinema Journal* 42, no. 4 (2003): 76–94.

12. "Dirt Craze Due to Women," *Variety* 103, no. 1, June 16, 1931, 1.

13. Ibid.

14. Emphasis in original. Samuel Goldwyn and Eric L. Ergenbright, "Women Rule Hollywood," *New Movie Magazine* 11, no. 2 (March 1935): 18.

15. Ibid.

16. The movie moguls who ran the Big Five vertically integrated major studios were Adolph Zukor at Paramount, the brothers Harry (head of the company) and Jack (as production chief) at Warner Bros., Nicholas Schenck at Loew's/MGM (with Louis B. Mayer as head of studio operations in Los Angeles and Irving Thalberg as head of production), and William Fox at Fox Film Corp. The other major studio, RKO, was a media conglomerate without any visible leader or mogul personality. Fox lost his company in 1930; it later merged with Twentieth Century, renamed Twentieth Century-Fox, led by studio executive Joseph Schenck (with Darryl Zanuck as head of production). The "Little Three" (which were not vertically integrated) studios were Columbia (headed by production chief Harry Cohn, who was also the chief executive officer of the Columbia Corporation); Universal, founded by Carl Laemmle, Sr.; and United Artists, the distribution company founded by Fairbanks, Pickford, Chaplin, and Griffith. Universal was later run by Laemmle's son, Carl Jr., as head of production from 1930 to 1936, followed by Charles Rogers (1936–1937), and Nate Blumberg and Cliff Work finished out the remainder of the decade and continued until the mid-1940s. Because Universal and Columbia lacked national theater chains, they distributed their films through the major studios. For more on the beginnings and solidification of the Hollywood studio system, see Douglas Gomery, *The Hollywood Studio System*.

17. McDonald, *The Star System*, 9; and see also *The Classical Hollywood Cinema*, by David Bordwell, Kristen Thompson, and Janet Staiger (New York: Columbia University Press, 1985), 91.

18. Production was conceptualized in terms of A and B films. Major stars tended to appear in A films that had larger budgets, generous shooting schedules, and relied on top producers, directors, writers, cinematographers, and other experienced personnel. The running time was normally eighty-five minutes or longer. By contrast, B movies were less expensive; adhered to a strict, shorter shooting schedule; and contained less-prestigious casts and personnel. Their running time ranged from fifty-five to seventy minutes. See Brian Taves, "The B Film: Hollywood's Other Half," in Balio, *Grand De-*

sign, 313–350; and Richard B. Jewell, *The Golden Age of Cinema: Hollywood 1929–1945* (Malden, MA: Blackwell, 2007), 69–71.

19. See Forty-Ninth Session of California State Senate, Chapter 705, Section 1493, approved by the governor on June 10, 1931, and put into effect on August 14, 1931.

20. Ibid.

21. See contract dated July 23, 1935, Ronald Colman legal file, DOSC, HRC, UT-Austin.

22. "Objections to 7-Yr. Contract," *Variety*, June 30, 1931, 3.

23. The Civil Code statute was later transferred to the Labor Code in 1937 as Section 2855 "pursuant to the Industrial Labor Relations Act." See Jonathan Blaufarb, "The Seven-Year Itch: California Labor Code Section 2855," *Communications and Entertainment Law Journal* 6, no. 3 (1983–1984): 656.

24. Balio, *Grand Design*, 145.

25. Ibid., 145–146.

26. Klaprat, "Bette Davis," 376.

27. See Bette Davis legal file, Warner Bros. Archive (WBA), University of Southern California (USC). In fact, Davis had been dropped from a prior option contract with Universal in 1931.

28. Klaprat, "Bette Davis," 376. See also See Bette Davis legal file, WBA, USC.

29. Ibid.

30. Ibid. Although she took legal action in 1936 against the studio in order to win more creative freedom and improved working conditions, the court ruled in the studio's favor, upholding Warner Bros.' firm suspension policy (which extended an actor's contract by the amount of time during which he or she refused to perform). See the summary of the Davis suit from RW Perkins to Freston and Lewis, November 11, 1936, and see also the British court's opinion, dated July 12, 1937, Bette Davis legal file, WBA, USC. For more on Davis's unsuccessful attempt to end her long-term contract with Warner Bros. and her 1936 suit against the studio, see Thomas Schatz, "A Triumph of Bitchery: Warner Bros., Bette Davis, and *Jezebel*," in *The Studio System*, edited by Janet Staiger (New Brunswick, NJ: Rutgers University Press, 1995), 79–82.

31. Schatz, "A Triumph of Bitchery," 75.

32. Schatz, *Genius of the System*, 220. See also Schatz, "A Triumph of Bitchery," 74–92, for further details on Davis's struggles as she evolved from contract studio "player" to contract studio "star." On Cagney's case see Cagney legal file, WBA, USC. I discuss de Havilland's case in Chap. 4.

33. Jane Gaines, *Contested Culture: The Image, the Voice, and the Law* (Chapel Hill: University of North Carolina Press, 1991), 152.

34. Balio, *Grand Design*, 143. See also Jewell, *The Golden Age of Cinema*, 255–257.

35. Richard B. Jewell, "How Howard Hawks Brought *Baby* Up: An *Apologia* for the Studio System," in Staiger (ed.), *The Studio System*, 47.

36. See also the Ruth Chatterton contract dated February 27, 1931, which outlines

her salary terms as follows: "Paid $675,000 per year for a period of two years in which artist will make three pictures a year. Artist paid $35,000 upfront after signing contract, and rest of $640,000 will be paid in eighty weekly installments" (approximately $8,000 a week), Ruth Chatterton legal file, WBA, USC. See also the Kay Francis contract dated October 15, 1931, WBA, USC. Francis and her agent, Selznick, renegotiated her salary twice more with Warner Bros. in 1932 and 1935.

37. Ibid. For more on Chatterton's career in 1930s Hollywood, see Emily Carman, "'Women Rule Hollywood': Ageing and Freelance Stardom in the Studio System," *Celebrity Studies* 3 (March 2012): 13–24.

38. See the Ruth Chatterton contract dated September 9, 1931, Ruth Chatterton legal file, WBA, USC. These salaries were in the minority after 1933, when Hollywood finally felt the economic impact of the Depression.

39. As noted in a studio memo dated January 3, 1935, Francis's new contract prevented Warner Bros. from using her name "in conjunction with any commercial advertising and/or exploitation of photoplays in which you appear for us." See Kay Francis legal file, WBA, USC.

40. See the interoffice memo dated April 26, 1933, from Thomas to Roy Obringer explaining Francis's objection to the use of her image to advertise leather shoes in conjunction with her film *The Keyhole*. Studio lawyer Obringer explains the situation as a "tie-up" ad for the picture and that "such ads" were "permitted" in their contract with the actress. He continues, stating that this "particular ad was placed in *Photoplay* in order to get a cover picture of Miss Francis on this important magazine, and also for other favors which we sought from them." He also underscores how the campaign would help bolster box-office performance. See Kay Francis legal file, WBA, USC.

41. Ibid.

42. See Balio, *Grand Design*, 157.

43. Ibid. Balio explains that when Warner Bros. hired Chatterton and others away from their rival studio, an outraged Paramount sued. However, Warner Bros. appeased the studio by agreeing to loan Francis out when Paramount needed her for the remainder of 1932; for example, Warner Bros. loaned her to Paramount for Lubitsch's *Trouble in Paradise* (1932). See also Warner Bros. studio memo dated June 14, 1932, on this issue, Kay Francis legal file, WBA, USC; and Alva Johnston, "Hollywood's Ten Percenters," *Saturday Evening Post*, August 8, 1942, 10.

44. Clark, *Negotiating Hollywood*, 47.

45. Ibid.

46. For more details on the studio's attempt to use the film industry NRA code to undermine star autonomy, see Clark, *Negotiating Hollywood*, 37–62; and Murray Ross, *Stars and Strikes* (New York: AMS Press, 1941), 149–175. For how the studios tried to use the NRA to curb the activities of agents, see Kemper, *Hidden Talent*, for the most thorough analysis.

47. Kemper's *Hidden Talent* is the leading authority on Hollywood agents in the 1930s. See also Gomery, *Hollywood Studio System*, 205–207. For more on Lastfogel see Frank Rose, *The Agency: William Morris Agency and the Hidden History of Show*

Business (New York: Harper Collins, 1995), and on Wasserman see Dennis McDougal, *The Last Mogul: Lew Wasserman,* MCA, *and the Hidden History of Hollywood* (New York: De Capo Press, 2001).

48. Johnston, "Ten Percenters," 36.

49. Kemper, *Hidden Talent*, 40.

50. Schatz, *Genius*, 177.

51. Selznick also represented directors (George Cukor, Alfred Hitchcock, and William Wellman) and writers (Ben Hecht, Gene Fowler, Dudley Nichols, and Casey Robinson). See Myron Selznick client notebook, HRC, UT-Austin. See also Thompson, *Showman*, 163–164.

52. Kemper, *Hidden Talent*, 41. For example, Kemper cites a memo "Important Points to Watch for in Studio Contracts," in which Selznick advises his staff to safeguard key contract provisions, such as defining employee duties, loan-out clauses, billing, and story approval, among others.

53. Kemper, *Hidden Talent*, 51.

54. Ibid., 74.

55. Ibid.

56. Kemper also notes how former Selznick clients moved to Feldman's agency later in their careers, including Ruth Chatterton, Constance Bennett, Miriam Hopkins, and others. For further details see *Hidden Talent*, 77.

57. To see more of Kemper's analysis on Feldman and his strategy with Dunne's career, see *Hidden Talent*, 88–93.

58. Ibid., 90. Universal's *High, Wide and Handsome* (1937) and Columbia's *The Awful Truth* (1937) were two such projects that Feldman developed for Dunne to showcase her comedic talent.

59. "Comedy Rated High for the Year," *Los Angeles Times*, November 24, 1937, 11.

60. See Balio, *Grand Design*, 157-158, for further elaboration.

61. Norbert Lusk, "Sensational Hit Made by Bette Davis," *New York Times*, July 7, 1934. Interestingly, *Variety* did not extol Davis's acting at all in this film, calling her role "totally unsympathetic" and saying she was perhaps "too honest with her own emotions," for playing the part realistically to a fault. But their downbeat review had more to do with her character's "lack of audience sympathy," which they felt would spell bad box-office returns. *Variety* did acknowledge the "new" Bette Davis of this film who played "the vamp" very well. *Variety*, July 10, 1934.

62. Ibid.

63. For more on Davis's struggles at Warner Bros. in the 1930s, see Schatz, "A Triumph of Bitchery," 74–92.

64. "John Barrymore Superlatively Funny in Film: Twentieth Century also a Triumph for Carole Lombard," *Los Angeles Times*, May 13, 1934, A3.

65. Frank S. Nugent, "The Screen: *My Man Godfrey*," *New York Times*, September 18, 1936.

66. "*My Man Godfrey*," *Variety*, September 23, 1936.

67. Ibid.

68. See contracts dated October 26, 1934, and January 23, 1936, Claudette Colbert contract file, Charles K. Feldman Collection (CKF), Louis B. Mayer Library (LBML), American Film Institute (AFI).

69. See contract dated November 13, 1933, Colbert contract file, CKF, LBML, AFI. See also p. 3 of 1934 renegotiated contract, as well as p. 4 of 1936 contract.

70. Clark, *Negotiating Hollywood*, 41.

71. For more on the genesis of SAG, see Ross, "The Stars Rise," in *Stars and Strikes*, 149–175. Ross's book still represents one of the best sources on SAG and collective bargaining among Hollywood actors in the 1930s.

72. For more on SAG, see Ross, *Stars and Strikes*; as well as Clark, *Negotiating Hollywood*, 37–62.

73. Clark, *Negotiating Hollywood*, 61.

74. Tino Balio, *United Artists*, vol. 1, and *United Artists*, vol. 2, *1951–1978: The Company that Changed the Film Industry* (Madison: University of Wisconsin Press, 2009).

75. Richard Koszarski, *An Evening's Entertainment* (Berkeley: University of California Press, 1990), 261. Other important stars who went into independent production and attained deals to release their films with studio distributors included Harold Lloyd (through Paramount), Colleen Moore (through First National), Buster Keaton, Norma Talmadge (whose producer husband, Joseph Schenck, was a partner and chairman of the board at UA, which released her films as well as Keaton's films), and fellow UA actress-turned-producer Gloria Swanson.

76. Charles Chaplin, *My Autobiography* (New York: Simon and Schuster, 1964), 223. See also Koszarski, *An Evening's Entertainment*, 265–268. Koszarski also cites Benjamin Hampton's *A History of the Movies* (New York: Covici, Friede, 1931)—one of the earliest histories of cinema—in which he devotes an entire chapter to Pickford and how her salary demands "created a precedent that soon altered the entire industry" (146).

77. For specific examples see Matthew Bernstein, "Hollywood's Semi-Independent Production," *Cinema Journal* 32, no. 3 (Spring 1993): 42–43.

78. Many of the Poverty Row studios, like Republic, specialized in low-budget Westerns or serial films such as the *Charlie Chan* series produced by Monogram in the 1940s. Poverty Row independents supplied the major studios with films to meet the demand of double-feature programming as well as of second-run theaters "for 208 films a year (two films for twice-weekly changes)." See Janet Staiger, "The Labor Force, Financing and the Mode of Production," in *The Classical Hollywood Cinema*, 319; and Brian Taves, "The B Film," 313–314, for further elaboration on this type of independent production.

79. Schatz, *Genius*, 176.

80. Bernstein, "Semi-Independent," 41–42.

81. See Balio, *Grand Design*, 105. For more information on UA, see also Balio, *United Artists*, vol. 1.

82. Goldwyn and Korda also sat on UA's board of directors, and in 1935 Selznick took over Joe Schenck's job as UA's chief executive, coordinating the production efforts

and schedules of the various producers working at the studio. After leaving his production chief position at Warner Bros. in 1933, Zanuck ran Twentieth Century Pictures and released films through UA before merging with Fox Film Corp. in 1935 with Schenck.

83. Bernstein, "Semi-Independent," 48.

84. Schatz, *Genius*, 177.

85. "News of the Screen," *New York Times*, January 25, 1937, 22.

86. "Poignant Stories Told on Screens," *Los Angeles Times*, August 20, 1937, 15.

87. "*Stella Dallas*," *Variety*, July 28, 1937.

88. "Ace Screenwriter Put to Work on Subject for Barbara Stanwyck," *Los Angeles Times*, April 19, 1937, 11.

89. Giuliana Muscio, *Hollywood's New Deal (Culture and Moving Image)* (Philadelphia: Temple University Press, 1997), 129.

CHAPTER TWO

1. David O. Selznick to Dan O'Shea, memo dated July 12, 1937, David O. Selznick Collection (DOSC), HRC, UT-Austin.

2. Jewell, "How Howard Hawks Brought Baby Up," 47. Jewell brings attention to this disparity in film history by focusing on the director Howard Hawks. I seek to expand his astute point by paying attention to stardom in this era.

3. Greta Garbo also fits within the list of semi-independent stars working solely at one studio; however, she is not a serious case study in this project because the MGM legal files were not available for research at the time of writing. Some of her contract negotiations are documented in Schatz's *Genius of the System*, 42–44. Loretta Young and Jean Arthur also went on to freelance by 1940, but not in the 1930s, and much of their freelance agreements are not readily available for scholarly research (Twentieth Century-Fox, Columbia, Paramount).

4. Their agreements, referred to as "minimum contracts," were known as "freelance minimum contracts" in industry parlance of the time. It designated only the minimal terms of employment (usually salary, number of weeks for employment, etc.) and no creative incentives or controls.

5. Stanwyck completed three pictures for Columbia by July of 1931: *Ladies of Leisure* and *The Miracle Woman*, directed by Capra, and *Ten Cents a Dance*. directed by Lionel Barrymore. She told Columbia she would film *Forbidden* (1932) if she received a $50,000 salary. Stanwyck received $25,000 and then $35,000 for her first two films for Columbia. See Al Diorio, *Barbara Stanwyck* (New York: Coward Mc Cann, 1984), 74; *Los Angeles Times*, September 11, 1931, found in the Stanwyck clippings file at the Herrick Library.

6. Ibid. See also September 4, 1931, letter from Columbia to Warner Bros., and Stanwyck legal files at WBA, USC.

7. *Los Angeles Times*, July 23, 1931.

8. See "Stanwyck-Col.-Peace," *Hollywood Reporter*, September 14, 1931, 1–2.

9. See contract dated September 29, 1930. Barbara Stanwyck legal file, WBA, USC.

10. See contract dated September 21, 1935, with RKO, and RKO-Barbara Stanwyck Twentieth Century-Fox legal agreement dated October 18, 1935. Barbara Stanwyck legal file, Twentieth Century-Fox (TCF), UCLA Performing Arts Special Collections (UCLA PASC).

11. See TCF memo from E. C. de Lavigne to Lew Schreiber, dated May 5, 1937. Stanwyck legal file, TCF, UCLA PASC.

12. Memo from E. C. de Lavigne at TCF to Lew Schreiber dated May 5, 1937. Formerly housed at UCLA PASC.

13. DiOrio, *Barbara Stanwyck*, 138.

14. See contract dated October 26, 1944. Barbara Stanwyck legal file, WBA, USC.

15. See Constance Bennett RKO payroll card, Box 96, UCLA PASC, April 9–May 14, 1932. On Pathé's sale to RKO, see Douglas Gomery, *Hollywood Studio System*, 8–9.

16. See Brian Kellow, *The Bennetts: An Acting Family* (Lexington: University of Kentucky Press, 2004), 147–148. See also Warner Bros. contract dated February 12, 1931, which highlights how Bennett fulfilled her commitment during her vacation time away from RKO. *Variety* reported that Bennett's vacation time was actually twelve weeks: "The overlap of the Constance Bennett Contract with Pathe, that occurs yearly during Miss Bennett's current three year term with Pathe is 12 weeks annually, not 10 as previously reported." "WB Star-Name Program," *Variety*, January 28, 1931, 34.

17. Warner Bros. contract dated February 12, 1931. Bennett legal file, WBA, USC.

18. "Litigation Due Over Bennett WB Contract," *Variety*, January 28, 1931. *Variety* went on to explain that RKO interpreted Bennett's five-year contract as an "exclusive" agreement. See also "Radio to Court in Bennett Case," *Hollywood Reporter*, February 4, 1931.

19. For example, see "WB Star-Name Program," *Variety*, January 28, 1931, 34, which even implies that Bennett's salary caused Paramount to back away from making a bid to purchase Pathé. See also "Harding and Bennett Contracts Indefinite," *Variety*, February 11, 1931, 2.

20. Bennett's RKO contract dated February 12, 1931, reveals the modifications made to her long-term contract in order to comply with her recent agreement with Warner Bros. Constance Bennett legal file, WBA, USC.

21. Later that year, in May, Bennett renegotiated her contract with RKO, increasing her salary from $2,750 to $5,000 a week, which would then rise in small increments to a cap of $7,000 a week until the completion of her contract in 1934. See contract dated January 6, 1931, Bennett legal file, WBA, USC.

22. "The Screen," *New York Times*, August 20, 1937.

23. Twentieth Century Pictures released *The Affairs of Cellini* through UA.

24. See contract dated June 30, 1933, with Twentieth Century Pictures. Constance Bennett legal file, TCF, UCLA PASC.

25. Ibid.

26. Gomery, *Hollywood Studio System*, 205. See also Kemper, *Hidden Talent*, 148–150.

27. Schatz, *Genius of the System*, 299. When the United States entered World War II in 1941, the tax burden on high-salaried individuals continued to increase, culminating with the US Revenue Act of 1941, which not only raised income taxes across the board but also lowered the top tax bracket to $200,000, meaning that individuals earning $200,000 would be taxed at a rate of 90 percent (resulting in a take-home pay of $20,000).

28. Kemper, *Hidden Talent*, 148.

29. By contrast, rival major studio MGM never lost money during the Depression because it maintained a smaller theater chain, and, consequently, the studio preferred to maintain a strong stable of stars under long-term contracts, as evidenced by their marketing slogan that promoted MGM as having "more stars than there are in heaven." It is not coincidental that they did not negotiate many freelance deals with talent.

30. See contract with RKO dated April 10, 1930. Irene Dunne Collection, USC Cinema-Television Library (USC CTL).

31. Ibid.

32. See contract with RKO dated September 1933. Irene Dunne Collection, USC CTL. The term "negative cost" is defined by RKO as "the total cost of producing" a film; see p. 3 of aforementioned contract for an extended definition. For more on her relationship with Feldman and his negotiations on the actress's behalf, see Kemper, *Hidden Talent*, 88–92.

33. See contract with RKO dated September 1933. Irene Dunne Collection, USC CTL, 1–2.

34. The last percentage earnings statement in Dunne's RKO files is from 1948, which states that her total cut of the profits was $161,969.09.

35. In contrast, Dunne's costars Astaire and Rogers had signed option contracts with RKO that did not have this financial incentive. Rogers signed a seven-year, long-term option contract with RKO in 1933; her weekly salary in 1934 was $1,100. See Ginger Rogers RKO payroll card dated May 24, 1934, Box 111, UCLA PASC. Astaire signed with RKO in 1933 at $1,500 per week, for two pictures a year in a four-year option contract. However, he jumped on the percentage bandwagon in 1936, renegotiating his contract to $3,000 a week and a 5 percent share of a film's gross after it earned $1.2 million, increasing to 10 percent should the film gross over $2 million. For details on Astaire's deals, see Kemper, *Hidden Talent*, 151. After Rogers's long-term contract expired in 1941, she attained a salary and percentage deal at RKO akin to Dunne's for *Tender Comrade*: $150,000 salary plus 10 percent of the gross earnings.

36. See contract dated December 3, 1939, with RKO, and October 28, 1937, three-picture agreement with Universal. Irene Dunne Collection, USC CTL.

37. RKO computed the negative cost of the productions as $800,000. See Irene Dunne RKO payroll cards, UCLA PASC.

38. The RKO revenue, profit, and loss figures were provided by Richard B. Jewell. The RKO legal files are housed by Turner in Atlanta and were not open to researchers as of 2015. See my article "Women Rule Hollywood," *Celebrity Studies* 3, no. 1 (2012): 13–24, for more on costar Cary Grant's percentage terms compared to Dunne's in *My*

Favorite Wife, which was not as lucrative. Grant earned $50,000 in salary plus $51,425 from a 2.5 percentage deal of the distribution gross.

39. Stahl eventually directed Dunne in *When Tomorrow Comes* (1939). See contract dated December 3, 1939, with RKO, and the October 28, 1937, three-picture agreement with Universal, Irene Dunne Collection, USC CTL.

40. Kemper, *Hidden Talent*, 91.

41. See letter to Columbia Pictures from Charles Feldman, dated January 20, 1943, Irene Dunne Collection, USC CTL.

42. Ibid.

43. Contrary to popular legend, Bow was not fired or dismissed in disgrace from the studio. See "CLARA BOW OUT AT PARAMOUNT: Film Contract Terminated by Mutual Consent," *Los Angeles Times*, June 9, 1931.

44. David Stenn's excellent biography of Bow vividly details her career in the early 1930s and unveils her comeback in 1933. See *Clara Bow: Runnin' Wild* (New York: Cooper Square Press, 2000).

45. Warner Bros. courted Bow for a long-term contract, as did Howard Hughes for a three-picture deal. UA, Universal, and MGM all offered her one-picture deals (all of which she declined due to what she perceived to be exploitative story material), while David O. Selznick, then head of production at RKO, offered her the lead in his exposé *What Price Hollywood?* (a role eventually given in 1932 to rising freelancer Constance Bennett).

46. See Stenn, *Runnin' Wild*, 239–241.

47. See contract dated October 1931 between Sam Rork and Bow, Jack Oakie Collection, USC CTL.

48. See memo between Columbia and Rork dated December 3, 1931, and memo dated January 16, 1931, from Columbia to N. Burden revealing that Bow appeared to be negotiating elsewhere. Jack Oakie Collection, USC CTL.

49. See contract dated April 16, 1932, and Fox memo dated October 23, 1935, Clara Bow TCF legal file, UCLA PASC.

50. Stenn, *Runnin' Wild*, 242.

51. Bow was diagnosed with schizophrenia in the 1940s and was unable to work. See Stenn, *Runnin' Wild*, for further details on Bow's life after Hollywood.

52. It appears that Bow authorized Rork to arrange deals on her behalf at Columbia and, later, Fox, and that she did not have an agent, which no doubt contributed to the sketchy percentage terms. A skilled agent would not have let this deal go forward without specific details on her $25,000 bonus.

53. Hopkins was released along with Charles Laughton and Fredric March in 1933. After a record loss of $21,000,000 caused Paramount to file for bankruptcy in 1932, the studio complied with their request and relinquished all three expensive stars to cut costs. For further elaboration on the Paramount stars' exit, see Swindell, *Screwball*, 134. On Paramount's dire financial situation in the early 1930s, see Balio, *Grand Design*, 16.

54. See contract dated September 25, 1934, with Pioneer Pictures, Miriam Hop-

kins legal file, Jock Whitney Collection (JWC), HRC, UT-Austin. Hopkins had previously worked with Mamoulian in *Dr. Jekyll and Mr. Hyde* in 1931.

55. "Actress at her own expense, may have any firm certified public accountants of standing equal to that of Price, Waterhouse & Co., examine the books and records of RKO insofar as they relate to said photoplay, not more than twice yearly, until expiration of 1 year after Pioneer's final remittance." See contract dated September 25, 1934, with Pioneer Pictures, Miriam Hopkins legal file, JWC, HRC, UT-Austin.

56. Excerpt of memo from Lowell Calvert to Kenneth MacGowen dated December 26, 1934, Miriam Hopkins legal file, JWC, HRC, UT-Austin.

57. See contract dated February 12, 1936, and Pioneer earnings summary ending May 28, 1938, Miriam Hopkins legal file, JWC, HRC, UT-Austin. Hopkins earned $31,645.83 for *The Story of Temple Drake* in 1933; see Paramount production files, Margaret Herrick Library. Pioneer's 1938 percentage earnings revealed that Hopkins's 10 percent cut amounted to $27,744.83 (nearly equaling her Paramount salary per picture when she was under long-term contract in the early 1930s), even though by this time she was no longer participating in the film's gross earnings.

58. Even though Hopkins was a lead female star under contract to Goldwyn, as an independent producer he distributed his films through United Artists, which did not have access to as large an exhibition market as the five major studios (MGM, Warner Bros., RKO, Paramount, and Fox). Consequently, she received less screen exposure.

59. *The Woman I Love* cost $725,000 but only grossed $553,000 domestically and $230,000 foreign, for a total loss of $114,000. While *Wise Girl* cost $448,000 to make, it only grossed $328,000 domestically and $162,000 foreign, bringing its loss to $144,000. Figures taken from C. J. Trevlin ledger from RKO, now unavailable for research; access generously provided to me by Richard Jewell and Cathy Jurca.

60. "Money Making Stars of 1937," *Motion Picture Herald*, December 18, 1937, 14–15. Exhibitors polled about two hundred Hollywood players and their films' performance in their theaters. "The ranking is based upon the number of points each player received, a mention for the first place receiving ten points, for the second place nine points, and so on down to one point for a tenth place on the ballot. The percentages are drawn from total points" (15).

61. Warner Bros. memo, Roy Obringer to Jack Warner, October 3, 1939, Miriam Hopkins legal file, WBA, USC. Obringer noted the unorthodox nature of this contract in this memo: "Hopkins' contract is not the ordinary contract because for a reduced compensation she obtained the right to do two outstanding pictures."

62. Ibid.

63. Ibid.

64. See Miriam Hopkins legal file, WBA, USC, for further detail on these situations.

65. See Mary Desjardins, "Not of Hollywood: Ruth Chatterton, Ann Harding, Constance Bennett, Kay Francis, and Nancy Carroll," in *Glamour in a Golden Age: Movie Stars of the 1930s*, edited by Adrienne L. McLean (Piscataway, NJ: Rutgers University Press, 2011), 22.

66. For a time after the merger, the studio released films as RKO Pathé.

67. See "All after Ann Harding Who May Have Contract Readjusted by Pathé," *Variety*, February 4, 1931, 3.

68. See "Ann Harding Rejects $840,000 Her Share New 3-Yr. Pathé Deal," *Variety*, March 25, 1931, 3.

69. See Ann Harding RKO payroll card dated June 13, 1934, UCLA PASC. See also RKO earnings ledger, figures taken from C. J. Trevlin ledger from RKO, now unavailable for research. Figures generously provided by Catherine Jurca.

70. For more on Hayward's hand in negotiating Hepburn's RKO deals, see Kemper, *Hidden Talent*, 150. It does not appear that Hepburn had story approval, although I cannot verify this because I did not have access to Hepburn's RKO contracts or legal files, only her payroll cards, which are available at UCLA.

71. See Myron Selznick client notebook, HRC, UT-Austin, and Katharine Hepburn RKO payroll card, UCLA PASC.

72. The second film, *The Little Minister*, cost a hefty $650,000, and RKO lost $9,000 at the box office. See RKO profit ledger figures taken from C. J. Trevlin ledger, generously provided by Catherine Jurca.

73. Additionally, Hepburn hoped to earn the following percentages on each film's box-office profits: 5 percent of $600,000–$750,000 earnings in film distribution gross; 7.5 percent of $750,000–$1,000,000 in profits; and 11 percent of any distribution profits grossing over $1,000,000. See Myron Selznick client notebook, HRC, UT-Austin; and Katharine Hepburn RKO payroll card, UCLA PASC.

74. Jewell, "How Howard Hawks Brought *Baby* Up," 42–43. For example, *Sylvia Scarlet* was a $363,000 loss; the biopic *Mary of Scotland*, directed by John Ford, lost $165,000; and so did the historical drama *A Woman Rebels* ($222,000 lost). Figures from Myron Selznick client notebook, HRC, UT-Austin; and RKO profit figures taken from C. J. Trevlin ledger.

75. Jewell, "Howard Hawks," 43.

76. Ibid.

77. The poor box-office performances of these films were not all due to Hepburn. RKO spent a considerable amount on its A-film budgets, which impeded their ability to generate a substantial profit. For example, *Stage Door* did earn a modest profit of $81,000 but failed to justify its high production cost of $952,000. Similarly, *Bringing Up Baby*'s $1 million–plus budget severely limited its box-office earning potential. As RKO production chief Samuel Briskin surmised at the time, Hepburn films costing more than $700,000 could not make a profit. See Jewell, "How Howard Hawks Brought *Baby* Up," 46.

78. By the 1930s exhibitors were also noting these disappointing box-office returns. Consequently, Hepburn was relegated in 1937 to the third-tier ranking by the *Motion Picture Herald* exhibitor poll and branded "box-office poison" by film exhibitors in 1938 due to her films' poor box-office results.

79. See Kemper, *Hidden Talent*, 150.

80. See contract dated December 21, 1932, Claudette Colbert contracts, Charles

Feldman Papers (CFP), American Film Institute (AFI), Los Angeles. The Feldman files do not precisely define what Paramount understood to be "excess gross receipts." Based on my research of other percentage earnings, it's likely Colbert would have started to participate in her films' distribution earnings once they exceeded the negative cost of the picture.

81. In fact, Colbert's salary for the film ($50,000) was one-sixth of the film's total budget.

82. The salary was distributed in weekly installments of $6,000 over two years. See Paramount contracts dated November 13, 1933, and October 26, 1934, Claudette Colbert, contracts, CFP, AFI. For more on the tact and negotiating style of Feldman and his influence on Colbert's career, see Kemper, *Hidden Talent*, 83–86.

83. Kemper, *Hidden Talent*, 84.

84. Ibid.

85. This would increase by 3 percent intervals on each additional $100,000 that the film earned in exhibition, culminating at 20 percent of the film's gross profits over $400,000. See Claudette Colbert contract dated June 10, 1936, CFP, AFI, Los Angeles.

86. Kemper, *Hidden Talent*, 87. Her salary totaled $426,944 in 1939.

87. Academy nomination procedures were not standardized until 1936; until then, actors could be nominated for multiple performances in a year (as was the case with Gaynor). See Emmanuel Levy, *The Politics and History of the Academy Awards* (New York: Continuum, 2001), 30–31.

88. See long-term contract signed September 18, 1926, Janet Gaynor legal file, TCF, formerly housed at UCLA PASC.

89. The Gaynor-Farrell musicals include *Sunny Side Up* (1929), *Delicious* (1931), *Tess of the Storm Country* (1932), and *Change of Heart* (1934). Her top box-office grossing films were *Sunny Side Up: The First Year* (1932), *State Fair, Carolina* (1934), and *Small Town Girl* (1935). Gaynor and Will Rogers were scheduled to work together again in *The Farmer Takes a Wife* and *One More Spring* (both released in 1935, the former being Henry Fonda's screen debut). Information on Rogers from AFI Catalog note entries for *Farmer Takes a Wife* and *One More Spring*.

90. As Douglas Gomery notes, Fox's downfall can be attributed to the overexpansion of his company (he tried to acquire Loews/MGM in 1929), the 1929 stock market crash, and a US government antitrust suit instigated by his creditors. This, coupled with his injuries from a near-fatal car crash on Long Island in July 1929, led to his ouster from the Fox Film Corporation board on April 8, 1930. See Gomery, *Hollywood Studio System*, 43–45.

91. Box office information noted in "Gaynor-Zanuck War," *Variety*, September 28, 1936, 1, 7. *Small Town Girl*, released by MGM, was the sole loan-out in Gaynor's ten-year tenure at Fox.

92. See contract dated August 1, 1933, for special provisions, and Fox memo dated February 6, 1934, on her salary specifics. Janet Gaynor legal file, TCF, formerly housed at UCLA PASC.

93. Ibid. The contract also specified that should Sheenan not be available, Gaynor would nominate a replacement.

94. Gaynor, Fox, and MGM reached an agreement to loan out her services for *Small Town Girl* in 1935. She retained all of her aforementioned contractual rights at MGM (including a written agreement that MGM producer Hunt Stromberg would supervise the film). See memo dated November 5, 1935, Janet Gaynor legal file, TCF, formerly housed at UCLA PASC.

95. See memo from George Wasson to Mr. JJ Gain, dated April 15, 1935. Janet Gaynor legal file, TCF, formerly housed at UCLA PASC; and "Fox Skeds [*sic*] Co-Star Policy for Gaynor," *Variety*, September 26, 1936, 1, 4.

96. "Fox Skeds [*sic*] Co-Star Policy for Gaynor," *Variety*, September 26, 1936, 1.

97. "Gaynor-Zanuck War: Player Calls Studio Pact Tactics False," *Variety*, September 28, 1936, 1, 7.

98. Ibid. See also "Janet Gaynor Seen as Through [*sic*] at 20th-Fox," *Variety*, September 29, 1936, 4.

99. "Gaynor Team with March for Selznick," *Hollywood Reporter*, October 3, 1936, 1; "Janet Gaynor will play in Selznick's Hollywood color picture, 'A Star Is Born' as her first freelance picture. . . . Miss Gaynor just terminated a career-long connection with the Fox Company."

100. See contract dated October 9, 1936, Janet Gaynor legal file, DOSC, HRC, UT-Austin.

101. See memo dated May 18, 1937, from O'Shea to David O. Selznick, Janet Gaynor legal file, DOSC, HRC, UT-Austin. SIP used the term "net profits" to denote that Gaynor would receive her cut of the distribution profits after the initial cost of the film had been recouped. I am unable to determine what SIP designated as the net cost of *A Star Is Born*; Gaynor's contract denotes that they would be determined by "a recognized auditing firm in accordance with the standard principles of motion picture accounting." It appears that Gaynor earned $6,156.25 from her percentage deal. See October 27, 1937, renegotiated contract as well as June 3, 1939, letter from SIP to Lloyd Wright. Janet Gaynor legal file, DOSC, HRC, UT-Austin.

102. *Variety*, April 28, 1937.

103. "Carole Lombard Asks Para [*sic*] Freedom or Boost," *Hollywood Reporter*, July 31, 1936, 1.

104. Adjusted for inflation, Lombard's top salary is equivalent to $7,597,743.

105. Lombard was paid $150,000 for nine consecutive weeks, at $16,666.67 a week. See contract dated November 1938 and studio memo dated August 30, 1937, and a letter to Warner Bros. from Myron Selznick dated August 18, 1937. See Carole Lombard legal file, WBA, USC. Lombard preferred working with Tetzloff because of his careful lighting to mask her facial scar from a 1925 car accident.

106. *Nothing Sacred* production file, DOSC, HRC, UT-Austin, p. 3: "Producer agrees to pay Artist, for Artist's services . . . salary at the rate of $18,750 a week" of eight weeks' salary, "or $150,000 by the end of the said term." See also "Selznick Terms Lombard on One-Pic-A-Year Deal," *Hollywood Reporter*, June 19, 1937, 1. Leo Rosten also

notes in 1941 that Lombard was among Hollywood's highest paid, with her salary of $150,000 per picture. See Rosten, *Hollywood: The Movie Colony, the Movie Makers* (New York: Harcourt, Brace, and Company, 1941), 341.

107. Memo dated December 1, 1936. Carole Lombard legal file, DOSC, HRC, UT-Austin.

108. See contract dated May 29, 1937, with SIP. Carole Lombard legal file, DOSC, HRC, UT-Austin.

109. "Lombard, Powell Set for Selznick Film," *Variety*, August 6, 1938, 6. There is also a press release from the Russell Birdwell file announcing this plan; see Box 6, Folder 1, JWC, HRC, UT-Austin.

110. From an interview with Gladys Hall, August 19, 1938. Gladys Hall Collection, Margaret Herrick Library, Beverly Hills. Portions of this article were published in "Lombard as She Sees Herself," *Motion Picture* (November 1938). Her comments on independent production, however, were not published.

111. Memo dated August 18, 1938, Carole Lombard legal file, DOSC, HRC, UT-Austin. Here Selznick proposes a sequel to *My Man Godfrey* or another screwball comedy, *American Sleeping Beauty*, as possible projects for this deal, which ultimately never came to fruition.

112. Various independent producers—including Sam Goldwyn, Walter Wanger, and SIP—expressed interest in the Lubitsch Company venture. Tom Kemper postulates in *Hidden Talent* that the trade publications' announcements were a preemptive publicity stunt on Myron's part, and that financing fell through due to the agent's erratic personality and alcoholism. David O. Selznick's biographer, David Thomson, claims that Myron's production venture failed due to his inability to secure guaranteed distribution. See Thomson, *Showman: The Life of David O. Selznick* (New York: Alfred A. Knopf, 1992), 274–275. The Lubitsch Company's proposed first project was to be *The Shop Around the Corner*, which Lubitsch eventually took to MGM.

113. Box-office figures provided by the William Schaefer ledger, WBA, USC.

114. Lombard also retained advertising rights that prevented SIP from using her likeness in commercial tie-ins with films. See memo dated October 21, 1937, from David O. Selznick to Dan O'Shea, Carole Lombard legal files, DOSC, HRC, UT-Austin. She remains the sole freelance star in this study to have hired her own publicist.

115. Production cost is referred to as "negative cost" in the contract; this provision means that before Lombard could collect her earnings, the film had to gross 1.7 times the cost of the film's production. This contract also had several provisions discussed in the introduction: story approval and costar status only if she agreed that the actor was of equal professional standing. See RKO deal dated April 10, 1939.

116. See Carole Lombard percentage reports, Myron Selznick Collection (MSC), Agency Files L-LON, HRC, UT-Austin.

117. Lombard received a $25,000 advance *against* her projected $150,000 interest and percentage share. See amendment to agreement noted on April 1, 1940, in Selznick ledger, Carole Lombard file, client notebook, MSC, Box 1, HRC, UT-Austin.

118. Carole Lombard file, client notebook, MSC, Box 1, HRC, UT-Austin.

119. See RKO profit ledger figures taken from C. J. Trevlin ledger and Carole Lombard file, client notebook, MSC, Box 1, HRC, UT-Austin.

120. See MRS Collection, Agency Files L-LON, HRC, UT-Austin. While *They Knew What They Wanted* brought in $932,000, its high production budget (the "negative cost") was $781,000, which equated to a $291,000 loss. This mirrors the budget problems of Katharine Hepburn's RKO films in the mid-1930s.

121. Kemper, *Hidden Talent*, 157.

122. Memo from David O. Selznick to Ginsberg dated April 30, 1938, DOSC, HRC, UT-Austin.

123. The memo goes on to note that RKO producer Pandro Berman seconded this observation on the gross potential for Lombard's films. Ibid.

124. See Jock Whitney Collection, DOSC, Box 45, Folder 1; and January 22, 1940, memo from David O. Selznick to Lombard, which released her from any contractual obligations. Carole Lombard legal file, HRC, UT-Austin. The memo is also published in *Memos from David O. Selznick*, edited and selected by Rudy Behlmer (New York: New York Modern Library, 2000), 270–272. Although *Nothing Sacred* opened to critical praise, the film's million-dollar budget, expensive freelance talent, and Technicolor costs hindered its ability to turn a profit. For reviews of the film, see *New York Times*, November 26, 1937, 27; and *Variety*, December 1, 1937, 14. For box office returns, see Earnings Report, November 1940, Folder 10, Box 628, DOSC, HRC.

125. Other clients who left Selznick before his death in 1944 included George Cukor, Errol Flynn, Gregory La Cava, and Joan Bennett, among others. For more on this and the end of Selznick's agency see Kemper, *Hidden Talent*, 189–198.

126. Arbitrators for *Myron Selznick and Company v. Carole Lombard* were William T. Coffin, Odele S. McConnell, and William C. Mathe, decision filed February 1941. Found in "Carole Lombard Correspondence" folder, Box 628, DOSC, HRC, UT-Austin.

127. Ibid. She was required to pay Selznick 10 percent of her income (up to $270,000) over the next five years from her RKO deal. After the suit, Nat Wolff became her agent and negotiated her last two freelance contracts.

128. After scouring the available studio archives for any contracts and/or legal material on Wong and Vélez, I have only been able to locate the RKO payroll cards for Vélez and a 1938 Warner Bros. contract for Wong. The disparity of legal material on these women's careers can partially be attributed to the lack of studio legal material available in libraries and archives. The MGM and RKO legal files at the Turner Corporation in Atlanta are not open to researchers, while the Paramount legal files appear to be missing as a result of the Gulf and Western corporate takeover in the 1960s. (They are not at the Margaret Herrick Library with the rest of the studio production files.)

129. While there has been much recent scholarship on the racially stereotyped Hollywood personae of Wong and Vélez (in other words, their onscreen images), very little has been written about their off-screen contractual labor in the studio system. Some of the work on racial stereotyping of these actresses includes Yiman Wang, "The Art of Screen Passing: Anna May Wong's Yellow Yellowface Performance in the Art

Deco Cinema," *Camera Obscura* 20, no. 3 (2005): 159–190; Ana M. López, "Are All Latins from Manhattan? Hollywood, Ethnography, and Cultural Colonialism," in *Unspeakable Images: Ethnicity and the American Cinema*, edited by Lester D. Friedman (Urbana: University of Illinois Press, 1991), 404–424; Charles Ramirez Berg, *Latino Images in Film: Stereotypes, Subversion, Resistance* (Austin: University of Texas Press, 2002); and Diane Negra, *Off-White Hollywood: American Culture and Ethnic Female Stardom* (Routledge: New York, 2001). Note that Negra's discussion is limited to mostly European women.

130. Description of the SAG basic "minimum contract" as described by the firm Freston and Files to Roy Obringer, Warner Bros.' studio lawyer, in which the law firm outlined the terms of Anna May Wong's freelance deal to make *When You Were Born*, January 21, 1938. See Anna May Wong legal file, WBA, USC. The basic minimum contract became official in 1937 when SAG was recognized by the studios; the contract also reduced the work week for actors from fifty-two to forty-eight hours. See Ross, *Stars and Strikes*, 172.

131. See Richard Caves, *Creative Industries: Contracts between Art and Commerce* (Cambridge, MA: Harvard University Press, 2000), 5, 12.

132. Ibid., 8.

133. Yiman Wang, "The Art of Screen Passing," 162.

134. Victoria Sturtevant, "Spitfire: Lupe Vélez and the Ambivalent Pleasures of Ethnic Masquerade," *Velvet Light Trap* 55 (Spring 2005): 21.

135. Vélez's agent is noted in her Fox Studio legal files in a memo dated March 26, 1932, found in the Twentieth Century-Fox legal files (TCF), formerly housed at UCLA PASC. Wong's legal file identifying her agency (Conlon-Armstrong) is found at WBA, USC.

136. This regulation mirrored dominant ideological beliefs of US culture at the time, especially in the segregated American South and major American cities with ethnically marked neighborhoods. To see the code in its entirety, see Thomas Doherty, *Pre-Code Hollywood: Sex, Immorality, and Insurrection in American Cinema* (New York: Columbia University Press, 1999), 361–364.

137. The film industry first formed its own self-censorship committee, the Motion Picture Producers and Directors Association (MPPDA), to thwart a national, government-controlled censorship institution in 1922. Former postmaster general Will Hays headed the organization, and beginning in 1924, the office began publishing moral guidelines for producers to follow, though they were not strictly adhered to until 1934, after Breen was hired to head the PCA.

138. Doherty, *Pre-Code Hollywood*, 339. In contrast, Lary May makes a compelling argument for a socially progressive brand of Americanism promoted by Hollywood in the 1930s that advocated for a redistribution of wealth, grass-roots activism, and interracial, cross-class coupling. May sees post–World War II society as the shift to a more monolithic, corporate American culture that idolized domesticity and whiteness as opposed to multiculturalism and social progressiveness. See *The Big Tomorrow: Hollywood and the American Way* (Chicago: University of Chicago Press, 2000).

139. Ruth Vasey, *The World According to Hollywood, 1918–1939* (Madison: University of Wisconsin Press, 1997), 219.

140. Engagement agreements were an early form of SAG's basic minimum contract agreement, which did not become standard in Hollywood until producers agreed to negotiate with SAG in 1937.

141. See contract dated February 5, 1927. Anna May Wong legal files, WBA, USC. Later that year she signed a separate Warner Bros. engagement agreement for $300 for seven days to play the supporting character Cherry Blossom in *The Crimson City* (1928).

142. "Anna May Wong Signed for Paramount Films," *Hollywood Reporter*, March 27, 1931, 1. The *Reporter* said that Wong's salary was rumored to be $1,500 a week.

143. MGM considered casting Wong in a sympathetic lead role—the dutiful Chinese-American woman in *The Son-Daughter* (1932)—but she lost it to Helen Hayes, a white actress. Lupe Vélez was also reportedly under consideration according to reports from *Film Daily* and the *Hollywood Reporter* detailed in the AFI Catalog entry for *The Son-Daughter.* A similar scenario occurred when Wong actively campaigned for the lead role of O-lan in MGM's adaptation of Pearl S. Buck's novel *The Good Earth.* She was instead offered the supporting role of the seductive concubine.

144. On this, see Tim Bergfelder, "Negotiating Exoticism: Hollywood, Film Europe, and the Cultural Reception of Anna May Wong," in *Film Europe and Film America: Cinema, Commerce and Cultural Exchange 1920–1939*, edited by Andrew Higson and Richard Maltby (London: University of Exeter Press, 1999), 314–315.

145. See contract dated January 17, 1938. Anna May Wong legal file, WBA, USC.

146. Ibid.

147. This conclusion is also sustained by the excellent 2013 documentary on Wong titled *Anna May Wong: In Her Own Words*, directed by Yunah Hong.

148. Headlines include "Para Skeds Dates for Anna Wong Pix," *Hollywood Reporter*, March 5, 1937, 4; "Anna May Wong's New Term at Paramount," *Variety*, April 3, 1937, 1; "Hayakawa Sought to Pair with Wong," *Hollywood Reporter*, September 1, 1937, 2; "Wong Stars in 'Orient,' Reis and Yost Script," *Hollywood Reporter*, October 6, 1938, 1; among others.

149. On B-movie qualities in the studio era, see Brian Taves, "The B Film: Hollywood's Other Half," in *Grand Design*, edited by Tino Balio (Berkeley: University of California Press, 1995), 314.

150. See Lupe Vélez, payroll cards, RKO Collection, UCLA PASC. She was employed for three weeks on the RKO production *Phantom Fame* beginning September 7, 1932, and between October 11 and November 18, 1932, for the RKO film *The Half Naked Truth.*

151. See Lupe Vélez payroll cards, UCLA PASC.

152. Ibid.

153. Sturtevant, "Spitfire," 21; and see also Charles Ramírez Berg, *Latino Images in Film: Stereotypes, Subversion, Resistance* (Austin: University of Texas Press, 2002),

90–97. Berg makes a persuasive case for Vélez's slapstick female comedic talents and the subversive nature of her performance in the *Spitfire* series, which he argues counters negative stereotypes of Latinos. This analysis is limited solely to the film text and does not take into account her contractual agency to make these films.

154. Profit figures taken from RKO profit ledger figures from C. J. Trevlin ledger. *The Mexican Spitfire* series budget ranged from $100,000 to $142,000.

155. Joanne Hershfeld, *The Invention of Dolores del Río* (Minneapolis: University of Minnesota Press, 2000), 13–15. Indeed, del Río did hail from an aristocratic family in Durango, Mexico, that traced their ancestry to Spain.

156. Sturtevant, "Spitfire," 22.

157. See payroll cards ranging from September 28, 1931, to October 25, 1933. Dolores del Río payroll cards, UCLA PASC.

158. See March 3, 1934, memo to Obringer from studio producer Hal Wallis, which underlines the details of del Río's contract. Dolores del Río legal files, WBA, USC.

159. See March 3, 1934, memo from studio producer Hal Wallis to Roy Obringer. Dolores del Río legal file, Warner Bros. Archive, USC. Her contract also gave her the "right to do one outside picture." See also Dolores del Río contract dated March 27, 1934, WBA, USC. *Bird of Paradise* was a concern for the Studio Relations Committee for some of its seductive scenes and its interracial love story, though it ultimately adheres to the Code when del Río's character "sacrifices" herself to the gods and dies by the film's end, believing that she caused her white lover's fever.

160. According to the studio's profit earnings provided by the William Schaefer ledger at WBA, USC, all of del Río's films at Warner Bros. made money. Hershfeld implies that the studio and actress could not come to an agreement. See Hershfeld, *Dolores del Río*, 49.

161. Ibid., 50.

162. Hayworth, who was born in the United States, underwent painful electrolysis to raise her hairline, lost weight, and dyed her dark hair red. "Hayworth" was, in fact, her mother's maiden name. To see Hayworth's physical transformation and an ideological analysis of it, see Lary May, *The Big Tomorrow*, 165–166.

163. Adrienne L. McLean, *Being Rita Hayworth: Labor, Identity, and Hollywood Stardom* (New Brunswick, NJ: Rutgers University Press, 2004), 31.

164. Ibid., 12–13. One of the few female producers in the studio era, Van Upp was made an executive producer by Harry Cohn in 1945. Additionally, Hayworth's 1946 contract with Columbia, negotiated by her William Morris agent Johnny Hyde, stipulated that she would receive 25 percent of the film's gross after the distribution and negative expenses. See McLean, *Being Rita Hayworth*, 221; see also McDougal, *The Last Mogul: Lew Wasserman, MCA, and the Hidden History of Hollywood* (New York: De Capo Press, 2001), 153–157; and Schatz, *Genius of the System*, 470–473, for further elaboration.

165. See December 13, 1940, SIP memo to Roy Obringer. DOSC, HRC, UT-Austin. For more on McDaniel's off-screen persona and career, see Vitoria Sturtevant, "'But

Things Is Changin' Nowadays and Mammy's Gettin' Bored': Hattie McDaniel and the Culture of Dissemblance," *Velvet Light Trap* 44 (Fall 1999): 68–79.

166. Memo from Selznick to LV Calvert, dated December 12, 1939. Carole Lombard legal file, DOSC, HRC, UT-Austin. In addition to Gaynor and Lombard, Selznick also had Ingrid Bergman, Vivien Leigh, and Joan Fontaine under contract to SIP, amplifying the gender costar dilemma.

167. For example, Thomas Schatz underscores how Edward G. Robinson achieved a lofty salary per picture in the early 1930s, while Paul Muni had unprecedented creative control guaranteed through his limited, non-option contracts at Warner Bros. prior to the 1940s. By comparison, Bette Davis and the other female talent at Warner Bros. "lagged" behind their male colleagues. See Schatz, "A Triumph of Bitchery," 79.

168. See Carman, "Women Rule Hollywood," 13–24, for more on Ronald Colman's and Cary Grant's freelance careers, which I analyze in regard to gender and ageism. Additionally, other male freelancers included notable character actors such as Edward Everett Horton and featured veteran actors such as John Barrymore, Walter Huston, and Adolphe Menjou.

169. For example, Myron Selznick negotiated March's contract for *A Star Is Born* for a flat-rate salary of $125,000 for eight weeks of work. In addition to project approval, his contract included two special provisions: that he receive either star or costar billing, and that he not be required to work on Sunday. See Myron Selznick, client notebook, Fredric March entry, MSC, HRC, UT-Austin.

170. In addition to his $75,000 salary, March's percentage deal earned him 7.5 percent of the film's gross up to $1 million and 10 percent of the gross after $1 million. See Myron Selznick client notebook and Fredric March contract dated August 22, 1938, MSC, HRC, UT-Austin. The deal was extremely lucrative for March, who earned more than $110,000 in his percentage; for more details see Kemper, *Hidden Talent*, 151.

171. Memo dated March 29, 1941, Fredric March legal file, WBA, USC.

172. For example, March was completely absent from the top fifty stars detailed in the *Hollywood Reporter*'s 1936 "Fifty Best Draw Names" poll gathered from 1,192 exhibitors (July 27, 1936, 1–2). The list is headed by Astaire and Rogers at RKO, but Irene Dunne was the highest-ranked freelancer at 13, followed by Carole Lombard at 17, Janet Gaynor at 20, Barbara Stanwyck at 34, and Ronald Colman at 35.

CHAPTER THREE

1. Joan Standish, "Barbara Stanwyck To Give Up Career for Husband?," *Movie Classic* (October 1931): 39.

2. Ibid.

3. Ibid.

4. For example, see *Los Angeles Times*, July 23, 1931; "Stanwyck Walks On Columbia," *Hollywood Reporter*, July 17, 1931, 1; W. R. Wilkerson, "Letter to Barbara Stan-

wyck," *Hollywood Reporter*, August 24, 1931, 1–2; "Stanwyck-Col. Peace: Three-Way Settlement Seen with Actress Making 3 Each for Columbia and Warners," *Hollywood Reporter*, September 14, 1931, 1.

5. Circulation figures from Balio, *Grand Design*, 170.

6. Another fruitful side project could investigate the paradoxical relationship between feminine empowerment and objectification that these magazines represent, although it ultimately transcends the focus of this chapter.

7. For example, see Sheila Worth, "At last! Ronnie Talks about Romance," *Modern Screen* (October 1936): 31, about freelancer Ronald Colman; Gladys Hall, "A Recipe for a Happy Marriage, as told by Fredric March," *Movie Mirror* (December 1932): 26–27; and Ben Maddox, "Leslie Howard and the Ladies," *Screenland* (November 1939): 28–29. See the Margaret Herrick Library in-house periodical index for a complete listing of fan magazine articles on these actors. The only male freelancer whose star persona actively integrated his independent stardom in similar fashion was Cary Grant, who like Lombard turned to freelancing after his talents were allowed to languish at Paramount through incessant loan-outs. In comparison to other male freelance stars, Grant's copy made use of his independent stardom. See, for example, "Cary Grant: $250,000 a Picture?," *Screenland* (February 1938): 45; and "Ascending," *Silver Screen* (April 1938): 27.

8. UA, as a distributor-only studio, did not have its own publicity director, whereas RKO and Columbia maintained smaller publicity departments and worked with independent publicists. The studio exchanges circulated these press reports and promotions to the film exhibitors, who in turn sent them to local newspapers to be featured in Sunday-paper fashion displays or local women's magazines. See Balio, *Grand Design*, 168–173, for further information on the studio publicity houses and their promotion of stars.

9. Carole Lombard, "Every Actor Should Take At Least One Week's Whirl at Publicity," in *Carole Lombard: A Bio-Bibliography*, edited by Robert D. Matzen (New York: Greenwood Press, 1988), 101. The press release was originally published in the *Hollywood Reporter*, October 24, 1938.

10. See Mary Desjardins, "As Told By Helen Ferguson": Hollywood Publicity, Gender, and the Public Sphere," *When Private Talk Goes Public*, edited by Jennifer Frost and Kathleen Feeley (New York: Palgrave Macmillan, 2014), 161–182, for more detail on Ferguson's career and those of other independent publicists in Hollywood.

11. Ibid., 150.

12. See Fuller, *At the Picture Show*, 133–168. See also Gaylyn Studlar's "The Perils of Pleasure?, 263–298.

13. See Stamp, *Movie Struck Girls*, specifically chap. 3, "Ready-Made Customers: Female Movie Fans and the Serial Craze," 102–153. These fan magazines offered a reflexive extratextual space not only for female stars, but also for women editors and writers. For example, female editors led *Photoplay* in the 1930s: Kathryn Dougherty (1932–1935); former treasurer of the *Photoplay* corporation, Ruth Waterbury (1935–

1941); renowned journalist Adela Rogers St. John; the popular novelist Faith Baldwin; and columnist and short-story writer Gladys Hall.

14. For more on the "insider information" provided by *Photoplay*, see Richard Griffith's introduction to *The Talkies: Articles and Illustrations from a Great Fan Magazine, 1928–1940* (New York: Dover, 1970) and the chapter by Katherine H. Fuller (chap. 8), "*Photoplay* Magazine, Movie Fans, and the Marketplace," 150–168.

15. See Eileen V. Wallis, *Earning Power: Women and Work in Los Angeles, 1880–1930* (Reno: University of Nevada Press, 2010), 5.

16. Specifically, female employment grew substantially in white-collar office jobs. See Alice Kessler-Harris, *Out to Work: A History of Wage-Earning Women in the United States* (New York: Oxford University Press, 1982), 224–225, 258. After the stock market crash in 1929, unemployment numbers among US workers began to steadily rise, culminating in its worst figure in 1933, when a quarter of the working population—13 million people—was out of work.

17. See Kessler-Harris, *Out to Work*, 254 and 259. The ranks of married working women also rose across the decade. In 1930, 28.8 percent of all wage-earning women were married; by 1940, the figure reached 35 percent.

18. See Nancy Woloch, *Women and the American Experience* (New York: Knopf, 1984), 454. On other noteworthy women who served as public officials, including the trendsetting first lady, Eleanor Roosevelt, who no doubt also elevated the public profile of career-oriented, politically minded women in the 1930s, see Woloch's chapters "Humanizing the New Deal," 419–438, and "Emergencies: The 1930s and 1940s," 439–478.

19. Woloch, *Women and the American Experience*, 272.

20. See Carole Lombard legal files, DOSC, HRC, UT-Austin.

21. See also my article titled "Independent Stardom: Female Film Stars and the Studio System in the 1930s," *Women's Studies* 36, no. 6 (2008): 583–615, in which I trace how the fan and publicity press evolved as female film stars achieved independent stardom.

22. For other studies grounded in extratextual popular discourses, see Danae Clark's *Negotiating Hollywood*; and Amelie Hastie, *Cupboards of Curiosity* (Durham, NC: Duke University Press, 2007).

23. Stanwyck hired publicist Helen Ferguson to manage her public persona at some point in the mid-1930s to 1940s, but I am not able to confirm when Ferguson became Stanwyck's publicist in any of her contracts available at Warner Bros. (1932–1935, 1940–1944, and 1945–1949), Fox and RKO (1935–1938), and with Hal Wallis. Mary Desjardins postulates in her article "As Told by Helen Ferguson," 161–182, that Stanwyck could have hired Ferguson in the early 1930s because she was a freelance artist and independent of studio publicity.

24. Adele Fletcher Whitely, "The Girl Who Has Hollywood's Number," *Modern Screen* 4, no. 1 (June 1932): 31.

25. Ibid.

26. Ibid.

27. Ibid.

28. Ibid., 104.

29. Gladys Hall, "Stanwyck Through the Looking Glass," *Modern Screen* 13, no. 5 (October 1936): 49.

30. Ibid.

31. Mary Desjardins also supports this view in "As Told by Helen Ferguson," 161–182, in which she analyzes a sampling of Stanwyck's interviews and campaigns that Ferguson oversaw.

32. Katharine Hartley, "Beloved Trouper," *Modern Screen* 14, no. 5 (April 1937): 126. For the industry trade coverage of Stanwyck's freelancing, see "WB Releases Stanwyck," *Variety*, November 27, 1934, 2 (in which the journal profiles Stanwyck's decision to "freelance"); "Stanwyck Wanted by 3 Studios," *Daily Variety* 5, no. 75, December 3, 1934, 1; "Stanwyck Wanted By Fox for Termer," *Daily Variety* 6, no. 7, December 13, 1934, 1; "Junior After Stanwyck," *Hollywood Reporter*, June 14, 1935, 1; and "Radio Pacts Stanwyck," *Hollywood Reporter*, October 1, 1935, 1.

33. Hartley, "Beloved Trouper," 126.

34. "Barbara Stanwyck's Advice to Girls in Love," interview with Gladys Hall. Gladys Hall Papers, Margaret Herrick Library, Academy of Motion Picture Arts and Sciences, Beverly Hills, CA, 1.

35. Ibid.

36. Ibid.

37. Helen Louise Walker, "Everything Under Control But Love," in *Silver Screen* (June 1936): 31.

38. Ibid.

39. Ibid.

40. Gladys Hall, "Sunny Side Up," *Modern Screen* (October 1939): 30.

41. Ibid. The subsequent Paramount picture was *Remember the Night* (Mitchell Leisen, 1940) costarring Fred MacMurray.

42. Brian Kellow, *The Bennetts*, 152.

43. Audrey Rivers, "Connie Bennett Huge Salary Starts Trouble," *Movie Classic* 1, no. 4 (December 1931): 4.

44. Ibid. See also the letter dated January 6, 1931, from Jack Warner to Constance Bennett, Constance Bennett legal files, Warner Bros. Archive (WBA), University of Southern California (USC).

45. Ibid.

46. Walter Ramsey, "How Constance Really Spends her Money," *Modern Screen* (August 1931); reprinted in *The Best of Modern Screen*, edited by Mark Bego (New York: St. Martin's Press, 1986): 78.

47. For example, *Modern Screen* claimed that rumors abounded that she spent over $250,000 *a day* on clothes alone.

48. Ramsey, "How Constance Really Spends Her Money," 78.

49. Ruth Biery, "Why Constance Is Unpopular in Hollywood," *Photoplay* (February 1932); reprinted in *The Talkies*, edited by Richard Griffith (New York: Dover, 1971), 114–115.

50. Ibid.

51. Biery, "Why Constance Is Unpopular," 115. I could not locate this provision in her Warner Bros. contract; however, Bennett did find herself in the middle of a battle between Warner Bros. and her agency, Selznick-Joyce, when she tried to get the studio to pay Selznick's 10 percent cut of her salary. When the studio only paid $15,000, Selznick came after Bennett for the rest. See memo dated November 9, 1932, Constance Bennett legal files, WBA, USC.

52. *The Common Law* (1931) earned a $150,000 profit, while *Born to Love* (Paul L. Stein, 1931) earned $90,000. (Each grossed over $600,000 and cost approximately $300,000 to produce.) *Two Against the World* (1932) earned $562,000 in profits for Warner Bros. Profit figures from C. J. Trevlin's RKO ledger and William Schaefer's ledger at WBA, USC.

53. Ibid.

54. Twentieth Century-Fox press release. Constance Bennett, clippings files, Margaret Herrick Library, Academy of Motion Picture Arts and Sciences, Beverly Hills, CA.

55. Kellow, *The Bennetts*, 227.

56. S. R. Mook, "'In Hollywood Women Maintain Equality with Men'—Constance Bennett," *Silver Screen* 4, no. 6 (April 1934): 22. Bennett's comments also present an interesting counterargument to the objectification that occurs on-screen and in these magazines in regard to women.

57. Ibid.

58. Ibid.

59. Ibid.

60. Gordon Crowly, "Why Hollywood Fears Constance Bennett," *Motion Picture* (July 1936): 43.

61. Ibid.

62. Ibid.

63. Elisabeth French, "The Indestructible Miss Bennett," *Modern Screen* 18, no. 6 (May 1939): 50.

64. Ibid.

65. Ibid., 79.

66. Ibid., 50. For more on her producer work, see Kellow, *The Bennetts*, 293. Bennett's cosmetics company fared well until she sold the company to a competitor as a franchise in the early 1940s, which undercut the product and decreased sales. She also started a clothing line, Fashion Frocks, in the mid-1940s, but this mail-order company also failed to take off. See Kellow, *The Bennetts*, 227–228, 255–256.

67. I am examining Bennett's venture into producing in a new journal article project, "Hard Bargainer: Constance Bennett's Multifaceted Career."

68. *The Story of Temple Drake* was a solid box-office success despite its portrayal of bootlegging, prostitution, and rape. See the PCA file on *The Story of Temple Drake* at the Margaret Herrick Library for more on the objectionable material in this film, as well as Lea Jacobs, *The Wages of Sin: Censorship and the Fallen Woman Film 1928–*

1942 (Berkeley: University of California Press, 1995), 36–37, 111. See also the American Film Institute Catalog entry on the film for its box-office popularity in 1933–1934.

69. For more on the threat of national boycotts, see Schatz, *Genius of the System*, 203–204.

70. Jay Brien Chapman, "My Movie Moral Code," in *Movie Classic* (October 1933): 72.

71. Ibid.

72. Ibid. Emphasis in original.

73. Ibid.

74. See Article 20 in Miriam Hopkins's contract with Samuel Goldwyn Inc., Ltd., dated August 31, 1934. Miriam Hopkins legal file, WBA, USC.

75. Ruth Rankin, "Glamour with a Grin," *Screenland* (November 1935): 55.

76. Desire Davis, "Becky Sharp Says It's Still a Man's World," *Motion Picture* (April 1935): 65.

77. Ibid.

78. Ibid., 65.

79. These two films were substantial losses for RKO: *The Woman I Love* lost $266,000, while *Wise Girl* lost $114,000. Figures from C. J. Trevlin, RKO ledger. Both are discussed in chapter 2.

80. Lois Svensrud, "Good News," *Modern Screen* (May 1938): 65.

81. Recall from chapter 2 that Hopkins reduced her asking price of $300,000 for four films with no story approval to $100,000 for two films with costar, director, and story approval. See Miriam Hopkins legal file, WBA, USC.

82. George Benjamin, "Low-Down on a High Up," *Modern Screen* (October 1939): 88.

83. Another possible reason for Hopkins's waning career was Hollywood ageism; by 1940 she was thirty-eight and facing competition from younger women. For instance, a deal to star in the Western *The Badlands of Dakota* at Universal fell through in 1941 after she lost the role to twenty-one-year-old Ann Rutherford. See my article "'Women Rule Hollywood'," 18, for more on how aging impacted Hopkins's career.

84. Biographer Robert D. Matzen cites more than a hundred contemporary 1930s and 1940s fan and popular magazine articles about Lombard in *Carole Lombard*, xiii.

85. Quotation from "Carole Lombard Day," SIP press release, July 9, 1939, DOSC, HRC, UT-Austin.

86. See contract figure no. 9 in interoffice memo to Dan O'Shea from David O. Selznick dated October 21, 1937. Carole Lombard legal file, DOSC, HRC, UT-Austin; and Myron Selznick Agency files, Carole Lombard file, client notebook, Box 1, HRC, UT-Austin. See also "Birdwell Leaving S-I for Own Firm," *Hollywood Reporter*, January 3, 1939, 2.

87. Lombard, "One Week's Whirl," 101.

88. Seymour Hart, "Carole Lombard Tells: 'How I Live by a Man's Code,'" *Photoplay* (June 1937): 12.

89. Ibid.

90. Ibid.

91. Ibid., 78.

92. Ibid., 12.

93. Ibid.

94. For more on Lombard's off-screen antics and personality, see Swindell, *Screwball*; and Matzen, *Carole Lombard.*

95. Hart, "Carole Lombard," 13.

96. This assessment is also sustained by Amelie Hastie, *Cupboards of Curiosity*, 164.

97. Hart, "Carole Lombard," 13.

98. "Four Part Biography on Carole Lombard," SIP press release. Russell Birdwell publicity file, Jock Whitney Collection (JWC), Box 6, HRC, UT-Austin.

99. Ibid.

100. Ibid.

101. See Russell Birdwell's memo to David O. Selznick dated October 20, 1938. Carole Lombard legal files, DOSC, HRC, UT-Austin.

102. Emphasis in original. Gladys Hall, "Carole Lombard—As She Sees Herself," *Motion Picture* (November 1938); reprinted in Matzen, *Carole Lombard*, 116.

103. Ibid.

104. Ibid., 113.

105. Noel F. Busch, "A Loud Cheer for the Screwball Girl," *Life*, October 17, 1938, 54.

106. Ibid.

107. See memo from L.V. Calvert to David O. Selznick about Lombard's *Life* cover story, dated October 17, 1938. Russell Birdwell file, JWC, HRC, UT-Austin.

108. Ibid. The *Life* article also publicized her aspiring independent production plans on a profit-sharing basis with Myron Selznick's new production company.

109. "'Tomboy' Lombard Earned $2,000,000," *Los Angeles Times*, January 18, 1942.

110. Alva Johnston, "Hollywood's Ten Percenters," *Saturday Evening Post*, August 8, 1942, 38.

111. Ibid. Also substantiated in "Arbitration between Myron Selznick & Company, Inc. and Carole Lombard," January 1941, in which the "phony" contract was referenced (p. 14). Myron Selznick files, DOSC, HRC, UT-Austin.

112. See Diane Waldman, "From Midnight Shows to Marriage Vows: Women, Exploitation, and Exhibition," *Wide Angle* 6 (1984): 40–48; see also Gaylyn Studlar, "The Perils of Pleasure," 263–298.

113. McLean, *Being Rita Hayworth*, 77.

114. Ibid.

115. Gable worked exclusively at MGM from 1930 until 1954, spanning most of his screen career. Only when the studio released him in 1954 did he begin to freelance. See Barry King, "Stardom as Occupation," in *The Hollywood Film Industry*, edited by Paul

Kerr (London: Routledge, 1986): 173. Taylor outlasted Gable, signing with the studio in 1935 and remaining on contract until 1958.

116. Elizabeth Wilson, "Carole's Colorful Career," *Screenland* (November 1935): 70.

117. Ibid.

118. Adela Rogers St. John, "The Story Behind the Stanwyck-Fay Break-up: A Great Human Document," *Photoplay* (January 1936): 100.

119. See Di Orio, *Stanwyck*, for more on the Fay-Stanwyck marriage and its inspiration for film projects.

120. St. John, "Stanwyck-Fay Break-up," 100.

121. Ibid.

122. Kirtley Basquette, "Hollywood's Unmarried Husbands and Wives," *Photoplay* (January 1939); reprinted in Griffith, *The Talkies*, 130.

123. Ibid., 321.

124. Samantha Barbas explains in *Movie Crazy* that this article caused a gossip scandal that compelled the studios to police the fan magazines so carefully "that they almost never contradicted the studios again" (99). Up to this point, the fan magazines had been relatively autonomous. See Barbas, *Movie Crazy: Fans, Stars, and the Cult of Celebrity* (New York: Palgrave, 2001) for more on the ramifications of this exposé; and Victoria Wilson, *A Life of Barbara Stanwyck: Steel-True, 1907–1940* (New York: Simon and Schuster, 2013), 757–759.

125. All the other couples eventually divorced, with the exception of Gable and Lombard, whose marriage ended with Lombard's death. The other couple cited in this article is George Raft and Virginia Pine.

126. Stanwyck and Taylor married on April 14, 1939. Wilson, *A Life of Barbara Stanwyck*, 758.

127. Ibid.

128. Gladys Hall, "Information if you please, about Barbara Stanwyck," *Modern Screen* (March 1940): 4–6.

129. Ibid. Indeed Stanwyck would never really retire. Her career spanned over eight decades in film, radio, theater, and television. She appeared in eighty-three films.

130. Elizabeth Wilson, "'Pretty Boy' Squares his Jaw," *Screenland* (August 1940): 32–33.

131. For example, see Charles Darnton, "All Right, I'll Fight," *Screenland* (January 1939): 24–25; and "Gable or Taylor?," *Screenland* (February 1938): 46–47.

132. Edward Doherty, "Can the Lombard-Gable Romance Have a Happy Ending?," *Modern Screen* 52, no. 6 (May 1938): 18.

133. Ibid., 95.

134. Ruth Biery, "Why Clark Gable says 'I am paid not to think,'" *Photoplay* (December 1932): 28–29.

135. Memo to Daniel O'Shea from David O. Selznick, undated. Folder 10, Box 628, DOSC, HRC, UT-Austin.

136. John Caldwell, *Production Culture: Industry Reflexivity and Critical Practice in Film and Television* (Durham, NC: Duke University Press, 2008), 1. Although Caldwell's discussion focuses primarily on below-the-line workers in contemporary Hollywood, his observations are equally illuminating for understanding the self-presentation of A-list talent in 1930s Hollywood.

CHAPTER FOUR

1. Thomas Schatz, *Boom and Bust: American Cinema in the 1940s* (Berkeley: University of California Press, 1997), 97, 102.

2. Ibid., 45–47.

3. Ibid., 46.

4. Such historians include Schatz, *Boom and Bust*, 46; Bordwell et al., *The Classical Hollywood System* (New York: Columbia University Press, 1985), 320–330; and Denise Mann, *Hollywood Independents* (Minneapolis: University of Minnesota Press, 2008), 67.

5. Both Harding and Hopkins reappeared in Hollywood as character actresses by the mid-1940s and 1950s. Harding appeared in *Mission to Moscow* (Michael Curtiz, 1943) and *The North Star* (Lewis Mileston, 1943), for example, while Hopkins was a featured player in William Wyler's *The Heiress* (1949) and *Carrie* (1952).

6. Many of their pre-code films were either denied rerelease or further censored by the head of the PCA, Joseph Breen, in the late 1930s. These films include *The Easiest Way* (1931), *Bed of Roses* (1933), *Dr. Jekyll and Mr. Hyde* (1931), *The Story of Temple Drake* (1933), and *Design for Living* (1933).

7. See Carman, "Women Rule Hollywood," 13–24.

8. Emphasis added. See Melvyn Stokes, "Female Audiences," 43–44; and Susan Ohmer, *George Gallup in Hollywood* (New York: Columbia University Press, 2006).

9. See Schatz, *Boom and Bust*, 469–472, for a complete listing of *Motion Picture Herald*'s exhibitor star polls. Cooper, Gable, Cagney, and Tracy all appeared in the top ten at various points throughout the 1930s as well, but on average, there were at least five or more female stars on the *Herald*'s poll in the 1930s.

10. For the top box-office earnings of Hollywood films in the 1940s, see "All-Time Film Rental Champs," *Variety*, February 24, 1992, 125–168.

11. Fred Astaire, Humphrey Bogart, James Cagney, Joel McCrea, and Spencer Tracy also entered the freelance class in the postwar years.

12. For example, Grant earned $100,000 per film with a 10 percent share once the total film gross exceeded $1.5 million at RKO in 1942, and he dropped his flat-rate salary to $50,000 in exchange for a larger stake in the distribution profits for his RKO work in 1946 (receiving a $75,000 advance against his percentage interest in gross receipts). See Cary Grant's RKO payroll cards dated March 6, 1944, and February 1, 1946. RKO Collection, UCLA PASC. Cooper's 1943 agreement with Warner Bros. was a packaged, one-picture deal specifically for the film *Saratoga Trunk* (released in 1946), and named

him as the star, Sam Wood as director, and Hal Wallis as producer. It included a profit-sharing deal for which Cooper accepted no upfront salary in order to secure 10 percent of the film's gross up to $1 million. See contract dated February 23, 1943, Gary Cooper legal file, WBA, USC, pp. 1–3, 7.

13. Schatz, *Boom and Bust*, 187; and Mann, *Hollywood Independents*, 34.

14. Schatz, *Boom and Bust*, 187.

15. Schatz, *Boom and Bust*, 57; and Richard B. Jewell, *RKO Radio Pictures: A Titan Is Born* (Berkeley: University of California Press, 2012), 220, 236.

16. Please note that de Havilland's name was misspelled by the court in issuing the "De Havilland Law." Section 2855 of the California Labor Code and the 1944 California Supreme Court verdict are still known among legal scholars as the De Haviland decision.

17. See California State court brief dated March 23, 1944, declaring de Havilland's contract null and void, and decreeing her a free agent. *De Haviland v. Warner Bros.*, 67 Cal. App. 225, 153 P.2d 983 (1944).

18. See Schatz, *Genius of the System*, 318.

19. See contract dated February 12, 1934 (effective February 28, 1935, and renewed with six successive options in 1936), WBA, USC.

20. Interview, "The Last Belle of Cinema," *Academy of Achievement*, http://www.achievement.org, October 6, 2006. Olivia de Havilland is one of the last living actresses of her generation (b. 1916).

21. Olivia de Havilland's suspensions resulted from her declining to appear in the following four pictures at Warner Bros.: *Saturday's Children* (Vincent Sherman, 1940), *Flight Angels* (Lewis Seiler, 1940), *George Washington Slept Here* (William Keighley, 1942), and *One More Tomorrow* (Peter Godfrey, 1946). This pales in comparison to the twenty-eight assignments she accepted between 1935 and 1943.

22. Memo to Jack Warner from Trilling, dated February 20, 1942, Olivia de Havilland legal file, WBA, USC.

23. Jonathan Blaufarb, "The Seven-Year Itch: California Labor Code Section 2855," *Communications and Entertainment Law Journal* 6, no. 3 (1983–1984): 666.

24. *De Haviland v. Warner Bros.*, 67 Cal. App. 2d at 235, 153 p.2d, 988.

25. Ibid., 668.

26. For the influence of the "De Havilland Law" in legal studies and legal precedent, see Blaufarb, "Seven-Year Itch," 653–693.

27. See Olivia de Havilland legal file, WBA, USC, as well as "De Havilland Sues For Work," *Variety*, July 14, 1944, 1.

28. Other talent nominees who were freelance artists in 1946 included Rosalind Russell for *Sister Kenny*, Laurence Olivier for *Henry V*, as well as the directors Frank Capra for *It's a Wonderful Life* and William Wyler, who won that year for *The Best Years of Our Lives*. In fact, Capra had founded the independent production company Liberty Films on January 29, 1945, with Samuel J. Briskin, Wyler, and director George Stevens. RKO agreed to distribute and finance three films from each director, the first being Capra's *It's a Wonderful Life*.

29. In 1946, nomination ballots were sent to 11,669 creative workers in the industry; however, the final award ballots were mailed only to the 1,600 Academy members. The change in the Academy's nomination and final voting procedures came in 1936, when then-president Frank Capra brought in the Screenwriters, Writers, and Directors Guilds to democratize the awards and make them representative of the entire film industry. This practice ended in 1957, when nomination voting was restricted to Academy members only. For more on this, see Levy, *Oscar Fever*, 25–26.

30. See contracts dated July 15, 1943, and April 10, 1944. Joan Crawford legal file, WBA, USC. Although her salary per picture was eventually raised to $100,000, and she received the right to make one outside picture, the only stipulation Crawford ever won was to have approval of her director of photography.

31. Jack Warner himself noted the irony in Crawford's action since she had no story approval. See memo dated February 11, 1944. Furthermore, Crawford asserted her agency when her agreement was renegotiated in 1947; the actress made two pictures a year for Warner Bros. at a salary of $400,000 and retained the right to make outside films. Even still, this agreement remained bereft of the creative provisions that were a staple of many of the freelance contracts analyzed earlier in this book. See contract dated March 28, 1947. Joan Crawford legal file, WBA, USC.

32. Schatz, *Genius of the System*, 422.

33. Moreover, the primary motivation for an overall decline in film production by the end of the decade (1948–1950) seems to be the uncertainty surrounding the impending breakup of the studio system. It is also worth noting that companies did not all divest their theater chains in 1948 after the Paramount decree. MGM, for instance, did not complete the divorcement of Loew's and MGM until 1959. See also Mann, *Hollywood Independents*, 66.

34. Annette Kuhn, "Introduction: Intestinal Fortitude," in *Queen of the B's: Ida Lupino Behind the Camera*, edited by Annette Kuhn (Westport, CT: Praeger, 1996), 2.

35. See contracts dated May 3, 1940, and June 10, 1940, as well as the letter from Warner Bros. lawyer Roy Obringer to Lupino dated June 10, 1940. Ida Lupino legal file, WBA, USC.

36. See contract dated April 1, 1941. Ida Lupino legal file, WBA, USC.

37. See letter from Roy Obringer to Lupino dated October 29, 1946. Ida Lupino legal file, WBA, USC. See also William Donati, *Ida Lupino: A Biography* (Louisville: University of Kentucky Press, 1996), chap. 8. Her contract was formally dissolved on February 18, 1947. See "Cancellation of Contract." Ida Lupino legal file, WBA, USC.

38. Donati, *Ida Lupino*, 126.

39. Ibid., 55.

40. Kuhn, *Queen of the B's*, 2.

41. For more on Bennett's career as a film producer, see "Hard Bargainer: Constance Bennett's Multi-Faceted Career," a project that I am working on for eventual publication.

42. See Benjamin B. Hampton, *History of the American Film Industry*, new ed.

(New York: Dover, 1970); and Lewis Jacobs, *The Rise of the American Film*, new ed. (New York: Teachers College Press, 1967).

43. Jewell, "How Howard Hawks Brought *Baby* Up," 39–40. The unappreciated artists in these examples tend to be Orson Welles or Erich Von Stroheim. Jewell, however, rightly points out that, in practice, the studio system never streamlined filmmaking into a "conveyor-belt business," even if it had aspired to such a strategy in theory, given that each film tended to present a set of unique problems that such an inflexible system could not easily remedy.

44. Ibid., 47.

45. See the introduction to Mann, *Hollywood Independents*. The independent-production trend among stars became more pronounced in the 1950s with Kirk Douglas's Bryna Productions, Burt Lancaster's various independent production companies with his agent Harold Hecht (Hecht-Norma Productions in 1948; Hecht-Lancaster, 1954–1955; and after producer James Hill joined in 1957, Hecht-Hill-Lancaster), as well as John Wayne's Wayne-Fellows Productions with producer Robert Fellows (later renamed Batjac after Wayne bought out his former partner). See also Paul McDonald, *Contemporary Stardom* (Malden, MA: Wiley-Blackwell, 2013), 107–116, for more extensive examples from the 1950s to the 1990s/2000s.

46. McDonald, *Contemporary Hollywood*, 119.

47. Ibid., 109.

48. Ibid.

49. Los Angeles was recently named "the best place in the U.S. for freelancers" in 2014 by the financing and investment blog *Nerd Wallet*, largely due to the entertainment industry's employment structure. See Maggie Clark, "Best Cities for Freelancers," *Nerd Wallet Finance*, February 25, 2014, http://www.nerdwallet.com/blog/2014/best-cities-freelance-workers/. At the same time, all film production is on a freelance, project-by-project basis (many of which are not in Los Angeles), which often results in a precarious professional path for individuals seeking employment in Hollywood.

50. See McDonald, *Contemporary Hollywood*, 121.

Bibliography

Aberdeen, J. A. *Hollywood Renegades: The Society of Independent Motion Picture Producers, 1942–1958*. Palos Verdes Estates, CA: Cobblestone Enterprises, 1999.

Allen, Robert C. "The Role of the Star in Film History [Joan Crawford]." In *Film Theory and Criticism*, 5th ed., edited by Leo Braudy and Marshall Cohen, 547–561. Oxford: Oxford University Press, 1999.

Balio, Tino. *Grand Design: Hollywood as a Modern Business Enterprise, 1930–1939*. Berkeley: University of California Press, 1995.

———. *United Artists: The Company Built by the Stars*. Vol. 1, 1919–1950. Madison: University of Wisconsin Press, 2009.

———. *United Artists: The Company That Changed the Film Industry*. Vol. 2, 1951–1978. Madison: University of Wisconsin Press, 2009.

Barbas, Samantha. *Movie Crazy: Fans, Stars, and the Cult of Celebrity*. New York: Palgrave Macmillan, 2001.

Basinger, Jeanine. *The Star Machine*. New York: Knopf, 2007.

Bean, Jennifer M. "Toward a Feminist Historiography of Early Cinema." In *A Feminist Reader in Early Cinema*, edited by Jennifer M. Bean and Diane Negra, 1–26. Durham, NC: Duke University Press, 2002.

Beauchamp, Cari. *Without Lying Down: Frances Marion and the Powerful Women of Early Hollywood*. Berkeley: University of California Press, 1998.

Bego, Mark. *The Best of Modern Screen*. New York: St. Martin's Press, 1986.

Behlmer, Rudy, ed. *Memo from David O. Selznick*. New York: Modern Library, 2000.

Berg, Charles Ramirez. *Latino Images in Film: Stereotypes, Subversion, Resistance*. Austin: University of Texas Press, 2002.

Bergfelder, Tim. "Negotiating Exoticism: Hollywood, Film Europe, and the Cultural Reception of Anna May Wong." In *Film Europe and Film America: Cinema, Commerce and Cultural Exchange, 1920–1939*, edited by Andrew Higson and Richard Maltby, 303–322. London: University of Exeter Press, 1999.

Bergstrom, Janet. "Murnau in America: Chronicle of Lost Films." *Film History* 14, no. 3/4 (2002): 430–460.

Bernstein, Matthew. "Hollywood's Semi-Independent Production." *Cinema Journal* 32, no. 3 (Spring 1993): 41–54.

———. *Walter Wanger: Hollywood Independent*. 2nd ed. Minneapolis: University of Minnesota Press, 2000.

Berry, Sarah. *Screen Style: Fashion and Femininity in 1930s Hollywood*. Minneapolis: University of Minnesota Press, 2000.

Blaufarb, Jonathan. "The Seven Year Itch: California Labor Code Section 2855." *Communications and Entertainment Law Journal* 6, no. 3 (1983–1984): 653–693.

Bordwell, David, Janet Staiger, and Kristen Thompson. *The Classical Hollywood System: Film Style and Mode of Production to 1960*. New York: Columbia University Press, 1985.

Caldwell, John. *Production Culture: Industry Reflexivity and Critical Practice in Film and Television*. Durham, NC: Duke University Press, 2008.

Carman, Emily. "Independent Stardom: Female Film Stars and the Studio System in the 1930s." *Women's Studies: An Interdisciplinary Journal* (Fall 2008): 583–615.

———. "'Women Rule Hollywood': Ageing and Freelance Stardom in the Studio System." *Celebrity Studies* 3 (March 2012): 13–24.

Caves, Richard. *Creative Industries: Contracts between Art and Commerce*. Cambridge, MA: Harvard University Press, 2000.

Chaplin, Charles. *My Autobiography*. New York: Plume, 1964.

Clark, Danae. *Negotiating Hollywood: The Cultural Politics of Actors' Labor*. Minneapolis: University of Minnesota Press, 1995.

Cones, John W. *Film Finance and Distribution: A Dictionary of Terms*. Los Angeles: Silman-James, 1992.

Curry, Ramona. *Too Much of a Good Thing: Mae West as Cultural Icon*. Minneapolis: University of Minnesota Press, 1996.

Custen, George. *Twentieth Century Fox: Darryl F. Zanuck and the Culture of Hollywood*. New York: Basic Books, 1997.

DeCordova, Richard. *Picture Personalities: The Emergence of the Star System in America*. Urbana: University of Illinois Press, 1990.

De Haviland v. Warner Bros., 67 Cal. App. 225, 153 P.2d 983 (1944).

Desjardins, Mary. "Not of Hollywood: Ruth Chatterton, Ann Harding, Constance Bennett, Kay Francis, and Nancy Carroll." In *Glamour in a Golden Age: Movie Stars of the 1930s*, edited by Adrienne L. McLean, 18–43. Piscataway, NJ: Rutgers University Press, 2011.

———. "As Told By Helen Ferguson: Hollywood Publicity, Gender, and the Public Sphere." In *When Private Talk Goes Public*, edited by Jennifer Frost and Kathleen Feeley, 161–182. New York: Palgrave-Macmillian, 2014.

DiOrio, Al. *Barbara Stanwyck*. New York: Coward McCann, 1984.

Doherty, Thomas. *Pre-Code Hollywood: Sex, Immorality, and Insurrection in American Cinema*. New York: Columbia University Press, 1999.

Donati, William. *Ida Lupino: A Biography*. Louisville: University of Kentucky Press, 1996.

Dyer, Richard. *Stars*. London: BFI, 1998.

Eckert, Charles. "The Carole Lombard in the Macy's Window." In *Stardom: Industry of Desire*, edited by Christine Gledhill, 30–39. London: Routledge, 1991.

Enstad, Nan. *Ladies of Labor, Girls of Adventure: Working Women, Popular Culture, and Labor Politics at the Turn of the Twentieth Century*. New York: Columbia University Press, 1999.

Eyman, Scott. *Mary Pickford: America's Sweetheart*. New York: Donald I. Fine, 1990.

Fischer, Lucy. *Designing Women: Cinema, Art Deco, and the Female Form*. New York: Columbia University Press, 2003.

Fischer, Lucy, and Marcia Landy, eds. *Stars: The Film Reader*. New York: Routledge, 2004.

Fuller, Kathryn H. *At the Picture Show: Small-Town Audiences and the Creation of Movie Fan Culture*. Charlottesville: University of Virginia Press, 2001.

Gaines, Jane. *Contested Culture: The Image, the Voice, and the Law*. Chapel Hill: University of North Carolina Press, 1991.

———. "Film History and the Two Presents of Feminist Film Theory." *Cinema Journal* 44, no. 1 (2004): 113–119.

———. "War, Women, and Lipstick: Fan Mags in the Forties." *Heresies* (1985): 42–47.

Gaines, Jane, and Charlotte Herzog. "Puffed Sleeves Before Tea Time: Joan Crawford, Adrian, and Women Audiences." In *Stardom: Industry of Desire*, edited by Christine Gledhill, 74–91. London: Routledge, 1991.

Gledhill, Christine, ed. *Stardom: Industry of Desire*. London: Routledge, 1991.

Gomery, Douglas. *The Hollywood Studio System: A History*. London: BFI, 2005.

Griffith, Richard, ed. *The Talkies: Articles and Illustrations from a Great Fan Magazine 1928–1940*. New York: Dover, 1970.

Hampton, Benjamin B. *History of the American Film Industry*. New ed. New York: Dover, 1970.

Hansen, Miriam. *Babel and Babylon: Spectatorship in American Silent Film*. Cambridge, MA: Harvard University Press, 1991.

———. "Early Cinema, Late Cinema: Permutations of the Public Sphere." In *Viewing Positions: Ways of Seeing Film*, edited by Linda Williams, 134–152. New Brunswick: Rutgers University Press, 1995.

———. "Fallen Women, Rising Stars, New Horizons: Shanghai Silent Film as Vernacular Modernism." *Film Quarterly* 54, no. 1 (Autumn, 2000): 10–22.

———. "The Mass Production of the Senses: Classical Cinema as Vernacular Modernism." In *Reinventing Film Studies*, edited by Christine Gledhill and Linda Williams, 332–351. London: Oxford University Press, 2000.

Haralovich, Mary Beth. "The Proletarian Woman's Film of the 1930s: Contending with Censorship and Entertainment." *Screen* 31, no. 2 (Summer 1990): 172–185.

Haskell, Molly. *From Reverence to Rape: The Treatment of Women in the Movies*. Chicago: University of Chicago Press, 1987.

Hastie, Amelie. *Cupboards of Curiosity: Women, Recollection, and Film History*. Durham, NC: Duke University Press, 2007.

Hershfield, Joanne. *The Invention of Dolores del Río*. Minneapolis: University of Minnesota Press, 2000.

Jacobs, Lea. *The Decline of Sentiment: American Films in the 1920s*. Berkeley: University of California Press, 2008.

———. *The Wages of Sin: Censorship and the Fallen Woman Film, 1928–1942*. Berkeley: University of California Press, 1995.

Jacobs, Lewis. *The Rise of the American Film*. New ed. New York: Teachers College Press, 1967.

Jewell, Richard B. *The Golden Age of Cinema: Hollywood 1929–1945*. Malden, MA: Blackwell, 2007.

———. "How Howard Hawks Brought *Baby* Up: An *Apologia* for the Studio System." In *The Studio System*, edited by Janet Staiger, 39–49. New Brunswick, NJ: Rutgers University Press, 1995.

———. RKO *Radio Pictures: A Titan Is Born*. Berkeley: University of California Press, 2012.

Kear, Lynn, and John Rossman. *Kay Francis: A Passionate Life and Career*. Jefferson, NC, and London: McFarland, 2006.

Kellow, Brian. *The Bennetts: An Acting Family*. Lexington: University of Kentucky Press, 2004.

Kemper, Tom. *Hidden Talent: The Emergence of Hollywood Agents*. Berkeley: University of California Press, 2010.

Kendall, Elizabeth. *The Runaway Bride: Hollywood Romantic Comedy of the 1930s*. New York: Knopf, 1990.

Kessler-Harris, Alice. *Out to Work: A History of Wage-Earning Women in the United States*. New York: Oxford University Press, 1982.

King, Barry. "Articulating Stardom." *Screen* 26, no. 5 (1985): 27–50.

———. "The Star and the Commodity: Notes towards a Performance Theory of Stardom." *Screen* 1, no. 2 (1987): 145–161.

———. "Stardom as Occupation." In *The Hollywood Film Industry*, edited by Paul Kerr, 154–184. London and New York: Routledge and Kegan Paul, 1984.

Klaprat, Cathy. "The Star as Market Strategy: Bette Davis in Another Light." In *The American Film Industry*, edited by Tino Balio, 351–376. Madison: University of Wisconsin Press, 1976.

Koszarski, Richard. *An Evening's Entertainment: The Age of the Silent Feature Picture, 1915–1928*. Vol. 3. Berkeley: University of California Press, 1990.

Kuhn, Annette. *Queen of the B's: Ida Lupino Behind the Camera*. Westport, CT: Praeger, 1995.

Levy, Emmanuel. *The Politics and History of the Academy Awards*. New York: Continuum, 2001.

Lewis, Jon. *American Film: A History*. New York: W. W. Norton, 2007.

Lewis, Jon, and Eric Smoodin, eds. *Looking Past the Screen: Case Studies in American Film History and Method*. Durham, NC: Duke University Press, 2007.

López, Ana M. "Are All Latins from Manhattan? Hollywood, Ethnography, and Cultural Colonialism." In *Unspeakable Images: Ethnicity and the American Cinema*, edited by Lester D. Friedman, 404–424. Champaign: University of Illinois Press, 1991.

Mahar, Karen Ward. *Women Filmmakers in the Early Film Industry*. Baltimore: Johns Hopkins University Press, 2008.

Maltby, Richard, and Melvyn Stokes, eds. *Hollywood's Audiences*. London: BFI, 1999.

Mank, Gregory. "Miriam Hopkins." In *Women in Horror Films, 1930s*, 83–102. Jefferson, NC: McFarland, 1999.

Mann, Denise. *Hollywood Independents: The Postwar Talent Takeover*. Minneapolis: University of Minnesota Press, 2008.

Matzen, Robert D. *Carole Lombard: A Bio-Bibliography*. New York: Greenwood Press, 1988.

May, Lary. *The Big Tomorrow: Hollywood and the American Way*. Chicago: University of Chicago Press, 2000.

Mayne, Judith. *Cinema and Spectatorship*. London: Routledge, 1993.

McDonald, Paul. *Hollywood Stardom*. Malden, MA: Wiley-Blackwell, 2013.

———. *The Star System: Hollywood's Production of Popular Identities*. London: Wallflower, 2000.

McDougal, Dennis. *The Last Mogul: Lew Wasserman, MCA, and the Hidden History of Hollywood*. New York: Da Capo, 2001.

McLean, Adrienne. *Being Rita Hayworth: Labor, Identity, and Hollywood Stardom*. New Brunswick, NJ: Rutgers University Press, 2004.

Mordden, Ethan. *Make Believe: The Broadway Musical in the 1920s*. New York: Oxford University Press, 1997.

Muscio, Giuliana. *Hollywood's New Deal (Culture and Moving Image)*. Philadelphia: Temple University Press, 1997.

Negra, Diane. *Off-white Hollywood: American Culture and Ethnic Female Stardom*. Routledge: New York, 2001.

Ohmer, Susan. *George Gallup in Hollywood*. New York: Columbia University Press, 2006.

Orgeron, Marsha. "Making It in Hollywood: Clara Bow, Fandom, and Consumer Culture." *Cinema Journal* 42, no. 4 (2003): 76–97.

Prindle, David. *The Politics of Glamour: Ideology and Democracy in the Screen Actors Guild*. Madison: University of Wisconsin Press, 1988.

Rabinovitz, Lauren. "The Future of Feminism and Film History." *Camera Obscura* 61 (2006): 38–44.

Rose, Frank. *The Agency: William Morris Agency and the Hidden History of Show Business*. New York: Harper Collins, 1995.

Ross, Murray. *Stars and Strikes: Unionization of Hollywood*. New York: Columbia University Press, 1941.

Rosten, Leo. *Hollywood: The Movie Colony, the Movie Makers*. New York: Harcourt, Brace, and Company, 1941.

Scharf, Lois. *To Work and to Wed: Female Employment, Feminism, and the Great Depression*. Westport, CT: Greenwood Press, 1980.

Schatz, Thomas. *Boom and Bust: American Cinema in the 1940s*. Berkeley: University of California Press, 1997.

———. *The Genius of the System*. New York: Henry Holt and Company, 1988.

———. "'A Triumph of Bitchery': Warner Brothers, Bette Davis, and *Jezebel*." In *The Studio System*, edited by Janet Staiger, 74–92. New Brunswick, NJ: Rutgers University Press, 1995.

Smoodin, Eric. *Regarding Frank Capra: Audience, Celebrity, and American Film Studies, 1930–1960*. Durham, NC: Duke University Press, 2004.

Sobchack, Vivian. "What is Film History? Or, the Riddle of the Sphinxes." In *Reinventing Film Studies*, edited by Christine Gledhill and Linda Williams, 300–315. New York: Routledge, 2000.

Stacey, Jackie. *Star Gazing: Hollywood Cinema and Female Spectatorship*. London: Routledge, 1994.

Staiger, Janet. "Individualism Versus Collectivism." In *Screen* 24, nos. 4–5 (July–October 1983): 68–79.

———. *Interpreting Films: Studies in the Historical Reception of American Cinema*. Princeton, NJ: Princeton University Press, 1992.

———, ed. *The Studio System*. New Brunswick, NJ: Rutgers University Press, 1995.

Stamp, Shelley. *Movie-Struck Girls: Women and Motion Picture Culture After the Nickelodeon*. Princeton, NJ: Princeton University Press, 2000.

Stenn, David. *Clara Bow: Runnin' Wild*. New York: Cooper Square Press, 2000.

Stokes, Melvyn, and Richard Maltby, eds. *Identifying Hollywood's Audiences: Cultural Identity and the Movies*. London: BFI, 1999.

Studlar, Gaylyn. "The Perils of Pleasure? Fan Magazine Discourse as Women's Commodified Culture in the 1920s." In *Silent Film*, edited by Richard Abel, 263–298. New Brunswick, NJ: Rutgers University Press, 1996.

Sturtevant, Victoria, "'But Things Is Changin' Nowadays and Mammy's Gettin' Bored': Hattie McDaniel and the Culture of Dissemblance." *Velvet Light Trap* 44 (Fall 1999): 68–79.

———. "Spitfire: Lupe Vélez and the Ambivalent Pleasures of Ethnic Masquerade." *Velvet Light Trap* 55 (Spring 2005): 19–32.

Susman, Warren. *Culture as History: The Transformation of American Society in the Twentieth Century*. New York: Pantheon, 1984.

Swanson, Gloria. *Swanson on Swanson*. New York: Random House, 1980.

Swindell, Larry. *Screwball: The Life of Carole Lombard*. New York: William Morrow and Company, 1975.

Taves, Brian. "The B Film: Hollywood's Other Half." In *Grand Design*, edited by Tino Balio, 313–350. Berkeley: University of California Press, 1995.

Taylor, Frederick Winslow. *The Principles of Scientific Management*. New York: W. W. Norton and Company, 1967.

Thomson, David. *Showman: The Life of David O. Selznick*. New York: Knopf, 1992.

Vasey, Ruth. *The World According to Hollywood, 1918–1939*. Madison: University of Wisconsin Press, 1997.

Waldman, Diane. "From Midnight Shows to Marriage Vows: Women, Exploitation, and Exhibition." *Wide Angle* 6 (1984): 40–48.

Wallis, Eileen V. *Earning Power: Women and Work in Los Angeles, 1880–1930*. Reno: University of Nevada Press, 2010.

Wang, Yiman. "The Art of Screen Passing: Anna May Wong's Yellow Yellowface Performance in the Art Deco Cinema." *Camera Obscura* 20, no. 3 (2005): 159–190.

Wexman, Virginia Wright. *Creating the Couple: Love, Marriage, and Hollywood Performance*. Princeton, NJ: Princeton University Press, 1993.

Whitfield, Eileen. *Pickford: The Woman Who Made Hollywood*. Lexington: University of Kentucky Press, 1997.

Wilson, Victoria. *A Life of Barbara Stanwyck: Steel-True, 1907–1940*. New York: Simon and Schuster, 2013.

Woloch, Nancy. *Women and the American Experience*. New York: McGraw-Hill, 1984.

Zuckerman, Mary Ellen. *A History of Popular Womens Magazines in the United States, 1792–1995*. Westport, CT: Greenwood Press, 1998.

Index

Page numbers in italics refer to illustrations.
For case studies on individual stars, see Appendix One.